MW00484264

The Four Musketeers

ABOUT THE AUTHORS

Kari Maund is a professional historian and writer. Her other books include *The Welsh Kings*, also published by Tempus. Phil Nanson is an amateur military historian who trained as a blacksmith and armourer. They both live in Cambridge.

The Four Musketeers

The True Story of
D'ARTAGNAN, PORTHOS, ARAMIS & ATHOS

KARI MAUND & PHIL NANSON

TEMPUS

To David and Margaret Nanson, for encouraging Phil's interest in things military, and to David N. Dumville, for putting the idea in Kari's head in the first place.

Tempus Publishing Limited
The Mill, Brimscombe Port,
Stroud, Gloucestershire, GL5 2QG

© Kari Maund and Phil Nanson, 2005

The right of Kari Maund and Phil Nanson to be identified as the Authors
of this work has been asserted in accordance with the
Copyrights, Designs and Patents Act 1988.

All rights reserved. No part of this book may be reprinted
or reproduced or utilised in any form or by any electronic,
mechanical or other means, now known or hereafter invented,
including photocopying and recording, or in any information
storage or retrieval system, without the permission in writing
from the Publishers.

ISBN 0 7524 3503 5

Typesetting and origination by Tempus Publishing Limited

Contents

Acknowledgements

Writing a book inevitably involves far more than sitting down at the word processor, and we would like to thank all those who have helped us along the way. In particular, we are indebted to: the staff of the inter-library loans service, Cambridge University Library; the Roger-Viollet Picture Library and their UK agent, Rex Features – and especially Glen Marks and Paul Brown; the Service Historique de l'Armée de Terre de France; the Maastricht Tourist Office; the staff of *La Botte Chantilly*, Lille; Patrick de Jacquelot, author of the wonderful Pastiches Dumas website; Nik Ravenscroft for much-needed elucidation on the Romantic movement; Austin Benson and Caro Wilson for allowing us to use their photographs; our splendid editor at Tempus, Jonathan Reeve; Emma Chapman; Austin and Caro (again) and Michael Abbott and Anne Wilson, for accompanying us around the homeland of the musketeers, Gascony.

Introduction

On the 14th March 1844, the city of Paris appeared almost to be in a state of uproar. Rumours were flying, and many people, seeing women running towards the nearest newsagent, and leaving their children crying at their open doors, hastily gathered up their coats and hats and directed their steps towards the offices of *Le Siècle*, outside which was gathered, increasing every minute, a compact group, noisy and full of curiosity.

The scenario is imaginary, yet something rather extraordinary was occurring that day. Paris – indeed, France – may not have realised it, but 14 March 1844 marked the beginning of a literary phenomenon. That day, in the pages of the newspaper *Le Siècle* (*The Century*), the first pages of a new novel, entitled *The Three Musketeers*, had appeared. The author was an established literary figure who had made a sensation with his stage melodramas: Alexandre Dumas. This new serial rapidly proved to be a huge hit, winning new readers to the paper, and adding to the renown of its author. The book was to spawn two sequels and two plays by the same writer, and a host of other works written by imitators and admirers. More than 150 years after its first publication, the story of d'Artagnan and the three musketeers is still in print in multiple languages and is read and loved all over the world. It has been filmed many times in different countries; it has been transformed into comic books and cartoons, its heroes used to sell products from wine to cologne to financial services. They are part of popular culture, not only in their native France, but worldwide.

But what most of those who have read and loved the book or seen the films do not know is that d'Artagnan and his three friends did not spring to life fully fledged from the brow of Dumas. Behind the story there were real men, who lived and fought and died under Louis XIII and Louis XIV. In France, several generations of scholars have worked to uncover the details of their lives, but to date there has been only one work about them in English, and that is out of print and now rather dated. The present book is intended to fill that gap. The musketeers lived through a turbulent age, and their lives encapsulate many of the themes that characterise France in the seventeenth century – the conflict between Catholics and Protestants, the struggle of the high aristocracy to maintain their power, the ambition of kings to expand their lands and influence, the rivalries of ministers and favourites. D'Artagnan, *confidant* of kings and ministers, was a witness to some of the most exciting events of the early years of Louis XIV's reign. This book looks at these events as the four experienced them. It examines the origins and history of the King's Musketeers, and shows how it was they came to be an elite and esteemed company whose members were often every bit as colourful and swashbuckling as their literary echoes.

After his death, d'Artagnan became the subject of a set of fake *Memoirs*, written by a professional hack named Gatien de Courtilz de Sandras: Courtilz's book provided Dumas with the idea for his novel, but each layer moved the four heroes further away from their real identities. *The Four Musketeers* looks at these two works and examines how they created and embroidered the musketeer legend. It goes on to lay out how that legend gathered momentum after the death of Dumas, and to chart the continuing adventures of d'Artagnan and his friends in further books and on the screen.

The Four Musketeers is the product of a life-long love for the novels and characters created by Dumas, and of an abiding fascination with the seventeenth-century France from which they emerged. Athos, Porthos, Aramis and d'Artagnan have become part of the tapestry of our modern world. This book hopes to show how they came to be there.

I

The Historical D'Artagnan

His name was not really D'Artagnan. It is a curious reversal of truth that, while in Dumas's famous version, Athos, Porthos and Aramis are pseudonyms and d'Artagnan alone bears his genuine name, in reality it was d'Artagnan who was pseudonymous. He was born Charles de Batz-Castelmore sometime between 1610 and 1615 in the small village of Lupiac in Gascony. His father's family were neither rich nor famous, and their claim to nobility was somewhat tenuous, probably dating from no earlier than the mid-sixteenth century. In 1565 the small château of Castelmore, five kilometres outside Lupiac, was bought by one Arnaud de Batz, a successful local tradesman. Although de Batz was a common name in Gascony, and although at least one branch claimed nobility going back to the thirteenth century, it is highly unlikely that Arnaud de Batz was anything other than a self-made man. Nobility was a desirable prize: it conferred not only status, but also exemptions from taxation, and Arnaud was only one of many comfortably-off commoners who sought means of self-elevation. In addition to

Castelmore, he purchased another noble domain, that of La Plagne, some two kilometres from Lupiac. It is not clear that Arnaud ever dignified himself with a noble title, but one of his descendants had begun to do so by the end of the sixteenth century.[1]

Charles de Batz was either the great-grandson or great-great-grandson of Arnaud. His father, Bertrand, inherited Castelmore towards the end of 1607.[2] By this time, the family was well-established locally, and had made a number of useful marriages, adding to their status, if not to their wealth. They were not particularly well off: they had abandoned their mercantile origins, and no especially lucrative local administrative offices had come into their hands. They probably lived off the revenues of their lands, which were not extensive.

Despite his debatable nobility and lack of funds, Bertrand de Batz-Castelmore managed to follow in the footsteps of his predecessors, and married well. On 27 February 1608, shortly after he had inherited Castelmore, he entered into a marriage contract with Françoise de Montesquiou d'Artagnan, daughter of Jean de Montesquiou, Lord of Artagnan, about thirty kilometres from Lupiac.

The Montesquiou family belonged to the ancient nobility, and its various branches and relations held considerable lands in the neighbourhood. For the Lord of Castelmore, this was a important alliance. Jean de Montesquiou d'Artagnan had served in the French Guards and was well known to the King of France, Henri IV. This familiarity of the crown with the name d'Artagnan was to prove invaluable to Charles de Batz-Castelmore. It is easy to imagine how desirable this marriage must have been to Bertrand II, promising as it did a wealth of influence and connections. At 5,000 *livres*, Françoise's dowry was not substantial, but it was respectable. It is harder to appreciate the marriage from the Montesquiou point of view. Bertrand was a neighbour, certainly, and Jean de Montesquiou had three daughters to marry off. There may also have been an existing connection between the two families: a Batz-Castelmore document recounts the marriage in 1654 of François de Batz (supposedly a son of Arnaud) to one Jeanne de Montesquiou.[3] It is notable that the arrangement followed quite quickly upon Bertrand's succession to the château of Castelmore. This seems to have been the senior holding of the family, and perhaps lent him more of the cachet required to aspire to a Montesquiou.[4]

Bertrand and Françoise had six children: four boys and three girls. Their birth order is not certain, but Charles seems to have been the second or third eldest boy. Nothing certain is known of his upbringing or education, although we know that he was literate, and received martial training. The estate at Castelmore was insufficient to support them in idleness: three of the four boys, including the eldest, Paul, embarked on military careers, while the youngest, Arnaud, entered the Church. Charles had left home before 1635, the year of his father's death: the inventory of Bertrand II's possessions made *post mortem* states that Paul, Charles and a third brother, Jean, were 'absent from the region and in the service of His Majesty'.[5]

In March 1633, one 'Charles d'Artagnan' was a member of the company of musketeers who paraded in review before Louis XIII.[6] All three of the brothers adopted their mother's surname on entering military service. The Montesquiou d'Artagnan family was well known and well established. Their name would open far more doors than that of Batz-Castelmore. Henceforth Charles de Batz-Castelmore would be known as Charles Castelmore d'Artagnan, or, as in the record mentioned above, simply Charles d'Artagnan. The first foundation stone of the legend had been laid.

The career options available to sons of the minor nobility were limited, especially if their families were impoverished. Anything related to trade or business was unacceptable – liable, indeed, to cast doubt upon the honour of any supposed gentleman who entered into it. The high aristocracy could hope to win favour – and with it lucrative sinecures – at court, and a handful of wealthy nobles could support themselves in whatever interests appealed. But for the lower nobility, and particularly for their younger sons, the choice was largely between the Church and the military. The Aramitz family, as will be seen in Chapter 2, had adopted this course over several generations, along with many others.

There is no evidence that any member of the de Batz-Castelmore family had military ambitions prior to their ascent to noble rank. Military service was, however, a tradition in the Montesquiou family, and it is more than likely that Françoise encouraged her sons to embark upon a martial career, and her family connections provided them with an entrée into the complicated world of the French army. A gentleman could not enrol in just any company: only certain regiments were suitably prestigious. Access to them was a complex web of blood-relationship, influence, family contacts, regional loyalties and favour. Charles, Paul and Jean all benefited from the standing of their mother's family in their entry into the military. Paul had probably preceded Charles to Paris, but our first record of him as a soldier comes from 1640, at which time he was serving in the musketeers. Service in this company was often a stepping stone to promotion to higher rank in other companies, and shortly afterwards Paul became a lieutenant in the French Guard. With the latter, he served in Italy, where he was twice wounded, and by 1643 he was a captain.[7] As the eldest son, he chose not to spend his whole life in the military, and in 1646 he retired to Castelmore, having acquired through his service the valuable office of Captain of the Forests of Mazous and Clarac. He later also became governor of Navarrenx, a fortified town with an important place in French defences against Spain.

While Paul's career is relatively well documented, we know very little of Jean. He survived a dangerous illness in 1646 at Paris, and in 1650 he, like Paul, achieved the rank of captain, serving in the Persan Regiment. No more survives, and it has been plausibly suggested that he probably died in service.[8]

As for Charles, there is no evidence for his activities between 1633 and 1646. He did not return to Lupiac at his father's death in 1635. It is probable that he did not serve in the musketeers throughout this thirteen-year period, as he is absent from its rolls after 1640. Rather, like Paul, he is likely to have transferred into some other guard regiment, perhaps at a higher grade.[9] Perhaps he saw active service in the French campaigns of the Thirty Years' War, as Courtilz de Sandras was later to claim. We simply do not know.

A lot had changed by 1646. In 1633, Louis XIII ruled France, aided by the famous Cardinal Richelieu.[10] By 1646, both were gone. Richelieu had died on 4 December 1642 and Louis a few months later, on 14 May. The new King, Louis XIV, was a minor. His mother, Queen Anne, served as his regent, with Richelieu's protégé,

Cardinal Mazarin, as her first minister. Mazarin was competent and intelligent, but he was not a native Frenchman, and he faced considerable hostility from the higher nobility, who had hoped for greater power after the death of Richelieu. One of Mazarin's enemies was Jean-Arnaud de Peyrer, Seigneur de Troisvilles, better known as de Tréville, captain-lieutenant of musketeers. Like Charles, Tréville came from a Gascon family with a tenuous claim to nobility, but he had prospered under Louis XIII, and possessed considerable influence. His opposition to Mazarin was to have serious consequences for the company of musketeers. On 26 January that year, Mazarin had the company disbanded on the grounds that there was no justification for maintaining so expensive a troop while the King was a minor. By this date, Charles may once again have been serving in the musketeers; certainly he had somehow attracted the attention of Mazarin by the first months of 1646. He is first recorded in Mazarin's service on 28 June that year, when he rode to the royal court in Paris from the army then in Flanders to bring news that Cambrai was expected to fall into French hands in the next few days.

Contemporary French reports often refer to Charles henceforth as a *créature* of Mazarin. In English, the word 'creature' could well be taken as having negative overtones, but it must be stressed that these are not present in French. The sense is less that of a henchman than of someone raised up or benefited by a patron. Charles had some family connections, but up to the mid-1640s he seems to have lacked a well-placed sponsor; henceforth in Mazarin he had one. It is a strange irony that the genuine Charles d'Artagnan owed his prominence to Cardinal Mazarin. Alexandre Dumas found the Italian minister unappealing, and in *Twenty Years After*, d'Artagnan is a very reluctant servitor. The reality was different, and Charles was to know a lasting gratitude and respect for the cardinal, and indeed for the Queen, Anne of Austria. The mid-1640s were politically turbulent for France, and Mazarin was the target of many plots and schemes to remove him. Many noblemen were arrayed against him; others changed loyalties according to their own advantage. Similarly, many of the senior office-holders and wealthy urban *bourgeois*, both in Paris and in the provinces, opposed the minister and his party. It cannot have been easy for Mazarin to find and retain men he could trust; in Charles Castelmore d'Artagnan he had found a notable and laudable exception.

Why would Charles choose the service of the unpopular minister over, say, that of the celebrated Prince de Condé or the charismatic marshal, Turenne?[11] Nearly twenty years later, after his death, the inventory of Charles's possessions revealed that he owned portraits of both Mazarin and the Queen; certainly this is testament to his loyalty, but it may also hint at some deeper admiration, perhaps particularly for Anne of Austria, with whom he had little direct personal contact. It may also be that he partook of the belief that Dumas would later attribute to Athos: that one should wherever possible remain loyal to the principle of royalty and to the King as its embodiment over all personal interests or tastes. Mazarin was unpopular, but Mazarin was nevertheless the first minister of the young King. Probably, also, Charles had his eyes on the long term. As a member of the lesser nobility, he was unlikely to benefit from the plots and rebellions of the upper nobles, who looked almost wholly to their own advantage; similarly, the office-holders were unlikely to offer him any lasting advances. Loyal service to the King and his minister, however, might well reap rewards in the future, when Louis XIV achieved his majority.

To begin with, Charles's role was essentially that of a military courier; he carried reports and instructions from the war-front to the court and back again. His efficiency and effectiveness evidently impressed Mazarin. In addition to affairs of war, the minister began to trust Charles with matters touching more directly upon his (Mazarin's) personal position and upon his sensitive relationship with the Queen.

The Thirty Years' War, which had formed the backdrop to Charles's early military career, came to an end with the Peace of Westphalia on 24 October 1648.[12] Wars were expensive and seldom popular, particularly with the tax-paying sections of the French populace (which included the wealthy office-holders and *bourgeois*, but excluded the aristocracy). Religion provided a further complication: the Thirty Years' War had opposed France to the Catholic Hapsburg Empire, and allied her with a number of Protestant states.

Certain influential factions in France were opposed to this policy, believing that it was a duty of Catholic powers to present a common front. Richelieu had been consistently opposed to this *dévot* stance, and Mazarin had followed his lead, thus, in some views, prolonging the war. This, combined with resentment against Mazarin as a foreigner, and with the clashing and powerful ambitions of nobility and office-holders, gave rise, in 1648, to the French civil war known as the Fronde.[13]

In June 1648, Charles was still acting as a military courier. We do not know exactly how he was occupied during the final peace negotiations, but he certainly continued in Mazarin's service. Paris, never the most peaceful of capital cities, rapidly became too insecure for the court to remain, and on 6 January 1649 the Queen Regent, the young King and the cardinal left for Saint-Germain under cover of darkness. Possibly Charles played a part in this retreat; Dumas certainly gave him one, and earlier biographers also liked to think so.[14] There is no evidence either way. Throughout 1649, however, negotiations were under way between Mazarin, his enemies and his uncertain allies. Charles is likely to have been involved as a courier. Certainly, in September 1650, he carried dispatches between Mazarin and Hugues de Lionne, the Queen's household secretary. In December of the same year, he took a letter of congratulation from Mazarin to Maréchal de Plessis, who had recently scored a victory over anti-Mazarin troops. Charles returned to the cardinal details of those killed, injured and taken captive. Despite this victory, things were going poorly for Mazarin, and he was facing probable exile. In the winter of 1651, the Queen was prevailed upon to banish the cardinal, and he sent Charles to Bonn to seek sanctuary for his master from the Elector of Cologne, Maximilian of Bavaria. Mazarin was offered the castle at Brühl, where he took up residence in April 1651. Anne remained attached to him, and contact between them was maintained, despite the disapproval of the rebel nobility. Mazarin also maintained correspondence with his supporters and ministers: Charles carried their letters, often in code. This was by no means a safe occupation: the correspondence was clandestine and potentially dangerous, and leading *Frondeurs* were anxious to intercept and prevent it. Speed and discretion were essential; so too was diplomacy. The recipients of the letters were frequently powerful or of high rank.[15] Moreover, loyalties were often unstable, with individuals switching sides from Fronde to cardinal and back again as their self-interest dictated. Charles maintained Mazarin's trust throughout this treacherous period, which speaks highly for his resourcefulness, ability and loyalty. The d'Artagnan myth depicts Mazarin as grasping and ungrateful where Charles was concerned, but a letter survives from Mazarin to Lionne in which the former speaks hopefully of persuading the Queen to reward Charles with a military promotion.[16]

The promotion did not materialise, but by November 1651, Anne was in a position to recall Mazarin to France. Charles was sent ahead of him to Paris, charged with contacting Mazarin's supporters there. This was a dangerous task, as Paris remained strongly anti-cardinalist. Despite the Queen's support, Mazarin's status was far from secure: although one significant military leader, Turenne, had returned to the royalist party, another great general, Condé, remained a *Frondeur*, and had adopted a warlike stance against the cardinal. Shortly before Mazarin's recall, the young King had reached his majority, but his power was limited, and his protection uncertain. King and cardinal joined forces at Poitiers in January 1652, and proceeded to regain control for their party over south-west France and then Anjou. Charles accompanied them, still in his role as confidential courier, bearing orders and instructions to and from the court. By April, the royalists had the upper hand, at least militarily, and Condé retreated to Paris, still a *Frondeur* stronghold, while the court settled once again at Saint-Germain. This return to fortune had its benefits for Charles: the same month he received a lieutenancy in the Vitermont company of guards. That this was a reward for his past services is clear from its sequel: the company had had its own preference for lieutenant, and registered displeasure at this royal imposition by refusing to recognise Charles as their new officer. Odile Bordaz has suggested that this resistance may also have been due in part to hatred directed at Mazarin.[17] This was symptomatic of a wider problem: in spite of royal victories, the King and his mother found that Mazarin remained unacceptable to the people, and Paris held out obstinately against them. Peace seemed impossible. The royalists received a military check in July, when a battle in the Faubourg Saint-Antoine was won by Condé. However, his popularity was short-lived: he was unable to hold onto the friendship of the city's civic leaders, and his collusion in a massacre at the *hôtel de ville* in August turned them decisively against him. A new cabal formed, centred on the King's uncle, Gaston d'Orléans, a development which was to prove to the advantage of the royalist party. When the King summoned the Paris *parlement* to him at Pontoise, also in August, they prevailed upon him to send Mazarin once again into exile, but on far less stringent terms.

This time, the place of exile was closer, at the château of Bouillon. Mazarin was away from court, but he continued to have governmental responsibilities.[18] In particular, he was still actively pursuing the suppression of the Fronde outside Paris. By now, the level of disturbance was greatly reduced. Early in 1653, Charles was summoned to Mazarin and entrusted with a new mission. During the summer and autumn of 1652, Turenne had been engaged upon putting down *Frondeur* activity in Champagne. Winter had put an end to the fighting, but Mazarin was already preparing for the summer. Charles was sent to this front carrying an order for the building of a new bridge over the River Aisne in the town of Pont-à-Verre (a previous bridge had been destroyed). Initially, the local *intendant*,[19] Champfort, made difficulties, but further negotiation convinced him, and royal forces were provided with a necessary crossing point to further their campaigns. That Mazarin was able to command the obedience of such officials demonstrates that his power remained considerable during this second exile. The risks in serving him, for Charles, were considerably reduced from the dangerous times of the first exile. His missions were concerned with matters of state, and not with coded – and forbidden – correspondence between minister and Queen.

While Mazarin was in the provinces, the young King had been negotiating with the leaders of the Fronde in Paris, and their influence over the people was waning.[20] Condé remained rebellious, taking refuge with Spain, but by early 1653 the King was secure enough to order the recall of Mazarin, who re-entered Paris in some style on 2 February 1653. Louis XIV was crowned with full ceremony and in the prominent presence of Mazarin on 7 June 1564.[21] The Fronde was effectively over.

Charles Castelmore d'Artagnan had remained loyal to Mazarin, the Queen and the young King throughout the disturbances. Like his former captain, Tréville, he could expect rewards and recognition for his services. It is likely he was well aware of this: in later years, his confidence in dealing with the King suggests that he knew he merited his status, and was not at all afraid to trade on it.

The first reward was not long in appearing. Like all early modern courts, that of France possessed a number of offices which granted financial and social advantage alongside minimal or no duties. One such was the office of Captain of the Royal Aviary. It was valuable, as although it seems not to have carried a significant stipend, it did confer upon the holder a residence close to the King, within the Tuileries Gardens in the Pavilion de la Volière. Several influential people sought this position, but Mazarin did not forget his loyal courier. In April 1654, the King signed the following letter: '[on account of] the good services which the Sieur d'Artagnan has rendered to him, and to oblige him to continue in them, His Majesty has made him a gift of the charge of Captain of the Aviary in his Garden of the Tuileries...'.[22]

Following his coronation in June, Louis XIV embarked on campaign against the Spanish Netherlands.[23] We know Charles was amongst the royal army: for him, the end of the Fronde marked a return to active military service. In the summer of 1654, French royal forces besieged the town of Stenay, and Charles was involved in the fighting. He received an injury which was serious enough to draw the attention of Mazarin, but from which he made a good recovery.[24] His behaviour during the battles seems to have pleased cardinal and King, as more rewards were soon forthcoming. His lieutenancy in the Vitermont regiment had never been comfortable: by July 1564 he had a new position as captain of the Guards of the Company of Fourille. There were some financial complications to this promotion. At this time, many military appointments were essentially venal, and Charles was not rich. Although the King had granted him this new rank, he nevertheless had to pay the sum of 80,000 *livres* to the outgoing captain. To fund this, he sold his office of Captain of the Royal Aviary, thus losing his official Paris residence.[25] With his new company, he fought in both the sieges of Landrecies and of Saint-Ghislain in the summer of 1655. The following year, he was at the siege of Valenciennes. It is likely that all these sieges and battles cost Charles friends or comrades: in the case of Valenciennes, we know that he was present at the death of Captain Vitermont, under whom he had formerly been a lieutenant. The two may have been close: certainly the dying captain entrusted Charles with looking after the interests of his heir.[26]

The year 1658 saw no let-up of campaigning for Charles, and again he was present at a number of important sieges. But 1658 saw his recall to Mazarin's side. The war still continued, but Mazarin had need of him. Louis XIV had decided to re-establish the musketeers and a new company had been formed on 10 January 1657. As with the old company, it was to be a prestige regiment, and places within it were both desirable and sought after. To please his minister and mentor, Louis had conferred the senior rank – at this time a lieutenancy – upon Mazarin's nephew, Philippe Mancini, Duke of Nevers. Nevers was only fifteen, and had neither experience nor interest in the military: he required an experienced sub-lieutenant to assist and guide him. An initial appointment of Isaac de Baas proved unsatisfactory and Mazarin remembered Charles.[27] On 26 May 1658, at Mardyck, Charles received his commission as sub-lieutenant of the musketeers from the hands of the King. The new company immediately found itself deployed in the fighting, and served with distinction in the battle of Dunes and the siege of Dunkirk. The summer campaign was highly successful and, in the autumn, five companies were sent back to Paris to guard the King. This included the musketeers. The new company was dear to the King, who was their honorary captain: he was keen for them to be well dressed, well presented and well disciplined. Their duties included escorting the King on journeys, as well as guard-duty at royal places. Since Nevers took little interest in the troop, actual command devolved on Charles, who thus found himself in close, regular contact with the King in person.

Louis probably knew of Charles before this, but it is unclear if they were personally acquainted. It is likely that, during the Fronde,

Louis would have seen Charles about court, but the closeness of
musketeer and child ruler, much loved by makers of films, is certainly
a myth.[28] In 1658, Charles was no longer a young man – he would
have been in his early forties, and his experiences and background
would have made him very different to the eighteen-year-old Louis.
On the other hand, his unquestioned loyalty to Mazarin and to the
Queen would have predisposed Louis to him, while his military skill
would have appealed to the King's martial tastes. We know from his
surviving letters that Charles retained his strong Gascon accent, and
from the *post-mortem* inventory of his possessions that he was not
of a literary or philosophical bent. Nevertheless, Louis soon grew
to appreciate and like him, and in later years would prove to be
surprisingly careful of Charles's opinions and feelings.

The new appointment also brought him to public attention. The
musketeers were an elite troop, prominent in their duties, closely
tied to King and court. Their drills and manoeuvres were a matter
of public spectacle, carried out where anyone could see them, and
they were fashionable amongst literary and court circles.[29] Charles's
official activities became worthy of notice in the official record of
the court, the *Gazette de France,* and he was welcome at aristocratic
salons and gatherings. What he thought of this we do not know:
his surviving letters carry no information on this point. We know
that he was proud and careful of his position, but it seems that his
manner of expressing this was not offensive, as he was spoken of
with respect and even affection by contemporary poets and writers. It had taken him something of the order of twenty years, but
Charles Castelmore d'Artagnan had succeeded in emulating his
countryman, Tréville.

His new prominence means that we know more of his career
henceforth, and somewhat more of his personality and interests. He
was now established in the world, and, with the conclusion of peace
between France and Spain in November 1659 at the Isle of Pheasants
on the River Bidassoa (the 'Peace of the Pyrenees'), his military
duties were reduced. The new peace laid out plans for the marriage
of Louis XIV; Charles decided that he, too, should marry.

There is little evidence of romance in his marriage. Rather, as
was customary at the time, he married for reasons of rank and

finance. He was not a young man, nor was he of high birth, and his choice of bride perhaps reflects this. Her name was Charlotte-Anne de Chanlecy, lady of Sainte-Croix. She was a thirty-five-year-old, childless widow. She was of good, but not prominent, family, descended from the ancient nobility of Burgundy. The barony of Sainte-Croix was her personal property, inherited from her father. She also owned a family townhouse in Châlon-sur-Saône, which was her main residence, along with various other lands and sources of income.

It seems likely that they met in November 1658. King and court were on a journey to Lyons, where Louis was to meet a potential royal bride, the princess Marguerite of Savoy. One of their stopping places was Châlon, where the governor, Charlotte's half-brother, gave a reception party for them. Perhaps Charlotte, having spent most of her youth in the provinces and hoping for a brighter future, was looking out for a suitable second husband. Her age and her relative obscurity barred her from looking at the ranks of the higher aristocracy, but Charles, with his prestigious position in the new elite corps of musketeers and his closeness to the King, would have seemed a good prospect. He was noble, he was influential, he was of middle age, and he was unmarried. The musketeers presented a splendid spectacle, with their new equipment and high standards of appearance. At first, she would probably not have known that he was almost permanently in debt. To Charles, the widow's fortune, if not her person – and we have no reliable information about that – must have appealed. Her relatives may well have promoted the match: Charlotte was of a litigious disposition, and her half-brother may have preferred for her to be further away from family lands.

Charles's hopes were to be disappointed. Charlotte soon discovered the true state of his finances. There is no indication that either side sought to back out of the marriage, but when the contract for the marriage was signed, on 5 March 1659, it contained provisions protecting Charlotte's property from her future husband's pecuniary difficulties. The extent to which their property was to become joint was strictly limited, while a second clause laid out that any debts contracted before the marriage remained the sole responsibility of the original debtor.

From Charlotte's point of view, the contract was highly satisfactory.[30] Not only was she safe from financial problems, but Charles's splendid connections were already making themselves felt. The contract was signed in a royal palace, the Louvre. The witnesses brought by Charles were some of the highest figures of the court – the Maréchal-Duc de Gramont, his wife, and two of their children, and François de Montlezun de Besmaux, Charles's old companion, now governor of the Bastille. Although they probably were not present, Louis XIV and Mazarin appended their signatures. The high esteem in which Charles was held is clear from this gathering. The marriage itself took place a month later, at dawn on 3 April at a Paris church, Saint-André-des-Arts.

Only official documents survive relating to this marriage: there are no personal letters, no souvenirs, and it is sadly likely that there was little or no sympathy between the couple. This was not uncommon at the period, with most marriages being made for economic or social purposes, and most spouses having little or nothing to do with each other after the careful provision of heirs. Charles and Charlotte adhered to this pattern: within a few short weeks, he left his now-pregnant wife in Paris and set off with the King to Vincennes. It would be more than a year before he returned.

The marriage project between Louis and Marguerite of Savoy had come to nothing: Mazarin had arranged a far more useful and important match. In August 1659, Louis and his court set out for the border with Spain, where he was to marry the Spanish Infanta, Maria-Theresa. This was intended to put the seal on the new peace with Spain, and to usher in a new period of cordial Franco-Spanish relations. The arrangements were complex, however, and Louis thus did not hurry on his way south. It was Charles's task to provide a military escort for the King and his family as they travelled in state across much of central France. Alongside its nuptial purposes, this long trip also served a second important function, that of permitting the young King to see and be seen as widely as possible throughout his kingdom. Progress was slow, marked by receptions, hunting trips and visits.[31] Protocol dictated that the marriage could take place in neither France nor Spain, so the place selected was on the border – the Isle of Pheasants in the River Bidassoa, which was thereafter known as the Isle of the Conference. The route from Paris lay through Gascony; the first time Charles had set foot in his home country since he left sometime before 1633. The cortège spent some days there – in the afternoon of 25 April 1660 it arrived at Vic-Fezensac, only a few kilometres from Lupiac. The honour guard provided by the town to welcome the King was led by one of Charles's relatives by marriage. It is probable that other family connections were also present.

The next day, the royal company was due to pass close to Lupiac and to Charles's childhood home of Castelmore. We do not know if he was granted permission to pay a visit to his family there. His mother had died in 1566, but his elder brother Paul was now Lord of Castelmore. It is tempting to speculate that Charles may have made at least a brief visit to catch up on family news, to show his brother the fruits of his new rank, and, perhaps, to discuss his marriage.

The long royal progress was far from simple for Charles. He was one of the senior figures responsible for the security of the King, not only during hours of travel, but also at every stop. This involved a long succession of new residences, each presenting its own security problems and challenges. He also bore final responsibility for his company, including ensuring that billets were acquired for them and discipline was maintained. It is very likely that it was during this journey that the King came to appreciate and respect the abilities of the sub-lieutenant of musketeers, and that the bond of understanding and trust between them was formed.

The formal solemnisation of the marriage was due to take place at Saint-Jean-de-Luz.[32] Louis entered the town in full pomp on 8 May 1660. The next month was spent in fêtes, expeditions, theatre visits, balls and celebrations. Charles doubtless was involved in guarding these, and in particular accompanying the King on the various outings. On 6 June, the peace between France and Spain was formally ratified.[33] The marriage ceremony itself took place on 9 June. The court did not linger once it was achieved, and the progress north was begun on 15 June. The return journey was swifter than the outward one, but for Charles it presented familiar problems of security. They reached Paris on 26 August 1660. The entry was remarkable for its splendour, and the musketeers were a noted part of it. The official lieutenant of the company, Nevers, was absent: Charles therefore took his place at its head. His presence and demeanour were noted by the *Gazette de France*: 'entirely well-presented and on a valuable horse'.[34]

For Charles it was a return to a familiar and regular routine. It was also a return to his wife, living probably in the house on the corner of the Quai Malaquais and the Rue du Bac, where he had been living at the time of his marriage. In his absence, a new member had been added to the household: his eldest son, born probably during the first months of 1660. We do not know for sure if Charles even knew he now had an heir: if letters passed between him and his wife during his long absence, they have not survived. His children are not known to have been formally named until 1674, after Charles's death, and there is no indication that Charles expressed much interest in them. Charlotte had had long months alone during her pregnancy, and however she may have felt at the return of her husband, she must have been pleased by the return of the court and its promise of a livelier time. She was probably ready to welcome Charles, and she was soon pregnant with their second child. However cordial their initial relations had been, however, friction seems soon to have developed. Perhaps Charlotte felt neglected, as her husband devoted most of his care and interest to his company of musketeers and to the King. Perhaps, too, she failed to achieve satisfactory entrée to court society. Charles was well known to the leaders of court and *salon* life, but he was not a courtier, nor did he have a literary bent. It is unlikely he was willing to escort her to social events, even assuming he would have had the time. Then, too, Charlotte was jealous of her inheritance, while Charles accumulated debts outfitting and supporting his men. His prodigality may have threatened her sense of security. In addition she may have harboured suspicions as to the intentions and behaviour of her family and neighbours back in Châlon-sur-Saône, if we may be guided by her later tendency to become involved in litigation with them. Before the birth of her second son, she had left Paris to return to her château at Châlon. On 5 July 1661, the child was baptised – but not given a name – at the parish church of Saint-Vincent. He had been born the same day, so perhaps he was considered frail. There is no mention of his father in the baptismal record, and the haste may suggest some anxiety over his health on behalf of his mother. In fact, he thrived: it is through him that Charles's line survived.[35] It is possible, too, that Charlotte had been intending to return to Paris and to her husband after the birth: she may have returned to her home simply for a visit. Events, however, were to conspire to prolong and exacerbate the separation.

Louis XIV had reached his majority in October 1651, but he had continued to rely upon his mother and especially upon Mazarin in matters of government. On 9 March 1661, Mazarin died. His health had been poor for some time, but he had nevertheless continued to exercise his ministerial powers with the full consent and involvement of the King.[36] In addition to his role as minister, Mazarin had served as political tutor to Louis, who had spent time daily working on governmental matters with him. It was a solid apprenticeship, and after Mazarin's death, Louis announced that henceforth he intended to rule directly, without the assistance of a first minister.

This was a startling decision from the point of view of the high nobility and office-holders. Both Louis XIII and his father, Henri IV, had worked closely with trusted first ministers, and while Mazarin had made no recommendations as to a successor, there were men in his government with considerable expectations. Additionally, some of the senior aristocracy hoped for a return to greater influence for themselves, something which both Richelieu and Mazarin had worked hard to prevent. After Mazarin, perhaps the most powerful men in office were Nicolas Fouquet, *surintendant des finances*,[37] Michel Le Tellier, the minister of war, Hugues de Lionne, formerly the Queen's secretary, and Jean-Baptiste Colbert, *intendant des finances* and a close associate of Mazarin.[37] Both Le Tellier and Fouquet were spoken of as potential first ministers. Le Tellier was an established and familiar figure, who had served the crown since the reign of Louis XIII, and had been minister of war since 1643. He was not a young man – he was born in 1603 – but he had many years of experience through both favourable and adverse conditions. Fouquet was twelve years younger and possessed of considerable charm. His career had been highly successful: he had achieved high office at thirty-three, which was very young by contemporary standards. This first appointment had been a very important one, that of *procureur général*, representing royal interests to *parlement*. His career had brought him considerable wealth, and he had a name as a patron of the arts and as a builder of splendid new buildings. He lived in the fashion of a great lord, and enjoyed considerable popularity amongst influential literary and *salon* society. Like the English Duke of Buckingham, favourite of both James I and Charles I, Fouquet was larger than life and easily perceived as a figure of romance. Dumas certainly found him so, depicting him as noble, charismatic and tragic. Scholarly opinion has often been more severe, and his methods of acquiring wealth were certainly questionable.[39] It is unlikely that he was as well loved by those who bore the burden of taxation as by the ladies of the *salons*, but it would nevertheless be unfair to dismiss him as wholly corrupt.

All the ministers sought to please the King and to consolidate their positions with him, Fouquet included. In August 1661, he gave a huge *fête* at his château of Vaux-le-Vicomte. It proved to be a misstep. The extravagance of the festivities and the splendour of the surroundings outraged rather than impressed the King. Colbert, who disliked Fouquet, had already begun to work on the King against him; the *fête* seems to have served to confirm Louis's distaste. That a subject might live in such state was offensive to him, and he believed that Fouquet had enriched himself to the detriment of the royal treasury. After the death of Mazarin, Louis had ordered an inventory of state finances. The results were not pleasing: the state was impoverished. Fouquet's large fortune looked suspicious, while his wide network of friends and his generosity to and patronage of writers and artists eroded the King's image of himself as supreme patron and pivot of society. For Colbert, directing Louis's attention towards Fouquet served a double purpose. The two were undoubtedly rivals, and Colbert had schemes for fiscal reform in which there was no place for Fouquet or for his office of *surintendant des finances*. Moreover, the disarray of state finances was embarrassing for all those who had been close to Mazarin, and concentrating on Fouquet allowed Colbert to distract interest from his own position. Louis determined upon the arrest and disgrace of Fouquet.

Charles Castelmore d'Artagnan had owed his own rise to Mazarin and by 1661 he was well established with the King. We do not know how he felt on learning of the cardinal's death.[40] Now, he found himself right in the middle of events. The King had left for Nantes on 29 August. Fouquet joined him on 30 August, despite illness. The plan to arrest him was a tightly-kept secret: Fouquet had many important friends, so absolute discretion was essential. Following the example of Mazarin, Louis turned to Charles. On 1 September, Charles, himself unwell, was summoned to the King. The King dismissed him due to his illness, but ordered him to return once he was well to receive a very important mission. Charles returned on 4 September and was received in private. Louis gave him the written orders to arrest Fouquet and to take him under guard to a safe place away from Nantes. The plan to arrest Fouquet was complex. Charles was to bring forty musketeers on horseback to the royal residence. Twenty were to patrol the courtyard, the other twenty were to wait outside the gate. Charles himself was to retain a small number who should accompany him everywhere. Fouquet would have been summoned to the King: once he had left the château, Charles was to arrest him and take him to the chamberlain's room to await a carriage. Fouquet was to be prevented from putting his hands into his pockets, lest he destroy any papers he had upon him. Once the carriage had arrived, Charles was to take him in stages to the castle at Angers under strict guard. Charles was to have complete control over the choice of guards throughout, and arrangements had been made for their board and lodging in Angers, and for the expenses associated with the journey.

The day for the arrest was to be 5 September, and at first all went according to plan. Charles had sent his men in small groups to the rendezvous, and had sent a brigadier and ten musketeers ahead to make arrangements at Angers. Having met with his ministers, Louis detained Fouquet until he could see Charles waiting in the courtyard outside. Then he sent the minister away. It was at this point that the plan began to go astray. Le Tellier had been sent to confirm the arrest order to Charles, but he was delayed en route by one of Fouquet's friends, who was suspicious. Meanwhile, Fouquet exited the building, gained his sedan chair,

and left. Charles sent to the King in alarm, and received the order
to find Fouquet as quickly as possible. It must have seemed at
that moment that news of the intended arrest had leaked, and
Fouquet's friends were conspiring to help him escape. On horseback and accompanied by a troop of his musketeers, Charles left
in search of his target. He caught up with him in the city in the
square before the cathedral. The musketeers surrounded the chair:
Fouquet got down and bowed. Charles showed him the royal
order, and then, wary of attracting too much attention, took him
for safekeeping to the nearest house. He also dispatched one of his
men to inform the King and to have the carriage sent to this new
place. Then, once it arrived, Charles boarded it with his prisoner
and set off on the route to Angers.

Neither man could have realised that this was to be the beginning
of a long association. Fouquet, certainly, knew himself in danger,
but it is doubtful that Charles was aware just how long it was to be
before he would return to his role at court. The arrest was politically
sensitive, and the King feared both a rising in Fouquet's favour by
the Parisians and the disappearance of key documents, vulnerable
to destruction by Fouquet's friends. While steps could be – and
were – taken to secure the papers, Louis nevertheless needed to feel
that Fouquet was in secure hands. It seems that he could think of
no one better than Charles. Charles certainly knew Fouquet, but
the two men were not close, and Fouquet had no claim on him.
Moreover, Charles was well known for his unswerving loyalty to
King and kingdom, and had no part in court factions. He was an
ideal guardian, at least from Louis's point of view.

Prisoner and guardian arrived at Angers on 7 September. Charles
now had the responsibility of installing his musketeers in their new
guard posts, and ensuring that the lodgings for the prisoner were
satisfactory. In addition to Fouquet, there were two of his household
– his valet, La Vallée, and his doctor, Pecquet. The château interior
was in poor condition, and Charles was put to considerable expense
in fitting out the rooms needed. The King had provided him with
money for the journey, but he soon found himself applying to
Colbert for further funds. Throughout his long tenure as jailer to
Fouquet, Charles was to be in regular correspondence with the

court, and his letters, concerned as they were with matters of state, have survived, providing us with a rare glimpse into his thoughts. His determination to perform his duties to the best of his ability is clear, but alongside this, he reveals a touching concern for the comfort and well-being of his prisoner. Fouquet might have been in disgrace, but he was also a fellow human being, and Charles never lost sight of that. His first letter, of 17 September, shows this: 'I am looking for a bed for him, that in which he sleeps not being satisfactory.'[41] Colbert sent him the money needed.

Another side of Charles is revealed by his letters. His education had been basic, and they reflect this. His handwriting was large and untidy. His spelling was erratic, although it should be remembered that spelling was not standardised at the period. Most notable, however, is that his letters demonstrate his Gascon origins clearly. He had lived his entire adult life away from Lupiac, yet his letters show that he had not lost his Gascon accent. Gascon pronunciation gave 'b' for 'v' and 'g' for 'c': Charles's letters, spelled phonetically, show that he had not adapted his manner of speech to that of the court. His situation alongside Fouquet was both delicate and important, yet his correspondence gives us another piece of information: Charles the soldier hated to write letters and sent them less frequently than Colbert and the King wished. It seems they were a chore to him, and one he put off until it was unavoidable.

Another prisoner was shortly added to his responsibilities. This was Paul Pellisson, a poet and close associate of Fouquet, who had been arrested on the same day at Nantes. Charles sent a troop of his musketeers to fetch him and escort him to Angers. This achieved, the King then ordered Charles to bring both Fouquet and Pellisson to Amboise, where Fouquet should remain under the guard of Talhouët, an ensign in the royal bodyguard. Charles was to continue with Pellisson to Paris, where the latter was to be delivered to the Bastille. Charles must have hoped that this would mark an end to his service as jailer and a return to normal duties – and perhaps a chance to persuade his wife to come back? He was soon to be disappointed. The convoy left Angers on 1 December. It was not an easy journey: angry crowds gathered along the route and mobbed the carriage to the extent that Charles feared the prisoners might be injured or even killed. His musketeers faced severe difficulties forcing their way through the people and clearing a route, as well as guarding the prisoners. The problems were so great at the city of Tours, where they arrived on 3 December, that Charles took the decision to cut short their overnight rest, and to depart at 3 o'clock in the morning. As a result they arrived at Amboise before it was fully day, and Charles was able, no doubt with relief, to install Fouquet in his new prison and into the charge of Talhouët. The remainder of the journey passed off more quietly, and Charles delivered Pellisson to the Bastille on 12 December.

He was to have less than a month before finding himself once again guarding Fouquet. Talhouët proved unsatisfactory: he had taken Fouquet to the prison at Vincennes in late December, but proved unable to get on with the guard lieutenant in charge there, Marsac. On 3 January 1662, the King ordered Charles to take over. He arrived at Vincennes with his musketeers the following day. Fouquet, at least, was probably pleased to see him: Talhouët had proved to be a far less considerate captor.

The legal process against Fouquet was by now under way, and in March two commissioners arrived, with their secretary, to begin his interrogation. Around the same time, certain privileges were accorded to the prisoner. At Charles's request he was permitted to hear Mass daily. He was allowed to write to his wife, under Charles's supervision, and, once the weather improved, to walk on the terrace of the castle in Charles's company. In June, he received the right to prepare his defence. Charles was responsible for all his needs, from food to ink and paper to clothing, and received funds every four months to provide for these. There survives a steady stream of letters and orders concerning this, most dealing with details which, for Charles, must have made a wearing routine.

In October, Fouquet was granted permission to receive lawyers to assist in his defence. This made for difficulties. The King ordered Charles to be present at all their deliberations, conflicting with the lawyers' desire to maintain confidentiality. They came up with a solution: Charles would not be in the room, but the lawyers would speak loudly, 'their very advanced age having made hearing a little difficult'.[42]

By now, his task of jailer, which had lasted well over a year, must have weighed heavily upon Charles. He might not leave his post, effectively cutting him off from his shaky marriage, his young sons, and from the military duties he loved. The job made him vulnerable: Fouquet continued to have many supporters, and there were persistent rumours that these were managing to keep Fouquet up to date with all new events at court and capital, that he was able to maintain regular clandestine correspondence with his allies and so forth. All such rumours touched upon Charles's efficacy as guardian and threatened to undermine the trust of the King and Colbert. His anxiety is plain from letters he addressed to the court, assuring them that he was taking all measures possible to prevent such things from happening.[43] He rapidly received reassurance that the King was fully aware that this was a matter of rumour and not of fact. Nevertheless, the volatile political circumstances of the times made for an uncomfortable environment for Charles, a man who preferred action over intrigue.

In June 1663, Fouquet was moved again, this time to the Bastille. Charles may well have hoped that this would put a term to his own service. The Bastille had its own governor, Besmaux, his former colleague. But Louis did not trust Besmaux, who had been a friend of Fouquet, and ordered Charles to take up residence in the prison alongside his prisoner.[44] He slept in an adjacent room, and the musketeers were set to provide a special guard for Fouquet, in addition to the prison's normal arrangements. It was a monotonous routine for all concerned. They remained at the Bastille until the summer of the following year. The King was moving to Fontainebleau, but he wished for the process against Fouquet to continue under his eye. Charles was sent to inspect the château at nearby Moret-sur-Loing to ensure that it was suitably secure. He found it satisfactory, and he escorted Fouquet there in June 1664. He had now been serving as jailer for almost four years. The letters that he wrote during this time bear testament to the care and thoroughness which he brought to this duty, despite its wearing nature. The King had nothing to complain about in his loyalty, trustworthiness and honesty. Everything was arranged effectively and openly, from the supplying of food to the prisoner – and Charles was also responsible for organising all these household details – to the details of security. Perhaps that was why, during the summer of 1664, he was granted some small relief from his duties: the King granted him leave to come to Fontainebleau when he wished and spend time at court. This relaxation lasted only for two months, but it was doubtless very welcome to him.

When the King returned to the capital, his prisoner was obliged to follow. By now, relations between Fouquet and Charles were marked by mutual respect and appreciation. Fouquet valued Charles's discretion and consideration, while Charles seems to have been struck by Fouquet's patience in adversity. The journey back to the Bastille occurred in August. Charles had been ordered not to stop: for once, he disobeyed. At Charenton, he permitted a break to allow Fouquet a brief reunion with his wife and children: the couple had not seen each other since September 1661. Perhaps Charles was thinking of his own wife and family, whom he, likewise, had not seen since the arrest. He might do nothing on his own account, but he was able to provide this short meeting for his prisoner.

Back at the Bastille, the familiar routine resumed. Charles visited his prisoner daily to find out if he had any requirements or wishes, and to check on his health. He would then escort him to meet with the representatives of the court. Charles also had to order the food for the day and arrange which dishes would be served. The governor of the Bastille, Besmaux, was disgruntled by the fact that he had not been trusted with the guardianship of Fouquet within the Bastille, and Charles also had to deal with this. Tact was not his strong point – a characteristic which had become more noticeable as he aged. He and Besmaux seem to have been on reasonable terms beforehand, but in the Bastille, relations rapidly cooled. The two men avoided each other, and engaged in a rather childish rivalry over dinner invitations to the magistrates and clerks.[45]

The final interrogations of Fouquet were to take place not at the Bastille, but nearby in the Petit Arsenal. Charles and fifty musketeers accompanied Fouquet on these short journeys, often made on foot. On at least one occasion, on 27 November 1664, a number of Fouquet's female supporters, including the renowned letter-writer Madame de Sévigny, went to watch Fouquet pass. She subsequently wrote:

> Monsieur d'Artagnan was next to him; fifty musketeers were behind by thirty or forty paces. He [Fouquet] seemed quite pre-occupied. As for me, when I saw him, my legs trembled and my heart beat so loudly that I could do nothing more. Approaching us in order to return to his prison, Monsieur d'Artagnan nudged him and pointed out to him that we were there.[46]

Her memory provides us with a brief glimpse of Charles at work, maintaining his vigilance, yet, at the same time, retaining his consideration for the prisoner.

The interrogations reached an end in early December. A few days later, a comet appeared over Paris. Some people saw it as a good omen for Fouquet. Perhaps Charles did, too: his sympathies for his prisoner seem to have grown slowly over their long association. Certainly, he woke Fouquet in the small hours to take him up onto the roof of the Chapel Tower in order to see the comet overhead. It seemed at first that the optimists were correct. The Chamber of Justice announced its sentence on Fouquet on 20 December. It was to be banishment. It was far more lenient that it might have been, and offered Fouquet the chance to live out his life with his family somewhere outside French borders. He might even be able to communicate with his friends and hope once again to influence events in France. Louis XIV was displeased: the Chamber had convicted Fouquet of what amounted to administrative malpractice, but the accusations had been far more serious.[47] The King interfered in the process of justice and had the sentence amended to lifetime solitary confinement. The prison was to be the fortress of Pinerolo in the Italian Alps, at the time a possession of France. Charles was asked to recommend a guardian, and nominated one of his senior musketeers, Bénigne Dauvergne, Comte de Saint-Mars.[48] Charles must have hoped that his own service as jailer was finally over.

He was once again to be disappointed. Saint-Mars was to take charge at Pinerolo, but Louis was not yet ready to dispense with the vigilance and experience of Charles. Pinerolo was a long way from

Paris, but Charles was ordered to escort Fouquet for this final journey. He was not happy. Olivier Lefèvre d'Ormesson, a councillor
to the *parlement*, who reported on the process against Fouquet, met
him at the Bastille on the morning of 22 December and observed
'He seemed morose about the journey which he was being made
to make to Pinerolo, from which he might have been spared.'[49]

It was a difficult day for Charles. He was obliged to separate
Fouquet from his valet and personal doctor, who had remained
with him since his arrest. These two were highly anxious, having no
idea as to what was due to happen to their master: it fell to Charles
to reassure them. Meanwhile, Fouquet was informed of his revised
sentence. The sentence was pronounced at around ten in the morning: the departure was scheduled for eleven. Fouquet was not to be
permitted to see his family before his departure. The sole familiar
faces were those of the musketeers, and in particular, Charles.

Charles likewise was given no chance to make any farewells. Who
was there that he might have visited? His wife remained at Châlon
with their two sons. There were friends, no doubt, although some
must have been amongst the ranks of musketeers who were to travel
with him. We know he felt guilty that he failed to pay a duty call on
Colbert, to whom he sent his apologies from Fontainebleau the following day. It seems that Charles, no less than Fouquet, had become
increasingly cut off from the world since September 1661. He could
take comfort from one thing, however: unlike Fouquet, he was not
condemned to remain at Pinerolo for the rest of his days.

They had a large distance to cover, and it was mid-winter.
Nevertheless, they made good time. Despite his dislike for writing, Charles sent full details of their progress to the King and his
ministers. Some of the details are sad. Madame Fouquet had written to her husband, but Charles had been unable to pass on her
letter: it was forbidden. At Grenoble, a local official refused entry
to the advance guard of the convoy, citing as grounds their lack of
a royal safe conduct. Charles, exasperated, had the man thrown into
prison for a day. The King approved. A few days later, at Gap, the
local consuls went to the other extreme, offering Charles a gift of
wine and giving him their personal escort to his lodgings.[50] It was
11 January 1656: they had covered the ground from Paris in twenty

days, but the worst section lay ahead. The Alps were snow-covered
and treacherous. They travelled in careful stages, Charles having
ensured that their arrival was notified in advance to each stopping
point. Five days later, on 16 January, they finally reached Pinerolo.
Fouquet's new jailer, Saint-Mars, was there ahead of them. Charles
inspected the new prison, and Fouquet was installed. He was to
remain there until his death in 1680.[51] Saint-Mars was ordered to
keep him under the régime created by Charles. We have no details
of any farewell between former jailer and prisoner. We do know
that works on the prison proceeded slowly, due to the weather.
We know also that Charles did not stay long. Perhaps the weather
helped hasten his departure, or perhaps he could support his own
quasi-imprisonment no longer. The town of Pinerolo had fêted him
as a grand personage, but not even such marks of respect could make
him linger. He had duties to return to with his musketeers. And
events at court were threatening his position, despite the fact that
the King was highly pleased with how well he had accomplished
his duty as jailer.

Charles was sub-lieutenant of the first company of musketeers.
In 1660, Mazarin had given to Louis a second musketeer company. Originally, the captain-lieutenant of the second company was
Monsieur de Marsac, but in January 1665 Colbert succeeded in
obtaining this position for his brother, Édouard-François Colbert
de Vandières, Comte de Maulévrier. At this point, Louis decided
to reorganise the second company and make it part of the royal
military household, alongside the first company. Henceforth, the
second company was known as the 'Little' or 'Black' musketeers,
to distinguish from the first – the 'Great' or 'Grey' musketeers.[52]
Moreover, Colbert wished for his brother to have overall precedence over both companies of musketeers, a status which accrued
to Charles, as the deputy of Nevers. Colbert was already working on
Nevers to surrender his office, but as yet had failed to find a suitable
alternative to offer him in replacement. A further complication was
created by the fact that it was known that Charles was unlikely to
accept anyone other than the hands-off Nevers over him: the King
was well aware of this and made it plain he would not have Charles
inconvenienced. But Colbert was determined, and took advantage

of Charles's absence. On 28 January, while Charles was still on his way back from Pinerolo, a review of both companies was held, and Maulévrier marched at their head. It was a worrying precedent. A rumour began to circulate that Maulévrier was to be given command of both companies, while Charles was to be pensioned off with the governorship of a town.

Colbert was ambitious for himself and his family. It has been suggested that his manoeuvrings against Charles were also rooted in some personal dislike, probably arising from the Fouquet affair. He may have taken Charles's concern for the prisoner amiss, and suspected him of becoming too much a partisan of the fallen minister.[53] If so, however, Colbert was not willing to take his designs too far, and subsequently his relations with Charles were harmonious. Furthermore, the King was not in favour of this scheme. Before the review, Minister Le Tellier had written to Charles informing him of the formation of the second company and assuring him of his own precedence over both companies. Perhaps Louis sought to undermine Colbert's scheme? A decision was made that ensured Charles would remain the overall commander: the King separated the grade of captain-lieutenant of the first company from its responsibilities – including overall precedence – and conferred these specifically upon the sub-lieutenant. Thanks to Louis's appreciation of him – and thus to his own loyalty and faithful service – Charles emerged triumphant over the schemes of Colbert.

Thus, on returning, Charles found his military duties expanded. A certain rivalry grew up between the two companies of musketeers, above all concerning the splendour of their appearance, which had serious financial consequences. Maulévrier was far wealthier than him, and was able to make a considerable show. Charles's own military stipend was far from adequate to meet such demands, yet, as commander, it was his responsibility to ensure that the appearance of his men was superb.

The musketeers were very much the fashion: the King favoured them greatly, and a place in their ranks was considered a key stepping stone on the route to a successful military career. Charles Castelmore d'Artagnan, a younger son of a poor Gascon landholder of dubious nobility, had under his command scions of some of the highest families in the land. He was a familiar and respected figure both at court and in Paris and enjoyed the confidence of the King, all without compromising his origins or his marked accent. His activities – reviews, parades, escorts – with his musketeers were remarked upon frequently by the *Gazette de France*. Such displays were expensive and Charles ended up in such financial straits that the King noticed. In May 1667, Louis arranged for him to receive 10,000 *livres* from the war fund as an advance to pay for the expenses of his company – for one month.[54]

Why was being sub-lieutenant of musketeers so costly? The answer lies in the practices of the time. The state paid soldiers a wage, but it did not pay for the main part of their costumes and equipment. Each man was expected to supply these from his own resources. Should anyone be lacking the necessary funds, the commander was their first recourse. For Charles, it was a matter of honour to assist his men when needed. The rivalry between the two companies led to an escalation of display and elaboration, moreover, which increased the expense: a simple matter for the rich Maulévrier, but a worrying burden for Charles. That the King was ready to help him in turn speaks volumes for the bond that had grown between them.

Certainly, he can have had no hope of obtaining assistance from his wife. It had been something over five years since he had even seen her, and the marriage was shaky. His new duties seem to have put a final seal upon it. On 16 April 1665, frugal Charlotte signed an act of renunciation of her marital community of goods with Charles. All mutual financial connection between them was ended, and with it, the marriage itself was as good as over. All that remained were their two sons – and we have no evidence at all as to whether Charles even tried to maintain contact with them – and their legal status as married. Neither might remarry, but apart from that, they were publicly separated. Such a situation was by no means unusual, and no stigma was attached to Charles as a result. He and Charlotte had had little enough time together even at the beginning of their marriage, and Charles's long absence had served only to reinforce his existing habits of solitary living. It is doubtful that he missed her.

His musketeers served in many ways as his family. He remained close to his men even while guarding Fouquet, and is recorded on several occasions as acting as godparent both to the children of his current and former soldiers and even to the soldiers themselves.[55] Additionally, at least one of his kinsmen was a musketeer under him. This was his younger maternal cousin Pierre de Montesquiou d'Artagnan, to whom he was both friend and patron. This Pierre was sometimes known as 'Little d'Artagnan', a comment not on his height but to distinguish him from the better-known Charles. The court of Louis XIV in the 1660s was a lively and eventful place, moreover: quite aside from his duties, Charles was seldom at a loss to occupy himself.

The musketeers also retained their role as an effective active force. March and April of 1665 passed in parades, but in May one company – which is unclear – was sent to the Vendômois region to assist in suppressing an anti-taxation revolt. It was unpleasant work, as many of the rebels were poor, untrained and desperate. Despite this, they succeeded in giving the musketeers who were sent there a nasty shock, driving them back when they attempted to assist officials trying to gather taxes. It is tempting to hope that it was Maulévrier's company – after all, as the brother of the fiscal reformer Colbert he was perhaps more likely to have been chosen where taxes were at stake. Perhaps, too, Colbert might have wondered whether Charles, himself relatively poor, might be tempted to leniency. On the other hand, Charles's loyalty and obedience to royal commands were unquestionable. The surviving evidence provides no grounds for knowing either way.

In the autumn of 1665, war broke out close to the borders of France. Charles II attacked the United Provinces – those parts of the Low Countries which were independent of Spain – in alliance with the bishop of Munster, Bernard von Galen. The conflict had begun as a naval affair, but the involvement of the bishop brought a land dimension also, and the United Provinces, who had only a small force available to them, called upon the French for aid. There had been an alliance between the two countries since the sixteenth century, based upon common hostility to Spain, whose territories of the Spanish Netherlands lay between them. In October, Louis sent an army under the command of Lieutenant General François de Pradel. It was made up of 4,000 infantry and 2,000 cavalry – amongst the latter 500 musketeers drawn from the ranks of the two companies of musketeers.[56] Both Charles and his opposite number Maulévrier were included in the expeditionary force. It arrived at Maastricht, which had been provisioned to receive it, on 26 October. Joining up with the forces of the United Provinces in November, the armies launched a number of attacks against the forces of the bishop of Munster. The companies from Louis's royal household – which included the musketeers – were placed in the vanguard. The bishop's forces proved evasive, but the French were able to capture a number of them after a short siege at Loken. The musketeers played a key role in breaking the siege: with Charles at their head, they rode close to the ditches that guarded the village, carrying the *fascines*[57] necessary to allow the foot-soldiers to gain entry. After Loken, they took a number of other villages nearby as well. Charles was doubtless satisfied with the performance of his men: he received the congratulations of the King.[58]

It was now close to winter, and conditions were becoming inhospitable. The bishop's men had followed a policy of destroying the countryside as they passed through it, which had serious provisioning implications not only for the local inhabitants but also for the French army. The result was a number of disagreeable incidents in which French troops resorted to plunder. The King was not pleased, and addressed stern letters to all the commanders, including Charles. Shortly afterwards, the weather became too severe to permit the campaign to continue, and the French withdrew to winter quarters. The musketeers were sent to Rheinberg, where they were made welcome. Charles ensured that they treated the townspeople well, and maintained excellent discipline.[59] At one point the district in which his men were quartered caught fire: Charles contributed to the fund for the payment of damages. The peaceful winter was followed by a peaceful spring, for the first company of musketeers at least. A peace was signed between the bishop of Munster and the United Provinces on 19 April 1666, before Charles and his men had seen any new action. The musketeers returned to Paris, where they were given a triumphal welcome at Fontainebleau by the court. The

King was very pleased with their performance and especially that of Charles:'Monsieur d'Artagan, wise and valiant/Was received with a gracious air' wrote the poet La Gravettte de Mayolas.[60] A summer of renewed parades and reviews followed.

Charles had served Louis loyally and well, and the King was sensible of this. It seems he wished to make his gratitude tangible. In September 1666 a valuable sinecure at court fell vacant, the office of Captain of Deerhounds. It carried an income, which would doubtless be useful, but subsequent events suggest a plot between King and musketeer to allow the former to reform his household. Charles resigned the post within three weeks; the King converted it into two lieutenancies concerned with hunting, and conferred one upon the Marquis de Raré, who had already been in negotiations with Charles over the captaincy. Perhaps Charles received a financial reward, too — it would be nothing unusual for the period.

Charles may also have been aware that a greater reward was now upon the horizon. Nevers had remained captain-lieutenant of the first company of musketeers since its re-formation in 1657, yet he had never developed any interest in the regiment or indeed in any military matter. He had spent much of his time in his homeland of Italy, and thus had had minimal contact with the men he supposedly commanded. Early in 1667, he finally resigned. A large number of potential replacements was put forward, many influential, most backed by one or other of the leading statesmen of the court. The King ignored them all, and bestowed it upon Charles. After nearly nine years as sub-lieutenant and *de facto* commander of the first company, he had finally achieved the rank to go with the duty, and equalled his former captain and fellow Gascon Tréville. On 22 January, Louis held a large fête at Houilles. In front of his entire company, Charles was formally installed as captain-lieutenant. His sub-lieutenant was to be Jean-Louis Castéra de la Rivière, one of his cousins. His elevation to captain-lieutenant was a notable event, widely reported, not only by the *Gazette de France,* but also by poets and writers of contemporary chronicles.[61]

Around this time he also began using the title 'Comte d'Artagnan', to which he had no real right. It was acceptable to King and court, however, and official documents henceforth refer to him thus.

The new captain-lieutenant and his company passed the rest of the winter peacefully, participating in numerous splendid reviews as well as continuing with their normal duties. These parades and mock battles served not simply to entertain the court, but also to impress upon rival states the military might of France.

Louis was about to go to war. There had long been a rivalry between France and Spain, and tensions were frequent. His marriage to Maria-Theresa had been intended to ease these and to bring about a new era of peaceful co-existence. But the mutual hostility was too deep-rooted and a marriage tie was no check to Louis's ambitions to expand both his borders and his sphere of influence. Events in Spain in the second half of the 1660s now provided him with an excuse to recommence hostilities. His grounds lay in the very marriage contract which had been intended to create peace.

The Spanish King Philip IV had died on 17 September, and his son and heir, Carlos II, was underage and in very poor health. He was not expected to live long. Moreover, he was Philip's son by his second marriage, to Marie-Anne of Austria. Louis's wife Maria-Theresa was Philip's eldest daughter by his first wife, the French princess (Louis's aunt), Elizabeth. The marriage contract between Louis and Maria-Theresa had stipulated that she renounced any claim that she might have to the Spanish throne, but this was supposed to be in return for a dowry payment of 500,000 golden *écus*, a vast sum, due to be handed over within eighteen months of the wedding. The payment had never been made. Louis now chose to make an issue of this.

Spain still held considerable territory in what is now Belgium, Luxembourg and the Netherlands, and these lands abutted on France to the north-west. Louis felt his border in this area was insufficiently fortified, and sought to extend his lands there and annex certain key towns and regions. He was aware, too, that lands belonging to Spain lay close to France on most of its borders, and this he considered to be an ongoing threat. He argued that, in default of the 500,000 *écus*, his wife was due land from the Spanish crown. Certain areas of the Low Countries held to an ancient Brabantine law, the law of devolution, by which female heirs of a first marriage preceded their male siblings by any second marriage as far as inheritance was concerned. Under this law, Louis argued, he was owed territory in the Low Countries by Carlos II. His lawyers sent a document developing this argument to the Spanish court in early May 1667.

The campaign began in May 1667. The King accompanied his army. It had almost the air of a pleasure trip: Louis took with him not only the Queen, but his two mistresses, the rising star Athénäis de Montespan and the fading Louise de la Vallière.[62] Overall command of the army was given to Marshal Turenne. Charles was appointed as cavalry brigadier, with five squadrons under him, including both companies of musketeers.[63] The army reached Amiens on 20 May, where the King set up camp. It was not long before fighting began.

Charles and his musketeers were in the thick of it from the start. The attack opened at Armentières. Charles and his men marched through the night to nearby Arras from where they joined the fighting. Armentières was defended by a small Spanish force, which chose to retreat. The French rapidly overran the town, and its commander was taken prisoner. A French garrison was installed, and Charles rejoined the main army. It was 24 May. On 2 June, Charleroi fell, without any conflict at all. The heavily fortified town of Tournai presented a more difficult target. The French army was divided: on 17 June one part, under Turenne, marched from the town on the Brussels side. Charles was sent with a smaller detachment to Arras, where he joined up with mercenary reinforcements under François-Marie de Lillebonne, Prince of Lorraine. This second part then moved on Tournai from the other direction, blocking its lines of retreat. By 21 June, the town was surrounded by the French. Charles and his men found themselves camped opposite the Saint Mark gate, on the left bank of the River Escaut. The King himself came to inspect their arrangements. As Charles was showing him the guard-posts, cannon were fired from the town, killing several horses being ridden by members of the King's entourage. Louis remained calm, despite the alarm of his officers. Accompanied by his captain of musketeers, he was confident of his safety, and continued his inspection.

Throughout the following day, the French made a series of attacks. A counter-attack by the defenders in the early hours of 23 June was repelled, and later that day a number of leading townsfolk came to Louis to sue for terms. They promised to surrender if the King would guarantee to uphold the existing privileges of the town. Louis agreed, but the town governor continued to offer resistance. A brief French bombardment accompanied by pressure from the towns-people rapidly changed his opinion. On 24 June, Tournai opened its gates. Charles and his men had distinguished themselves by their efficiency, and on 25 June they escorted the King as he made his formal entry to the town.

The next goal was Douai. Once again, the army was divided, and once again Charles found himself leading part of the force designed to cut off the enemy line of retreat. While the main army proceeded from the Cambrai direction, Charles, his musketeers and four other brigades crossed the River Scarpe by night and encircled the town from the direction of Condé. Douai was another fortified town: the French invested it on 2 July and a two-day siege ensued. The musketeers were granted two days to recover from their night manoeuvres. On 5 July, they rejoined the fighting. To the sound of their own tambours and fifes, the musketeers charged over the trenches, taking the counterscarp, crossing the ditch, and driving the defenders from a *demi-lune* to plant their own flags on the advance works of the fortifications. The noise of their musicians combined with their coolness under fire terrified the defenders: as the musketeers entered the town itself, the inhabitants fled. Douai surrendered the next day, largely due to the heroics of Charles and his men.

This victory was followed, for Charles, by a respite from fighting of two or three weeks. The King, accompanied by his captain-lieutenant, took a break to inspect certain of his new properties and to rendezvous with the Queen and court ladies.[64] By now, the Spanish had marshalled larger forces against the aggressors, but the existing line of French conquests now formed a formidable barrier. In late July, Louis set his sights on the strongest town of the region: Lille. Both a trade centre and a key military location, Lille was a highly desirable prize for both sides, and the Spanish were anxious to retain it. The town was well garrisoned: 2,000 soldiers, around 100 cannon, and well-armed townsmen, all under the command of an experienced captain, Spinola. It was well equipped to withstand a siege, with its fine defences and provisions for up to a year.

Charles found himself stationed in the Fives district, with his musketeers plus his brigade, now made up of two regiments of royal guards of the body, the regiments of Enghien and Monaco, and the Queen's light horse. The besieging army began to build their own fortifications to protect their positions, under the direction of a rising young military engineer, Sébastien Le Prestre de Vauban. It was Charles's first experience of Vauban and his team: no evidence survives as to their relations at this point, but engineers were to form a noticeable part of his life in the future. Later events may suggest that his initial impressions were less than favourable. Perhaps, man of action that he was, he preferred less defensive styles of warfare. Perhaps the activities of the engineers inconvenienced him as he went about his duties. Perhaps he felt their activities delayed the attack. Given his later relations with Vauban, however, one gathers the impression that Charles regarded the engineers with a certain degree of impatience. The digging of trenches – fifteen miles in total – and construction of defences went on for most of the first part of August, while Charles's soldiers mounted guard and protected the King, who continued to travel about the camp visiting the men.[65]

The area around the Fives gate was to be the first place of attack. Vauban and his men opened trenches to either side. The garrison of Lille responded by making a sortie on 19 August. Charles was ready for them: together with a battalion of Swiss guard, two extra guard regiments and several units of cavalry, he and his brigade drove them back, and held on to his position through a night of bombardment. Further sorties and heavy firing continued throughout the next two days, and Charles and his brigade were able to advance closer to the Fives gate and its guardian bastion, guarding the lines of advance. Cannon were moved up to support them and to threaten the town fortifications. On the night of 24 August, the French took the counterscarp and made a first assault on the *demi-lune*, briefly taking it. The following night was chosen for the final attack.

The musketeers played a principal role in this assault. While the main infantry force attacked the front of the strong *demi-lune* that protected the gate, men from the two musketeer companies attacked its sides, one from the right, the other from the left. They were commanded by Montbrun, lieutenant from the second company. Charles was supposed to remain in reserve with the rest of the companies. He did not. Around ten o'clock in the evening he left his reserves and flung himself into the thick of the fighting, restless with inaction and unwilling to allow his men to face dangers without him. Perhaps he sought to further their efforts and encourage them to higher achievement through his presence. He was apparently unarmed — one hopes he rapidly picked up something with which to defend himself. As a result, he received a minor wound, but no reprimand was forthcoming. For a man probably aged around fifty, it was no mean feat. The swashbuckling bravery of his Gascon heritage had not deserted him, nor had he grown in caution as he had in experience.

The defenders were greatly alarmed by the ferocity of the attack. The governor of Lille wished to continue its defence, but the leading townsmen were now arrayed against him. A group of burghers were sent to Louis to negotiate for surrender. Formal capitulation was made the following night, with Louis guaranteeing to the town its traditional rights and freedoms. The garrison and governor were permitted to leave, and Louis made his entry to his new possession on 28 August. Charles accompanied him at the head of the musketeers.

Lille was a key capture, but the campaign was not yet over. Spanish reinforcements under the Comte de Marsin had arrived nearby. The King now dispatched part of his army to block the Spanish advance. The Marquis de Bellefonds had been sent to secure the area around the Bruges canal: Charles's brigade accompanied him. On the night of 29 August, the Spanish troops marched straight into those of the French, already arrayed for battle. One of the French commanders, Créqui, was seriously injured in the fighting, but the result was a French victory and a Spanish rout. The encounter put an effective end to the campaign for the season, and Louis returned to Paris, via some of his new conquests, including Lille and Arras. The campaign had been a resounding success in French eyes and the King was everywhere received as a hero. For Charles it was a return to his regular peace-time duties and to the round of parades and reviews.

Hostilities resumed early in 1668. The political map had changed somewhat over the preceding months. French success in Flanders had alarmed the Netherlands, and they had signed a peace with the English (with whom they had continued fighting during 1667). Sweden, formerly an ally of France, now joined with the Dutch and the English in what is known as the Triple Alliance against Louis. Meanwhile, Louis had been preparing to move against others on his borders. Franche-Comté, now the area to the north and east of Lyons, was at the time not fully part of France. While Louis had been occupied in Flanders, his representative in Franche-Comté, the Prince of Condé, had been engaged in negotiations with the Comtois on behalf of the crown. The ostensible purpose of this was to ensure that Franche-Comté remain neutral, but it was in fact a blind. Louis intended to conquer the area, and secure yet another route against possible Spanish attack. Under cover of the talks, Condé raised an army for this purpose. In February 1668, he invaded Franche-Comté. Charles was with him, commanding a combined force of the musketeers and dragoons. The first goal was the capture of the town of Besançon, which surrendered without a fight on 6 February. On 9 February, the French army laid siege to the region's capital, Dôle. The musketeers led the attack, with two guard regiments. They rapidly overran the town's defences and it surrendered on 10 February. Within a few days all remaining resistance had been overcome and Louis was master of Franche-Comté after only twelve days of campaigning.

In May, a treaty – that of Aix-la-Chapelle – was signed between France and the powers in the Low Countries. Louis was in a strong negotiating position: he was able to use Franche-Comté as a bargaining chip, and in return for surrendering it, he secured possession of Armentières, Tournai, Courtrai, Oudenarde, Douai, Lille, Charleroi and Bergues. He was now in place to create a strong defensive network along the north-east border of France. The French court celebrated with a summer of fêtes, plays and military reviews.

Charles was once again entirely occupied with regular duties; the peace was to endure until 1672. The King had not lost his taste for military parades and fake battles, and Charles must have spent much of 1668 and 1669 ensuring that his men were well drilled and presented. In addition to these duties, the musketeers continued to guard and to escort the King. The court was often on the move: Louis was in the process of building his grand palace at Versailles and thus had no settled place of residence. In 1670, he decided to take the Queen and his heir, the Dauphin, on a ceremonial tour of their new holdings in Flanders. They were inevitably accompanied by the great nobles of the court. Once again, it was a round of celebrations and formal entries. As on Louis's marriage trip, Charles was charged with maintaining the security of the royal family as they travelled from place to place and as they stayed in a variety of lodgings. It was potentially a more dangerous journey than that to the Spanish border: the inhabitants in the conquered territories were not uniformly content to be under French rule, and Charles could not be sure that an attempt might not be made on the King's life. The long procession reached Lille on 22 May 1670, and the musketeers paraded before the King and Queen as they made their grand entry. This tour once again served a double purpose: it reminded the inhabitants of the conquered territories of the might and glory of France, and it allowed Louis to inspect the new fortifications that he had had commenced under the direction of Vauban. It is likely that Charles accompanied the King as he toured the partly constructed new citadel at Lille. He would find himself there again, in even more trying circumstances.

King and court were enjoying the fruits of their power, but all was not well within France. The winter of 1670 had been unusually harsh, and had resulted in great hardship in many rural areas, especially for the poorest. The peasants already bore the bulk of taxation and the King's wars had been expensive. The combination of a bad winter, a poor spring and the continuing burden of taxes now led to a revolt in one of the worst-affected areas, the Vivarais – the territory around Villeneuve-de-Berg in Languedoc. A rumour had circulated in the area that the King intended to introduce new taxes, on clothing, on children and on labour. In late April, the peasants began to arm themselves and marched to the town of Aubenas, where a tax collector had recently arrived. The town was pillaged and the office-holders of other nearby towns began to demand military help from the governor of Languedoc. The rebels moved through the territory, plundering and burning as they went, and their numbers grew. On 23 May, the rebels arrived at Villeneuve-de-Berg, demanding to meet with representatives of the King. The governor was able to pacify them temporarily with various concessions. The situation was worrying, however, and despite the concessions, the rebels continued to roam and to pillage. At court, the minister Le Tellier, now Marquis de Louvois, decided that firm action was needed. He organised a military force of 4,600 men. Their commander was to be Le Bret: Charles was appointed as one of his two brigadiers and placed in charge of the cavalry. Both companies of musketeers were included. They were to be supported by local troops drawn up by the nobility of Languedoc, so that the total number was between 7,000 and 8,000.

For Charles, it must have been a difficult assignment. His opponents were not the soldiers he was used to fighting, but rather a jumble of untrained and inexperienced peasants, often also ill-equipped, and fighting out of desperation. Some of the lower gentry were also involved: men whose background was very similar to his own. He was close to Gascony, moreover; the local accent and habits may have been a painful reminder of his childhood. It is easy to imagine that his loyalty to King and duty was at war with his early memories, and the prospect of fighting such an ill-assorted and ill-prepared enemy may have compromised his sense of honour.

The presence of a large and well-armed army did not deter the rebels. Minor encounters between groups of the professional soldiers and rebels ended badly for the latter, until on 25 July the two sides met. It was less a battle than a rout: unpleasant work for Charles and his musketeers, conditioned as they were to seek glory and honour through the profession of arms. We know that at least one man under his orders, the musketeer and memorialist Pierre Quarré d'Aligny, felt sorry for the victims, referring to their leader de Roure as 'that poor general'.[66] It is perhaps surprising that of the 2,000 or so rebels, only around 130 were killed. A considerable number fled: perhaps the professional soldiers withheld their full might. Losses to the royal army were minimal – thirty-two. Most of the rebel leaders were captured. De Roure escaped, but was caught later in the year and executed. Those of his former followers who were also captured fared little better. The King would accept no excuses for resistance to his will, however good the reasons for opposition might be, and however pitiable. Charles and his men were obliged to remain in the region throughout most of the process of justice, to mop up remaining rebellion. The presence for several months of so many soldiers only served to increase the suffering of the local population: the army pillaged and plundered widely, destroying crops and seizing such food as there was. How did Charles behave during this time, and what did he think of the whole affair? We do not know. It was not a compassionate age, and the behaviour of soldiers was often highly reprehensible. It is likely that, however much Charles may have disdained the nature of his current employment, he considered that the rebels merited the treatment they received. He returned to court at the end of the summer, to make report to the King and to resume his usual duties. In spring 1671, he accompanied the King on a new tour of France's possessions in Flanders.

It was a very different court to that of Charles's youth. Louis XIII had preferred hunting and private occupations to lavish fêtes and celebrations. Richelieu had curbed extravagances. Louis XIV was a far different proposition: his was a glittering, young court, fond of pleasure and display, with the King at its centre. His mother, Anne of Austria, to whom Charles perhaps had once had a sentimental attachment, had died in January 1666. Queen Maria Theresa received little attention, but Louis's mistresses – first Louise de La Vallière, then Madame de Montespan – were courted and admired. Louis had continued his father and Richelieu's policy of keeping the great nobility away from major office, and encouraging them to look to him for advantage and favour, rather than trying to seize it as of right. His was a court in which a man might rise – or fall – according to royal attitude.

One such man was Antonin Nompar de Caumont, Comte de Lauzun. Lauzun, like Charles, was a Gascon. His family were minor, but well-connected, and he had made good use of this to establish himself at court. He was witty and clever and adept at extricating himself from trouble, but he was also ambitious and incautious, and after some years of favour, he had succeeded in offending the

King. Although considered physically ugly, he had enjoyed considerable success with the court ladies, and he sought to turn this to considerable advantage. He had been paying court to Louis's first cousin, Anne-Marie-Louise-Henriette de Bourbon, Duchess of Montpensier, known as 'La Grande Mademoiselle'. She was a considerable heiress, but her very proximity to the King, combined with the chequered record of her late father, Louis XIII's brother Gaston d'Orléans, had meant that none of the state marriages considered for her had come to anything. In 1671 she was forty. She was headstrong and confrontational, and known to be dissatisfied with her lot. Courting her was risky, but potentially very rewarding. How far Lauzun intended his courtship to go is unclear: what is clear is that La Grande Mademoiselle decided that she would marry him.

Lauzun had enemies at court, including Louvois and Madame de Montespan. He was also far from a suitable husband for the King's cousin. On 25 November 1671, the King had him arrested by the captain of bodyguards, Rochefort.[67] The following day, he was sent on the first stage of the long journey to Pinerolo. His escort and guardian was Charles, accompanied by 100 of his musketeers.

Charles certainly knew Lauzun: indeed, the two had quarrelled during spring 1670 over matters of military precedence and behaviour during the court tour of French Flanders.[68] They had reconciled only a few days before Lauzun's arrest, which must raise the question as to whether Charles had advance knowledge of Lauzun's imminent disgrace. He was not a man who liked to be at odds with his prisoners, and he was close to the King: perhaps he was ensuring that relations were smooth ahead of a duty which would require tact and care? We do not know, but it seems possible. As escort, Charles behaved with dignity and grace towards his prisoner. As when he made the same journey with Fouquet, Charles ensured that their arrival was expected at each nightly destination, and took careful precautions in all circumstances. Charles was treated with great respect by local officials: at Gap, which they reached on 14 December, he was formally greeted by the governor and consuls of the town. At Briançon, he received almost a festival welcome in the main square, and was presented with four bottles of good wine. Much of this attention was directed to him as representative of the

King, but it was highly gratifying to the proud captain of musketeers. They arrived at Pinerolo early on the evening of 19 December.
Charles inspected the new residence prepared for his prisoner, and
dispatched a messenger to inform the King of their safe arrival. He
did not see Fouquet, although he had the chance to talk with the
prison governor, Saint-Mars. The messenger he sent was his cousin,
Pierre de Montesquiou d'Artagnan, 'little d'Artagnan', who had
been one of the officers of the escort, travelling with Charles and
Lauzun in the carriage. He was thus in a good position to inform
Louis of all the details of Lauzun's demeanour, behaviour, and even,
perhaps, conversation. Charles himself set off a few days later, reach-
ing court sometime in January 1672. La Grande Mademoiselle had
already questioned Pierre about Lauzun; now she took the chance
to speak with Charles. He reassured her as to Lauzun's health and
well-being, and dealt with considerable sensitivity with the fact that
Lauzun had sent her no message. Her account of their conversation
shows that Charles, often abrupt in his dealings, could nevertheless
sometimes be gentle – a side of him also displayed in his relations
with Fouquet.[69]

Charles was once again at court, pursuing his regular peacetime
duties, but another disruption was looming. Louis was once again
about to go to war, this time against the Dutch.[70] Once again, he had
an eye to increasing his lands and strengthening his frontier. There
was also an issue of royal pride. Louis felt personally offended by the
Triple Alliance and desired to punish the Dutch for breaking their
former closeness to France. He succeeded in detaching the English
from the Triple Alliance with a judicious mixture of bribery and
influence, and in March 1672 England launched a naval attack on a
Dutch convoy. On 6 April, France declared war. Charles was made
marshal of the camp of the royal army, but before he could march
with his musketeers, he found himself presented with an entirely
new set of responsibilities.

Louis had installed as governor in Lille Louis de Crevant, Marquis
d'Humières and Marshal of France. Humières was an effective
governor, but early in 1672 he succeeded in incurring the displeasure of the King. In overall control of the army Louis had placed
the distinguished Marshal Turenne. Humières, along with several

others of the marshals of France, refused to serve under Turenne
on grounds of protocol. Technically, they possessed the same rank
as Turenne and should not be subordinated to him. At this period,
rank and precedence were of great personal importance: Humières
and his colleagues had chosen, essentially, to take offence.[71] There
may also have been issues of jealousy and perhaps some resentment
that Turenne, who had had a somewhat chequered past, had now
achieved such glory.[72] Their resistance, in turn, offended the King,
who ordered all the objectors to retire to their lands and reflect
upon their conduct. This left Lille, a key fortress in Louis's strategy
in Flanders, without a governor. Someone of unquestionable loyalty
and trustworthiness was required: Louis once again called upon his
captain of musketeers.

For Charles, this was undoubtedly an honour and a clear sign of
how high he had risen from his lower-gentry origins. But it was
probably also something of a mixed blessing. As we have seen, his
heart lay with the army. War offered great chances not only for acts
of personal heroism but also for his beloved musketeers to shine. In
Lille, he would be performing an important duty, but he would be
separated from his regiment, and far from active service. He must,
as well, have remembered the months after the sentencing and
final imprisonment of Fouquet, when court gossip had hinted he
was to be pensioned off with a governorship. This current mission
might turn into the beginning of an attempt to push him into
retirement.

He arrived in Lille in early May, while his musketeers accompanied the royal army. This new office was unlike anything he had
previously undertaken: he would be dealing not with military men
and high court ministers, but with the office-holders and leading
citizens of a wealthy town. He would be dealing with unfamiliar
rights and customs, much of the local population was not well-
disposed to France and French interests, and Flemish was spoken
alongside French. The local accent was probably difficult for him,
and his own Gascon accent probably presented problems for the
townspeople. Charles had been amongst the besiegers of the town
and had played a noted part in its capture. He would have to manage
a staff of a far different nature to that to which he was accustomed.

He would have to deal with outside officials, also – those responsible for the finances, administrations and defence of the region. The town was in the process of being re-fortified, and there was a resident group of French engineers who looked to Vauban for their commands and were thus outside the regular town hierarchy. The governorship was a post requiring reserves of diplomacy and tact, as well as skill in negotiating the complex waters of local politics. Charles could be sensitive and careful in his dealings with individuals for whom he felt sympathy, and his devotion to the King was above question, but he was no politician, he was impatient, and he was frequently not tactful. It is impossible not to wonder why he was chosen for this role: perhaps Colbert, never well disposed towards him, had influenced the King, nursing a private hope that Charles would embarrass himself in some way. Certainly, Charles was out of his depth. He may have longed for his brother Paul, who had been governor of the small Gascon town of Navarrenx since May 1667, and would thus have valuable experience and advice to offer.

The months in which Charles was governor provide us with our richest record of his actions, ideas and feelings. Over the years, he had become more accustomed to writing frequent letters, and many of these have survived relating to Lille. On arriving in Lille, he was greeted by the *intendant* for French Flanders, Michel Le Peletier de Souzy, and by the local magistrate. Le Peletier was one of the few people who was pleased to see Charles: his relations with Humières had been poor, and Charles represented a welcome relief. The two got on very well throughout Charles's governorship. The magistrate may have been a different matter; he had considerable local responsibilities and may have regarded the newcomer with suspicion. Nevertheless, Charles was welcomed with a reception in the Palais de Rihour, Lille's town hall, part of which still stands.

Charles would have had to resume his new duties immediately: one hopes his staff were helpful. He probably used the official residence of the governor, the Hôtel de Santes, at least for business purposes; it is no longer extant. He may, however, have chosen to find less elaborate – and more familiar? – personal lodgings elsewhere in the town. Local tradition in Lille holds that he lived on Rue Grande Chausée, in an apartment behind what is now a shoe

shop.[73] Perhaps it provided him with a retreat from the weight of
his new public role.

He was governing on the edge of a war zone as the representative of a conqueror King. Almost immediately on his arrival he
was faced with an incident of anti-French feeling. A small group of
armed men attacked the royal office at Deulemont, a few kilometres
from Lille. One man was killed, the local royal administrator was
injured and a soldier taken prisoner. There were grounds to suspect
that the attackers were Dutch soldiers: the Dutch army had two
local garrisons, at Saint-Omer and at Ypres. Charles immediately
sent out men to collect as much information as possible about
the incident and the aggressors. He also wrote to inform Louvois,
the Minister for War. The information Charles gathered tended to
confirm Dutch involvement: in particular, the raiders had been
spotted in an inn on the Ypres road, and there had been movements
of small numbers of Dutch troops between their garrisons, which
might easily have disguised the dispatch and return of a raiding
party. Charles sent a troop of cavalry in the direction of Ypres to
hunt for the attackers and reinforce local military posts. The issue
was becoming sensitive, as, despite the information he had received,
Louvois was concerned that the attackers may in fact have been
soldiers from Spanish Flanders, not Dutch. If this were the case,
then Franco-Spanish relations were endangered. No proof could
be discovered either way, and the problem continued to rumble
on. A few weeks later a group of Lille horse-sellers were harassed
while travelling through Spanish Flanders by a group of Dutch. Le
Peletier, who throughout this affair had co-operated closely with
Charles, protested to Louvois and asked that Charles be allowed to
make a formal complaint to the local representative of Spain. Before
Louvois had made a decision, however, the Spanish took action and
issued an order forbidding both Dutch and French troops from
entering their territories.

Such skirmishes were the closest Charles was to come to military action for long months. But he was far from unaware of the
progress of the war. As governor, he received regular letters from the
royal administration recording the victories of Louis's army. It was
the custom to make formal acknowledgement of major victories

by holding a *Te Deum* in major churches. While officially giving thanks to God for the good fortune of the King, these had a clear political purpose. Such an public act of thanksgiving, particularly in a recently conquered city like Lille, made a bold statement to the King's new subjects that God was on his side. Charles was ordered to hold such events twice during June and July 1672, plus a third to commemorate the birth to Louis of a son.[74] For Charles, accustomed to being in the thick of the action, these celebrations must have been bittersweet.

His greatest test as governor was looming. Although he had charge of the city and its environs, he did not have command over the fortified citadel which Louis was having built there. Governorship of the latter had been conferred in June upon its main designer, the engineer Vauban. This division of authority was to have complicated – and, for Minister of War Louvois, irritating – consequences. Charles may not have wanted to be governor, but now that he was, he was determined that his position be respected and his control unquestioned.

Vauban was not present at Lille in person: the fortification works were under the supervision of his deputy, Augustin Le Haguais, Chevalier de Montegivrault. In Charles's opinion, as governor of Lille, he had the right to be informed of everything to do with the construction of the citadel and the fortifications. The letter of commission he had received from the King had stated that Charles was 'to command in our said city and citadel of Lille and in the lands and lordship of Lille, Orchies and the territory of Laloue'.[75] To Charles, this meant that while Vauban – or, rather, his deputy – was in charge of the building of the citadel, he, Charles, was in overall control. Montegivrault did not see it that way.

The latter was every bit as stubborn, determined and proud as Charles, and the two rapidly fell out. Like Charles, Montegivrault was jealous of his power and position. In his own eyes, he was the expert – the veteran soldier probably seemed to him old-fashioned and stiff-necked. On the other hand, to Charles, the young Montegivrault seemed impertinent and disrespectful. Charles expected to be informed of every little detail regarding the construction, which irritated Montegivrault. Charles's justification was that he was responsible for the defence of the city, and that changes in the fortifications affected his deployment of his garrison. In the summer of 1672, their mutual dislike erupted into a quarrel.

Charles had formed the habit of going for a daily ride around the old ramparts that encircled the city. This allowed him to inspect the guards and to be seen about his duties, as well as to take air and exercise. At some point in late July, he set out on this round, only to find that Montegivrault's engineers had cut through the ramparts, breaking the circuit. This was undeniably necessary for the progress of the construction project, but to Charles it was an insult. He had not been informed: more, he had been inconvenienced. He went to Montegivrault's lodgings to demand an explanation. Not finding the engineer, he commanded that the major who was with him write to request that Montegivrault provide Charles with an alternative route by which he might complete his daily rounds. After eight days, no reply was received. Charles decided to write a complaint to Louvois.

To some extent, he was attempting to justify himself. Montegivrault had already sent a letter of complaint to Louvois about Charles, accusing him of unfairness. On 13 August, Louvois had written to Charles reprimanding him for his behaviour and requiring him to make peace with Montegivrault. Charles, as we have seen, was not willing to accept this. Hence his own protest to the minister. 'Since I have been in Lille,' he wrote, 'I have lived with the chevalier de Montegivrault as fairly as possible, and I even believe that I have been too much so. Ever since I've been here, he has not told me a word of what he is doing here, apart from telling me that he has orders from you not to give an account to either the governor or the *intendant*...'.[76] He went on to recite the incident of the ramparts, and to complain that in addition to this interference with the ordering of the guards, Montegivrault had caused the city's river to dry up, to the inconvenience of the inhabitants. Far from making peace with Montegivrault, Charles was determined that his annoyance be registered in the highest circles, and hoped that his protest would bring down a reprimand upon his rival. It was typical behaviour for the proud musketeer, but it was hardly the tactful, conciliatory manner that his position in Lille required.

Complaining was a somewhat risky business: the fortification of Lille was dear to the King's heart and of great importance in his war strategy. Charles's actions could disrupt its progress. Either he was not aware of this, or he felt it was of lesser importance than the maintenance of his own authority. For whatever reason, he was prepared now to trade heavily upon his long relationship with Louis – and to assume that the King would not reach an irrevocable level of irritation.

He won the first round, but it was a thin victory. A few days later, Montegivrault presented himself before the governor. By his own account, Charles was on his loftiest behaviour. He demanded to know why Montegivrault had come; on hearing that it was simply to see him, Charles responded that this was hardly necessary, that he himself did not merit it. When Montegivrault attempted to explain, Charles observed that he could see no reason why Montegivrault might have any complaints, and left. It is likely that Montegivrault had come to try and make peace; by allowing his pride to overcome him, Charles had ensured that their future relations would be as difficult as possible. Again, it is typical of Charles, but hardly ideal for the governor of such an important city. A few days later, meeting Charles in the city ditches, Montegivrault avenged himself by failing to salute him. Charles, who had already reported his own minor revenge to the King and Louvois, at once wrote to complain of this new insult, which he represented as a slur on the King. 'I am persuaded, Monseigneur, that the King would be angry with me if I suffered a little fly-by-night engineer to show contempt for the role which His Majesty has done me the honour of giving me here…'.[77] He also complained to his friend, the *intendant* Le Peletier, to whom he confided his intention to come to blows with Montegivrault should any further such incident occur. It is clear that he saw nothing wrong in his own behaviour, but it is more reminiscent of the young and quarrelsome d'Artagnan of *The Three Musketeers* than of a distinguished and high-ranking officer in his fifties. Indeed, he went so far as to repeat the threat in his letter to Louvois.

Was he simply being headstrong? The ending of the letter provides a clue. He finished, 'If I might dare, Monseigneur, to implore you to work on the King so that he wishes to cut short my commission and to recall me back to him, I would be very obliged to you.'[78] Undeniably, Charles had let his temper get the better of him, but he was quick to see how he might turn this to his advantage. He had made requests to be relieved of his post before; now, he reinforced them with this demonstration of his problems and even his weaknesses in the role. One must wonder if, to some degree, he had deliberately escalated the quarrel to provide himself with a reason to cease to be governor. It was not the safest of strategies: he might incur royal wrath, but it may have been that he felt secure enough in Louis's good graces to take the risk. His friend Le Peletier was clearly aware of the dangers and wrote to Louvois also, endeavouring to calm the situation. As a result, Louvois wrote to Montegivrault requiring him to remember to salute Charles, but he also reconfirmed the chevalier in his role as director of the fortification works.

The dislike between governor and engineer nevertheless continued to make trouble. In early September, Montegivrault complained to Louvois that Charles was impeding the progress of the fortifications because he was making difficulties over the demolition of part of the old rampart. As Bordaz has pointed out, this particular grievance may have been fabricated; in July, Charles had abandoned this section of rampart as part of his defences, so he was clearly aware that it was to be removed.[79]

By September, Charles had embroiled himself in a quarrel with yet another member of Vauban's team, Monsieur de la Vercantière, the lieutenant who commanded the citadel in Vauban's absence. Like Charles, La Vercantière was a soldier, but this did not form a bond between them. Late in August Charles went on a tour of inspection of three districts of Lille, and was late in returning to his lodgings. As a result, La Vercantière did not send anyone to him to receive the day's orders. He failed to do so also on the following day, perhaps assuming that Charles was still busy. Charles took umbrage, sensing a slight to his authority. He went to discover what had occurred, and, it being late in the day, found the city gates closed, even though he had not given orders for this. He had the gates reopened and sent one of his officers to the citadel for an explanation. La Vercantière's response did not satisfy him, and he went in person to see the lieutenant. At first, La Vercantière protested that the oversight was not his, but rather that of one of his subordinates, but to Charles this was nit-picking, and he threatened to inform Louvois. La Vercantière, doubtless aware of the escalation of the quarrel between Charles and Montegivrault, decided that discretion was the better part of valour, and apologised, promising to be properly respectful in future. For the time being, Charles was satisfied.

His content did not last long, however. Several days later, a deserter was apprehended. According to military regulations, it was up to the governor to convene a military court and to oversee its proceedings. La Vercantière made the error of having the sentence against the deserter carried out without first informing Charles. Then, adding insult to injury, La Vercantière removed a number of soldiers from the prison, again without informing Charles. To the latter, this was yet another example of the citadel officials ignoring his authority. He wrote in complaint to Louvois: 'I believed, and I hope, Monseigneur, that you will not approve of the behaviour of monsieur de La Bergantière [*sic*], and it is for what he has done, Monseigneur, that I demand justice from you…'.[80] The letter provides a charming example of the persistence of Charles's Gascon accent – B for V – but by this time, Louvois must have been rueing the day when Charles had been appointed governor of Lille. La Vercantière likewise wrote to complain of the high-handed treatment he had received from Charles and asked, not directly for justice, but for a clarification of the local hierarchy.

Louis XIV himself now got involved. Despite the demands on his time presented by the Dutch War, he read through the Lille correspondence. His conclusion was that Charles – his 'dear d'Artagnan' – had allowed himself to be somewhat carried away in his expectations as a result of his impulsive nature: a tactful way of saying that Charles was behaving arrogantly. The King further observed that a little flexibility on behalf of the governor would put a stop to these annoyances. On his instructions, Louvois wrote to both Charles and La Vercantière. He required of La Vercantière that he respect Charles's authority, but reassured him that he had done

nothing wrong in the present case. Charles, however, received a
rather sterner missive, reprimanding him for allowing himself to be
overly strict in his requirements of local officers. The tone of the
letter hinted that Charles had verged upon usurping royal prerogative: a clear warning that patience with his complaints was wearing
thin. Louvois also, however, reassured him that he was still in the
King's good graces and that the King would not allow him to be
undermined.

It is clear from all this that Louis retained his affection for Charles
even in trying circumstances, and, indeed, that he was willing to be
tolerant when his captain tried to trade upon royal favour. It was
an extraordinary position for the younger son of a minor Gascon
family, and a tribute to Charles that, even on his worst behaviour,
Louis valued and trusted him. But this was not enough for Charles,
whose pride was still stung by La Vercantière's actions. Far from
accepting Louvois's judgement, on 10 September he fired off yet
another letter of protest, denying that he had in any way acted
improperly and accusing La Vercantière of misrepresenting the facts.
He ended the letter with the familiar request that he be released
from his duties of governor and returned to military service. Once
again, it seems that he was trying to be as troublesome as possible, in
the hope of escaping a job he disliked. Louvois was not taken in: his
response evaded Charles's demands while delivering compliments
upon Charles's suitability as governor. For the time being, Charles
was obliged to let matters rest.

If Louvois and the King were prepared to be tolerant, Vauban
– who was, after all, official governor of the citadel of Lille – was
not. The persistent irritations that had arisen between his subordinates and Charles had not escaped his attention. He had been in
Holland with the army during the summer, but in mid-September
he returned to France and had time to turn his attention to affairs
in Lille. He had been kept informed of events there, and now he in
turn complained to the King. Charles, he protested, was usurping
his, Vauban's, authority as regards the citadel. Perhaps Vauban should
resign his position, if this was to be the new state of affairs.

This was the last thing that Louvois wanted: Lille was a crucial
point in the new defences of France, and Vauban was essential to

the construction of those defences. Fortunately for Vauban, Charles's designated term of service as governor was drawing to a close: Louvois wrote to Vauban asking him to be patient.

In truth, although Charles succeeded in stirring up a great deal of trouble in his personal dealings with the high officials in Lille, he had carried out the rest of his duties satisfactorily. Throughout his quarrels with Montegivrault and La Vercantière, he had continued to maintain order in the city and its environs, to deal with matters of military justice, and to handle incursions into the area by enemy soldiers. On 17 October, a group of Dutch soldiers attacked a redoubt at Steenstraat on the Ypres canal. Of the French soldiers guarding it, three were killed and around twelve others taken captive. Charles immediately sent reinforcements, although the culprits could not be apprehended. As ever, the army was his first priority: desertions had proved to be a problem, and at around this time he also arranged for a new company to be sent to strengthen the garrison at Comines, near the site of the Dutch incursion.

His time was doubtless also taken up with administrative and bureaucratic matters, and, as governor, he will have had to attend a number of functions and parties given by local dignitaries. He also made friends. The *intendant* Le Peletier frequently invited him to dine, or to go on hunting expeditions. Another friend was a local nobleman, Michel-Ange, Baron de Vuoerden, who was Bailiff of the Estates of Lille, a position he had received from the King. Vuoerden had been a regular visitor to the French court as part of the train of the Spanish ambassador, and was probably already acquainted with Charles as a result. The two men were very different: Vuoerden was an accomplished scholar and highly qualified in law, yet a close friendship arose between them. We also get a small glimpse of Charles in a novel circumstance. His interests had always been military: he took little interest in literature nor, it seems, in romance. However, innovation in warfare fascinated him (one cannot help feeling that, along with duty, his regular tours of the new fortifications were inspired by a desire to see how they were progressing). During his term of office in Lille, a Swiss captain named Grosjean presented to him an invention, a new grenade which exploded on contact with the ground, without having to be lit first. According to Le Peletier, Charles was highly enthused by this novelty and wished to have it for his musketeers.[81] He wished Louvois to inspect the new invention also, and suggested sending Grosjean to him. Louvois, very busy, managed to head him off, and there the matter rested. Perhaps the new grenades proved unreliable, or perhaps Charles simply lacked the funds to pursue further action regarding them. It is charming, however, to learn that even in the midst of his responsibility as governor, his musketeers were still very much at the forefront of his mind. It also proved to be one issue on which Charles and Vauban found themselves in agreement; the engineer also recommended the grenades to the King.

Charles's term as governor was drawing to an end. His original commission had been until the end of October, but by 26 October he had had no orders. He wrote to Louvois, only to learn that he was to remain through November. With a certain date set, Charles settled down a little, avoiding quarrelling with any more of Vauban's men. His extended service allowed him to participate in one of the traditions of Lille, known as *La Loy*, 'the law'. This was in fact the renewing of the city's magistracy, a procedure which originated in a fourteenth-century charter granted to Lille by a countess of Flanders. Charles, as governor, was one of the commissioners appointed to choose new incumbents in a ceremony held on 1 November. After examining the list of candidates and announcing the new nominees, the commissioners attended a special service in the church of Saint-Étienne. There was also a feast. Charles had reserved his quarrelsome side for the officials of the citadel: this town ceremonial probably both entertained and flattered him. His friend Le Peletier reported that the townspeople were highly satisfied with the conscientious way in which Charles carried his responsibilities to *La Loy*.[82] The rest of November passed off peacefully, and on 6 December 1672, Charles finally stepped down as governor of Lille. D'Humières was reinstated, having, in the royal view, done sufficient penance for his obstinacy regarding Turenne.

All parties concerned were relieved. For Charles, this was a return to the duties he enjoyed and the musketeer company he loved. For Humières, it put an end to his disgrace. For Vauban and his sub-ordinates at Lille, it marked a return to peaceful coexistence with an experienced governor. But perhaps the most relieved of all was war minister Louvois, whose duties and responsibilities would no longer be interrupted by a seemingly endless stream of complaints, protests and demands from the stubborn and touchy captain of musketeers.

Back at court, Charles once more occupied himself with his familiar duties with his musketeers. His sub-lieutenant, Jean-Louis Castéra de la Rivière, had done a poor job of maintaining order, and there had been numerous incidents of insubordination and even desertion. Charles took rapid steps to re-impose proper discipline. It seems that his men fared as badly without him as he did without them. One matter may have pleased him: his old rival Maulévrier was gone, retired as a result of wounds received at the siege of Candia.[83] His replacement was Monsieur de Montbron. The French army had made significant advances during the campaign of 1672, and had only been prevented from threatening Amsterdam when its inhabitants deliberately flooded the land surrounding it to block the access routes. Turenne was pursuing the advantage into the winter months, besieging Charleroi. Charles and his musketeers remained with the King, first at Compiègne, then at Saint-Germain. Security was still of high priority to Louis, and he had now set his eyes on the heavily fortified town of Maastricht, which occupied a key location. By now, the Spanish had been drawn into the war, on the Dutch side, while Sweden had returned to alliance with France. Louis was undaunted by this escalation of war, determined as he was to reduce Spanish influence and expand his own.

Louis set out with his court and part of his army to join up with the troops under Turenne and Condé on 1 May 1673. He was also to meet up with an army sent by his ally, Charles II of England, under the command of the latter's illegitimate son, the Duke of Monmouth. The goal was Maastricht, which was occupied by a Spanish army of around 11,000 men, plus extensive artillery. In addition, the fortifications of the town were famous: the oldest parts were medieval, but these had been rebuilt and expanded according to modern practices after 1632. Charles accompanied the King at the head of his musketeers, but his responsibilities were wider than that. Louis had appointed him *maréchal de camp*, making him responsible for the overall logistics of the army, and second only to the lieutenants-general and generals.

Preparations for the siege were made carefully, and considerable efforts were expended upon disguising French intentions. Turenne had used the last months of 1672 to launch attacks along the Rhine and the Moselle, devastating the countryside and thus reducing the resources available to the enemy. During early 1673 he threatened Ghent, considerably to the north of Maastricht. His fellow general, Condé, remained in Dutch territory, distracting their forces. The route taken by Louis and the main army in May also served to hide their true aim: the Spanish were to be given the impression that their target was Brussels. Further feints were designed to encourage the Spanish to reinforce existing garrisons to the north, all of which meant that the number of men they would have readily available to come to the relief of Maastricht was considerably reduced. As part of this strategy, the musketeers were involved in a feint against Dendermonde in mid-May.

Louis's army arrived outside Brussels in early June. On 4 June, the musketeers were sent to begin the assault on Maastricht. The rest of the army followed. Turenne's men were sent to encamp on the east bank of the River Meuse, which provided the city with part of its defences, while the royal force settled in to the west. The King arrived on 8 June, and the work of entrenchment began. He had assembled a huge force – around 19,000 cavalry and 26,000 infantry, with fifty-eight cannon – nearly four times the number garrisoning Maastricht. The French were well supplied, too: they carried with them resources sufficient for six weeks. They also had the benefit of a new strategy, Vauban's system of parallels, inspired by Turkish practice, which they now used for the first time.

Parallels were a significant advance in the conduct of siege warfare.[84] It involved the construction of trenches running parallel to that section of fortifications which was to be attacked, and set within the range of enemy cannon fire. A first ditch was established and furnished with protective artillery, and then a second trench constructed even closer to the walls, and again supplied with artillery. A final trench was dug right at the base of the *glacis*.[85] This allowed the attacking force to advance in a well-defended fashion, while making it necessary for the defenders of the fortress to spread their efforts over a comparatively wide area. Conditions for construction were not ideal – much of the work had to be carried out at night, and the weather was rainy – but it nevertheless proceeded quickly. The musketeers were amongst those chosen to protect the sappers. The defenders tried to disrupt the work: one such attack was launched from the Tongres Gate, on the west side of the city. A group of around twenty musketeers found themselves attacked by a force of two squadrons of cavalry. The musketeers were drawn from both the companies, and included one of Charles's maternal cousins, Joseph de Montesquiou d'Artagnan, a member of the first company. Heavily outnumbered, the musketeers inflicted heavy casualties on their attackers, and succeeded in driving them back within the fortress. Two musketeers were killed, one of them the commander of the small group, *Maréchal de Logis* (Sergeant) de Paygnan. Charles must have been very proud of this performance, reflecting as it did not only a high level of military skill but also swashbuckling bravery.

The town was to be attacked from three points – the gate of Tongres to the west, the nearby gate of Brussels, and the Wick district to the east, on the right bank of the Meuse. On 16 June, the King ordered a display of strength close to the Tongres Gate, with troops parading and trumpets blaring. The artillery assault on the gate began two days later, on 18 June. It continued without cease for thirty-six hours, working on the nerves of both sides, and doubtless destroying hopes of rest. During this time the French succeeded in taking the Saint-Pierre fort between the Meuse and the River Jaar, which commanded a key line on Maastricht itself. This long bombardment was not without its dangers: at least one musketeer, a tambour, fell victim to enemy shot on 23 June, close to the Mass tent beside the royal camp.

Charles, as *maréchal de camp*, had been attached specifically to one of the lieutenants-general, the young Duke of Monmouth. This was a mark of respect from Louis to his ally, but it also served to ensure that the inexperienced Monmouth had a trustworthy advisor close to hand. Louis determined to open a full assault on the town on the night of 24–25 June. Command of this fell to Monmouth.

Artillery fire was begun from the Saint-Pierre fort to distract the defenders from the assembling of the French force close to the base of the ramparts and defensive works of the Tongres Gate. This gate had considerable defences: a *demi-lune* sited between the arms of a horn-work in front of a *glacis*. Meanwhile, further troops massed near the Brussels gate and the Wick district, under the command of the King's brother, the Duc d'Orléans. The second musketeer company formed part of Orléans's force. This concentration was in fact intended as no more than a distraction from the assault on the Tongres Gate.

The King himself was with the troops preparing for the main assault. Accompanied by Charles, he had come to inspect the force, which consisted of four battalions of the royal regiment, 300 grenadiers, 100 musketeers of the first company, and a group of lifeguards and gentlemen belonging to Monmouth – this latter including John Churchill, later the famous Duke of Marlborough. The advance began at around ten o'clock, to the beating of tambours and with all standards flying. The goal assigned to the first company of musketeers was to take the *demi-lune*. Fighting went on all night, and Charles was in the very thick of it. They took the *demi-lune* and succeeded in raising the French standard on its parapet. Twenty-five musketeers were injured or killed, including the ensign, Maupertuis, whose hand was run through. Of the assault on the Tongres Gate, Pierre Quarré d'Aligny noted, 'I was lucky not to have been injured, as was M. d'Artagnan, although we did not spare ourselves, such that the King was very pleased.'[86] In fact, Charles had received a light wound, but it was nothing that concerned him. He and his company were stood down on the morning of 25 June, and retired back behind their lines. Monmouth arrayed troops to defend the new gains. While Charles's men rested, he found himself embroiled in new problems. The commander due to relieve Monmouth, Monsieur de Lafeuillade, had apparently decided that it was necessary to build a barrier to protect the *demi-lune* from potential enemy reprisals. He wished to erect this as soon as possible. Someone had come to inform Charles of this plan: he was opposed, knowing that French forces were already in place on the *demi-lune*, and felt it would be better to allow them some rest, and to build the new defences that evening. Moreover, any men sent to work on a new barricade in the daylight would make easy targets for the defenders. He went to find Monmouth to put his point of view. He was overruled, and the building went ahead, under heavy fire. The French sustained heavy losses.

What was worse, however, was that the commander of the Maastricht garrison decided that this presented him with a good opportunity to try and retake the *demi-lune*. They succeeded in driving the French back to the very edge of the work. After their long night, and the labour of building the barricade, the French were unable to repulse them. Monmouth decided to call for reinforcements.

Charles had just finished his lunch when the sound of renewed fighting reached him. He sent Quarré d'Aligny with thirty musketeers and sixty grenadiers to attack the *demi-lune*. He must have been bitterly aware that his men were tired, and that this activity might well have been unnecessary if Monmouth and Lafeuillade had listened to him. Charles himself took a second group of men to the barricade, where he met up with Monmouth. There was an area of open ground between the barricade and the *demi-lune*: as a result of the barricade, only one man at a time could move out into it. Monmouth decided that the best way to proceed was to attack directly across this space, a highly dangerous strategy. The more experienced Charles counselled against it, as it would leave them open to enemy fire. Monmouth was determined, however. With his small number of lifeguards, he began the advance; Charles was obliged to follow. The fighting was intense and brutal, but the French forces succeeded in retaking the *demi-lune*.

It was around five hours before the musketeers were once more able to retire behind the lines and a roll-call was taken. Sixty of them were dead or wounded. It was at this point that they realised they were without their captain-lieutenant. Charles may have exasperated Louvois and made trouble for Vauban, but the affection of the first musketeer company for him was unquestionable. The first sergeant, Adrian Malaisé de Saint-Léger, immediately set out for the scene of the fighting, accompanied by many of the uninjured men. Four were killed by enemy fire as they advanced, but they continued onwards to the middle of the *glacis* where they found their captain. Alongside him lay the company standard. He had been shot through the throat, dying instantly. Saint-Léger carried his body back to the camp.

The King was informed of the death, and was greatly distressed by it. He rewarded Saint-Léger richly for his courage, and had a funerary Mass said for Charles in the privacy of his own chapel. Five days later, on 30 June, Maastricht surrendered.

Where was Charles buried? No one knows. There is no known record of his body being taken back into France, but if this was arranged privately, then such records probably would not survive. Certainly, it was a long way to Gascony, which might have prevented his brother for asking for the body. Charlotte was nearer, but her actions after the death are well documented, and there is no reference to his burial. It is perhaps most likely that he was buried somewhere in or around Maastricht, perhaps close to where he fell. In the spring of 2004, seven skeletons were uncovered in a Maastricht garden, close to the site of the Tongres Gate. Associated small finds gave strong indications that these were seventeenth-century in date: buttons, moreover, suggested that the remains were those of members of the French musketeers. That these were men who fell during the actions of 20–25 June is highly likely. Is one of them Charles Castelmore d'Artagnan? It seems unlikely. He was a notable figure, his body was identified and recovered: mass burials are usually the fate of the rank and file and the unrecognised. But it is possible that he lies somewhere nearby, under the streets of the modern city. He is no more forgotten in Maastricht than at Lille or Lupiac, and two statues of him stand amidst the remains of the seventeenth-century defences.[87]

Louis XIV sent an official messenger to inform Charles's brother Paul of the death: their cousin Joseph de Montesquiou d'Artagnan sent a more personal letter. He wrote, 'There is no-one in the world who feels this sorrow more strongly than I do. It is not because of what I had hoped in terms of my fortune, but because of the loss of a father whom I have lost in losing him.'[88]

Charles's main mourners were at court and in the musketeer company he had loved. The poor recruit from Gascony had become a man of repute, if not of substance. The King continued to speak of him frequently and with affection. The *Gazette de France* carried the news to the wider world. His wife Charlotte must also have been informed, but we do not know when or by whom: nor do we know how she reacted to the news. Charles's two sons were still young, but certainly old enough to understand the idea of a father. But they had seldom, if ever, seen theirs, and his death must have seemed a remote thing. Upon learning the news, however, Charlotte came to Paris, probably to discover what, if anything, her sons might inherit. Perhaps, too, she intended to have Masses said for her husband's soul.

Charles did not die a rich man, and he left no will. Legal practice in Paris required that upon death an official inventory should be made of the deceased's possessions. That of Charles Castelmore d'Artagnan was carried out in December 1673, and the document still survives.[89] His residence on the Rue du Bac had been sealed on his death and its contents preserved. On entering, the notaries were struck by the untidiness: perhaps Charles the soldier saw no need for order at home. Or perhaps, in his absence at the front his two servants had seen no need to set things to rights. Charles had owned nothing of any great value, although he clearly lived comfortably. His walls were hung with tapestries to keep out draughts; his kitchen was well equipped – one remembers his rivalry over fine dining with Besmaux when he was forced to stay close to Fouquet in the Bastille. His furnishings were more comfortable by far than those of his youth: his guests could rest on tapestry-seated chairs, and he slept in a large, pillared bed with no fewer than three mattresses. There were clear traces of his military occupation, too – boots, uniform cassock, richly-decorated horse equipment, and two swords, one with a gold guard. He had no family pictures, but in his bedchamber was hung a portrait of Anne of Austria. Perhaps, as Bordaz has suggested, he continued to cherish an affection for the late Queen.[90] A portrait of Charles's first great patron, Cardinal Mazarin, hung in the antechamber to this room. These dated, perhaps, from the late 1640s or 1650s, but Charles had not forgotten the minister to whom he owed his good fortune. There was no picture of Louis XIV: perhaps, seeing the original on an almost daily basis, Charles felt no need of one.

There were also papers. A considerable number were official,
dating from his time as Fouquet's jailer. Charles was no fool: this
was still a sensitive matter and he was well advised to retain proofs
that his own actions had been carried out with official sanction.
He may have had Colbert in mind: the influential minister had
never warmed to him. After Charles's death, the papers came into
Colbert's hands; the latter found nothing objectionable and had
them filed in the State Archive. Other papers dealt with his marriage
– the contract and the legal separation – and with his debts, plus
papers reflecting on his administrative functions with his company.
There were no love letters and no personal writings – certainly no
memoirs. Charles had had no interest in literature; he possessed no
books. The whole of his estate was valued at 4,539 *livres*, of which
the bulk was made up by the tapestries, his clothing, and two car-
riages. He had had no gold or silver vessels, no jewellery, no *objets
d'art*. Moreover, he had left debts of over 20,000 *livres*. The King,
still solicitous of his captain-lieutenant, paid them.

Louis was also concerned for Charles's two sons. This payment
of debts protected them from a considerable burden. Charlotte had
renounced any claim she might have had on his estate, doubtless
concerned by these same debts. Guardians were appointed for the
children in December 1673, at around the same time as the inventory was made. The principal guardian was to be Charles's older
brother Paul, but given his age and his residence in distant Gascony,
the main role devolved onto the shoulders of a deputy, Jean-
Louis Castera de la Rivière, Charles's cousin and formerly his
sub-lieutenant of musketeers, who had retired from service on a
large pension. The guardianship arrangements were made in the
presence of Charlotte's cousin, who had a court appointment, and
Charles's younger brother, the priest Arnaud, who had made the
journey to Paris to assist with his brother's effects. In January 1674,
Charlotte was granted an audience with the King, a mark of respect
for her late husband. Louis still had one concern about Charles's
sons: they had not been baptised, despite their age. He wished
to confer upon them a notable honour: royal godparents. The
baptisms were held at Versailles and officiated over by the distinguished churchman Monseigneur de Bossuet. For the elder boy,

the godparents were the King and Queen; for the younger, Louis's eldest son and the Grande Mademoiselle. Louis further honoured the boys by conferring upon them both his own name, Louis. At last, too late, Charlotte had achieved entry to the glittering world of the King's inner circle. She recognised, however, that it could not last, and soon returned to her home at Châlon-sur-Saône. She died on 31 December 1683, a little over ten years after her husband.

Charles's two sons continued to benefit from the affection of the King for their father. The elder Louis became a page of the royal stable and later an officer of guards, where he had a reputation for courage, before inheriting the domain of Castelmore from his paternal uncle Paul. He used the title 'Comte d'Artagnan', however: it was far more recognisable. He died in 1709, unmarried, aged forty-nine. The younger Louis also pursued a military career in the guards, and became a gentleman to the Dauphin. He was his brother's heir, both to family lands and to the title Comte d'Artagnan. Marrying in 1707, he left two sons on his death in 1714. His younger son seems to have died in childhood, but the elder continued the family's military tradition, serving in the musketeers before becoming a captain of dragoons. He was to be the last of Charles's descendants to use the name d'Artagnan: his son Louis-Constantin reverted to de Batz-Castelmore. Louis-Constantin was also a soldier, serving in the Royal Foreign regiment. He died childless, last of the line of Charles de Batz-Castelmore, captain-lieutenant of musketeers, known as Comte d'Artagnan.

But perhaps Charles's best epitaph is that written in 1673 by the poet Juliani de Saint-Blaise: 'D'Artagnan and *la gloire* have the same coffin'.[91]

2

Athos, Porthos, Aramis – and Monsieur de Tréville

D'Artagnan and the three musketeers: the image created by Dumas is indelibly printed on the western imagination, and has found its echoes all across the world. The names – Athos, Porthos and Aramis – have a legendary air, and Dumas himself had at least a suspicion that they could not be real.

In some ways, he was right: the personalities, the quirks and traits, the daring deeds and complex histories with which he endowed them were indeed fictional. But despite their names, and despite Dumas's own words, Athos, Porthos and Aramis were as real as Charles Castelmore d'Artagnan, if far less well documented in our surviving historical records. Dumas had found their names in the pseudo-memoirs of d'Artagnan by Courtilz de Sandras and seems to have taken them to be at best pseudonyms, if not outright fictions. He had a robust attitude to history, selecting from it those incidents and events that might enhance his narrative, and was never afraid to sacrifice fact to excitement. Did he accept Courtilz's account as genuine? Certainly, he adopted a free hand in adapting it to his work, and, experienced romancer as he was, it seems likely that he recognised the unreliable and propagandistic qualities of the text in front of him. The information provided by Courtilz on Athos, Porthos and Aramis was very thin – one must suspect that Courtilz himself knew almost nothing about them aside from their names. It is certainly to the golden imagination of Dumas that the three musketeers owe their immortality. But behind the apparently unlikely names and the swashbuckling legend lie three real men, all of whom pursued the career of arms at around the same time and in the same environment as Charles Castelmore d'Artagnan.

Their names were Armand de Sillègue d'Athos d'Autevielle, Isaac de Portau and Henri d'Aramitz. All three, like Charles Castelmore d'Artagnan, belonged to the minor gentry, and like him, they came from the south-eastern corner of France. In general terms, they were Gascons, but more accurately, they were Béarnais – inhabitants of the uplands formed by the foothills of the Pyrenees. Again, like Charles, all three sought to advance themselves and perhaps add to family income by following the career of arms in Paris, although not all were younger sons. Courtilz de Sandras described them as brothers; this is not so, but they were all distantly related to one another through one man: Louis XIII's commander of musketeers, Monsieur de Tréville.

They had something else in common along with Tréville: they belonged to that group known as the Gascon *cadets*. There was a specific identity attached to such men, and with it almost a legend. The word *cadet* now refers to a younger son or a junior line of a family, but in the past it carried wider implications. In origin, it probably referred to a local leader, a lordling with powerful ties to his territory and community.[1] It thus had implications of pride. It came to be particularly applied to Gascons in the wake of the accession to the French throne of King Henri IV – a Gascon himself.

So what was meant by 'Gascon cadet'? They were impoverished, certainly; they carried strange or convoluted names;[2] they were fiercely proud of their lineage (however debatable it might seem in the eyes of the northern French aristocracy). They were boastful and swaggering and short-tempered, quick to avenge a slight, however small – or imaginary – and equally quick to recite their own achievements. They were brave, be it in warfare or in duels, and they had a strong military bent. They were clannish, helping and supporting each other in their careers. Many Gascons served in the armies of Henri IV, Louis XIII and Louis XIV, and several highly regarded regiments were a Gascon prerogative: so strong was the latter notion that one famous soldier, Cyrano de Bergerac, pretended to be a Gascon to gain admission to the company of his choice.[3] They were strongly attached to their homeland, retaining a marked regional accent. The image is dashing and romantic to some degree – one thinks of British notions of Scottish Highlanders or Welsh archers – but, like those notions, it had a darker side, embodying prejudices based on class and regional stereotypes. The popular view of the Gascon certainly encompassed the bold, courageous, larger-than-life Henri IV, but it also carried with it negative images of social-climbing country bumpkins.[4] The idea of the Gascon cadet was well established by the time of Dumas, and his depiction of d'Artagnan is both a homage to and a cornerstone of the legend. The reality was probably less swashbuckling – and the prejudice far harder to deal with. Yet there was a special quality to these young men who came from Gascony to serve the kings of France with courage and loyalty, and the myth is to some degree mirrored in the lives of Charles Castelmore d'Artagnan, Armand de Sillègue d'Athos d'Autevielle, Isaac de Portau, Henri d'Aramitz and Captain de Tréville.

DE TRÉVILLE

We have seen how Tréville played a part in the early career of Charles. In terms of the other three, his influence was probably greater, because of the bonds of kinship. His own career is almost the epitome of the ambitions and aspirations of martial Gascon gentlemen in the first half of the seventeenth century.

Tréville was born Jean-Arnaud de Peyrer in 1598 in the small Béarnais town of Oloron-Sainte-Marie.[5] His father, Jean, was a prosperous merchant who had acquired considerable military experience in the Wars of Religion. Subsequently, Jean de Peyrer engaged in trade with Spain, which not only brought him wealth, but also gave him considerable influence: in 1607, he bought a seigniorial property, the manor of Troisvilles in the foothills of the Pyrenees. Jean-Arnaud was a child of Jean's second marriage, to a young woman of local, minor, but established nobility, Marie d'Aramitz. Jean de Peyrer was probably a Catholic, and his children were raised in that religion, although Marie was from a Protestant background. The Huguenot Protestant faith was strong in Gascony and Béarn, but a considerable number of its more prominent inhabitants had followed the example of their ruler Henri of Navarre and become Catholic for political reasons by the beginning of the seventeenth century. Being Catholic made life easier, particularly if one had ambitions to serve — and to rise — at the royal court. Like the forebears of Charles Castelmore d'Artagnan, Jean de Peyrer had bought himself a toehold on the ladder of nobility; he wanted more for his son. Jean-Arnaud entered the army in 1616, as a cadet in a guard regiment, a position for which his father had probably had to pay a fee. He remained with this regiment for some years; in 1622, he became an ensign. In 1625, he achieved entry to the musketeers, already a prestige regiment, and served with them as a cornet. In this capacity, he was present at the famous siege of La Rochelle in 1629; d'Artagnan and the three musketeers, whom Dumas was to endow with such brave exploits at that siege, were still at home in Gascony. Jean-Arnaud clearly served with some distinction, as his progress was relatively rapid, despite his fairly obscure origins. In 1632, he became lieutenant of the musketeers, and, on 3 October 1634, he was made their captain. He was an adept courtier as well as a soldier, and at the same time as becoming lieutenant, he was made one of the King's gentlemen of the bedchamber. Unlike Charles, Jean-Arnaud was not averse to mixing in politics and was very sensible of the power conferred upon him by his military position.

He made a useful marriage, in 1637, to Anne de Guillon, sister of another career soldier, the Baron de Guillon des Essarts.[6] Not only was Essarts a useful contact, but Anne's dowry was sufficiently large to allow him to purchase further lands around Troisvilles, plus the additional manor of de Peyre. Jean-Arnaud had inherited his father's desire to enhance and improve their family status. Essarts was a close friend, in all probability, and certainly the two men shared a common political agenda. Both disliked Richelieu, and were on poor terms with him. In 1642, this led Jean-Arnaud into dangerous waters.

Louis XIII had had a number of favourites during the course of his reign, most of whom were denied access to government and discouraged by the King from attempting to influence policy.[7] The last – and perhaps the most dangerous – of these was Henri d'Effiat, Marquis de Cinq-Mars.[8] Cinq-Mars had been brought to court in 1635 at the age of fifteen through the influence of Richelieu, and by 1639 he was established as royal favourite. Richelieu may initially have hoped that the young man would be grateful to him, and bear him no ill will – the preceding favourite, Marie de Hauteforte, was a devoted friend of the Queen, Anne of Austria, and thus no friend to Richelieu. Cinq-Mars, however, was stubborn, self-centred and relentlessly self-aggrandising. He also sought to exploit the King while bearing him little or no affection. He rapidly came into conflict with Richelieu. The relationship of Louis XIII and his first minister was complex and sometimes seemingly hostile, and Cinq-Mars allowed his own wishes to lead him into believing that Louis would prefer him over Richelieu should a choice be necessary. In 1642, a cabal formed around Cinq-Mars with the intention of over-throwing – and probably assassinating – Richelieu. The conspirators, who had a wide range of ambitions and hopes, included some major figures, not least the King's brother, Gaston d'Orléans, and the Duc de Bouillon. Jean-Arnaud, as commander of an elite regiment, was a valuable potential ally, and at some point in the first part of the year the conspirators approached him to join them.

Jean-Arnaud was well acquainted with Cinq-Mars and was one of his regular associates at court, along with Essarts. He was broadly in sympathy with the anti-Cardinalist aims of the faction. However, he was considerably older than Cinq-Mars, and far more experienced in the ways of the court. He had seen Richelieu weather a number of plots against him led by members of the great nobility – and even by Louis's mother, Marie de Medicis – and he was well aware of the unreliability of some of the key conspirators, notably

Gaston. While allowing his sympathy for the plotters to be known, he seems to have avoided allowing himself to be drawn in too deeply, stating that he would associate himself with the plot only if he was assured that the King approved it. This proved to be a wise position: in mid-June 1642, Louis had Cinq-Mars and his closest associates arrested. Richelieu was seriously ill, and suspicious that his King might have allowed himself to be influenced by the cabal; as a result he made a number of demands of Louis, intended to reaffirm his own position.[9] These included the removal from court of a number of his enemies, including Jean-Arnaud and Essarts. Their punishment was restricted to exile: nothing serious could be proved. Cinq-Mars himself went to the scaffold on 12 August 1642.

Jean-Arnaud went into exile on 1 December 1642, but it was not to last long. Richelieu died on 4 December, and, shortly afterwards, Louis recalled several of the friends he had sent into exile, including Jean-Arnaud and Essarts. Perhaps, after all, Louis had something of an uneasy conscience over the plot.

Jean-Arnaud's opposition to Richelieu had derived partly from his sympathy for Anne of Austria, whom the minister had kept very much in obscurity. This was to serve him well in the next few months. Louis XIII himself died on 14 May 1643 and, after some political manoeuvring, Anne became regent for the young Louis XIV. In October, she made Jean-Arnaud a count. However, Jean-Arnaud had transferred his dislike of Richelieu to the latter's successor, Mazarin, and the two soon came into conflict. Mazarin naturally did not wish to have his enemy in a position of influence and soon began what was to be a long campaign to remove Jean-Arnaud from the captaincy of musketeers. Jean-Arnaud proved stubborn, but in 1646 Mazarin found another way of undermining him. The King was a minor; Mazarin used this as an excuse to suppress the musketeer company on the grounds that they were unnecessary. Anne did not prevent this – one of the complaints regularly levelled against her by her former friends was that, once regent, she forgot those who had supported her in her youth.[10] She did not wholly abandon Jean-Arnaud, however, and he was compensated with the governorship of the city and castle of Foix in Languedoc. Over the next decade, he divided his time between

Foix and Paris. His career during the Fronde was unremarkable, but he served the royal side loyally.

Neither he nor the musketeer company had been forgotten, however. After the end of the Fronde, the newly secure Mazarin returned to his scheme to see his nephew, Philippe Mancini, Duc de Nevers, as captain of a musketeer company. Although the King's musketeers had been suppressed, Jean-Arnaud, as their last captain, retained the right to that position. In order to re-establish the company in the way he wished, Mazarin still needed to persuade him to step down. Jean-Arnaud by this time was almost fifty, and well settled in Foix and its environs. Perhaps his desire for military glory had faded, perhaps his family brought pressure to bear upon him, but this time he conceded to Mazarin and, on 10 January 1657, the musketeer company was re-formed, with Nevers as their new captain – an appointment which was to prove very much to the advantage of Jean-Arnaud's former subordinate, Charles Castelmore d'Artagnan. Jean-Arnaud did not go unrewarded for his co-operation. His elder son had religious tendencies, and was thus promised the abbey of Montier-en-Der.[11] His younger son was made a cornet in the new musketeer company, and was promised that he would inherit the governorship of Foix from his father. Jean-Arnaud received the prestigious Order of the Holy Spirit, conferred on him on 1 January 1658.

His interests by now were concentrated in the south, and he spent most of his time on his Béarnais properties. He was now a wealthy man, able to afford considerable building programmes, and between 1660 and 1663 he had a splendid new manor house built at Troisvilles, which stands to this day.

He was not forgotten at court. By August 1667 he had been promoted to the rank of lieutenant-general, probably a consequence of the King's presence in southern France on the long marriage journey of 1659–60. Perhaps, too, Charles Castelmore d'Artagnan, now at the right hand of the young Louis XIV, persuaded his King to recognise his former captain. Jean-Arnaud lived out his remaining years in peace, buying the barony of Tardets to add to his lands in 1671. He died on 8 May 1672 at Troisvilles, leaving his two sons to enjoy the benefits his career had garnered.

Jean-Arnaud de Peyrer de Tréville had been a popular captain of musketeers, and his name has survived as part of the legend both of that company and of the central years of the seventeenth century. He has often been seen as a model for other young men of the minor Gascon nobility – a theme particularly highlighted by Dumas in *The Three Musketeers*. As will be seen, he was part of a complex network of kinship which he was more than willing to use to the advantage of his kinsmen, who followed him to Paris. Perhaps Charles Castelmore d'Artagnan had him in mind when he set off to the capital in about 1633. But that particular young soldier was to surpass the career of his former captain and come to replace him as a symbol of the courage, bravery and ambition of the *cadets* of Gascony.[12]

Jean-Arnaud and Charles were certainly acquainted. It is less certain that there was friendship – or, in one case, even acquaintance – between Charles and the men who are commemorated as the three musketeers. Nor do we know for sure that they knew each other. Dumas's story of the Three Inseparables who had formed their bond before d'Artagnan came to Paris and who then expanded their ranks to include him is one of the great myths of friendship, and it has proved hard for historians and biographers to let go of. The earlier writers – Jean de Jaurgain, Charles Samaran – who laid the groundwork for modern analyses of these men and their careers certainly wished to retain the myth and worked hard to fit the facts around it.[13] Modern novelists have followed suit.[14] We do not know enough of the personalities of Athos and Porthos to know if they would have dealt well with the proud and stubborn Charles: in the case of Aramis, there are hints of potential political divergence between their views – something Dumas probably did not know, but which his later books uncannily echo.

ATHOS

During the five or six years in which he had lived in the greatest intimacy with his companions Porthos and Aramis, they remembered having seen him smile frequently, but they had never heard him laugh. His words were brief and expressive, always saying what they wished to say and nothing more: no embellishments, no embroideries, no flourishes. His conversation was all fact with no stories.

Although Athos was barely thirty and had great beauty both of body and of spirit, nobody knew him to have a mistress. He never talked of women. Only, he did not stop anyone from talking of them in his presence, though it was easy to tell that this type of conversation, in which he never involved himself save with bitter words and misanthropic insights, was extremely disagreeable to him. His reserve, his unsociability and his silence had almost made him an old man...[15]

The Athos familiar to us from the novels of Dumas is a striking figure: the epitome of nobility, honour and grace, the touchstone for the behaviour of all those around him, and the pivot for a bloody and melodramatic love story. Morally, he stands head and shoulders above his companions, disdainful of worldly ambitions and riches. Yet his is a protected elevation: the author has conferred upon him the advantages of inherited wealth, privileged education and a sort of inherent beauty of soul which supposedly comes to him by right of his blood. He represents an ideal of the nobleman: a status which grows as the novels progress and which has as a consequence his near-absence from the action of the final volume. In age, he becomes so perfect as to be impossible as a hero in a melodramatic tale: the flaws which made him engaging in earlier books – his vengefulness, his heavy drinking, his bouts of melancholy – have been replaced with a religious certainty which confines him to inaction. There is something rather incredible about the older Athos – and, to modern eyes, perhaps also something rather priggish. No man can be so perfect without becoming uncomfortable for those around him – one thinks of Sir Galahad in the Arthurian romances. This edifice of nobility and high-mindedness comes from Dumas's imagination, and perhaps from his own mixed feelings about the aristocracy. His family had revolutionary connections and he was proud of that, yet at the same time he had a romantic love of titles and status and a yearning after what he perceived as their qualities. This found its expression through his writing – many of his heroes are nobly born – and its strongest representative in the person of

Athos. Yet it is likely that the real Athos was far removed indeed from this image.

Armand de Sillègue d'Athos d'Autevielle is the most shadowy of the three men who underlie the three musketeers – he is little more than a name and a date. We know more about his family than about the man, as he died young and apparently made little mark on the world.[16]

Dumas's Athos came from the area around Blois, and was thus unmarked by regional accent or supposed character.[17] Armand – like Charles and Jean-Arnaud – was a Gascon, or, more properly, a Béarnais. His family was probably very like Charles's in origin and aspiration, although probably less successful in its social climbing. The village from which he took his famous surname, Athos-Aspic, is now little more than a hamlet – a handful of farms lying around a church. It lies in the upland close to the major fortified town of Sauveterre-de-Béarn, and was probably originally dependent upon that town for its defence. Smaller than Lupiac – or Aramitz, or Porthos's home village of Lanne – it can never have been a major or wealthy holding. It was not the family's first holding, nor their largest, but somehow it has come to be the one by whose name they are remembered.

The hamlet belonged to a man named Pé-Bernand de Gestas in 1386, but by the sixteenth century his family had failed in the male line, and Athos passed via an heiress, Quiterie d'Athos, to the La Lanne family. Quiterie and her husband sold the hamlet to a near-neighbour, Tamonet de Sillègue, and his eldest son Peyreton, on 8 July 1557.

Sillègue was another small hamlet, close to a larger settlement, Autevielle. The latter lay on a crossroads, and was better situated in terms not only of access but also of the revenue that it might hope to garner. Peyreton de Sillègue had acquired Autevielle in the summer of 1553, buying it from its previous owner, Gabriel de Béarn. The de Sillègue family were, like the de Batzes of Lupiac, merchants, and had made sufficient funds to embark on land-purchase through the fur trade. The three villages made a neat block of territory which could provide food and agricultural revenues as well as money from travellers and from exploitation of the river that ran through

Autevielle. There was a château at Autevielle, and another, probably smaller, at Athos, although neither now survive. The house at Athos is almost entirely gone, its remains probably plundered for building materials by local farms. All that can be seen today is a small section of wall. The chateau at Autevielle, a compact gentry home which was probably the main residence of the de Sillègue d'Athos d'Autevielle family, survived into the twentieth century, but was destroyed by fire in 1942 or 1943.[18] Peyreton married twice: by his first marriage, he had a son, Bertrand. His second marriage seems to have been late in life, as his new wife, Marie de Munein, was the sister of his son's wife. From this second marriage he had two further sons, Simon and Daniel, and a daughter, Catherine.

We know nothing about the identity of Peyreton's first wife, not even a name, and thus we cannot know how she affected the complex bonds of kinship that tied family to family throughout Gascony. However, through her son Bertrand, she was the grandmother of our Athos, Armand. Bertrand was his father's heir, and thus succeeded to the lands at Athos, Autevielle and Sillègue, although we do not know when. In around 1607, he married, and his wife was a member of the du Peyrer family, which, it will be remembered, was that of the future captain of musketeers, de Tréville. Unfortunately, the personal name of Bertrand's wife is not recorded, so we do not know exactly how she was related to Jean-Arnaud du Peyrer de Tréville, but her sons were considered by him to be cousins of some kind. Definitions of kinship spread over a much wider range in the seventeenth century, so one must not assume that Armand's mother and Jean-Arnaud's father were siblings. They might equally have been cousins, at one or more remove, or members of two different generations (aunt and nephew, uncle and niece, or cross-generational cousins). What is important is not how they were related, but that they considered the relationship to be of significance. Bertrand and his wife had at least two sons, Jean and Armand. Jean seems to have been the elder, and in turn inherited the lands and lordships of Athos, Autevielle and Sillègue. He married Jeanne de Bachoué, sometime before June 1633. Through him, the family line survived down to the end of the seventeenth century – Jean's son Pierre married (Charlotte de Vigner, apparently from the

Toulongeon area) and had died by January 1674. His son, Jean, was
in possession at least of Autevielle in 1675 and again in 1685, but
by 1689, when we last encounter him, his title was Lord of Icharre.
What became of the lands around Athos is not known.[19]

What of Armand? Aside from the details of his family, we know
only two things about him: that he had entered the company of the
King's Musketeers through the good auspices of his cousin Tréville
by 1643, and that he died in Paris on 21 December 1643.

How and why did he die? We know very little, but luckily, the
register of the church of St Sulpice, where his burial service was
held, survives. An entry in it reads:

> Funeral procession, service and burial of the late Armand Athos
> Dautubiele [sic], musketeer of the King's guard and gentleman of
> Béarn, taken close to the Pré-aux-Clercs' covered market.[20]

What can we learn from this brief notice? Certainly, it would seem
from the wording that Armand did not die a natural death, nor did
he perish from an illness or an accident. The verb 'taken' suggests
a violent aspect – an ambush, a robbery gone wrong, or a duel.
Of the three, perhaps the latter is the most likely. He is highly
unlikely to have been wealthy, although in a city like Paris in the
mid-seventeenth century, degrees of wealth were highly subjective
and an impoverished minor nobleman might well have seemed well
off to some of the urban poor. Ambush cannot be ruled out: we
know next to nothing about his character, but he may have won
enemies somewhere, or perhaps incurred bad debts. Given his age
– probably in his twenties – his background, his occupation and
his career choice, as well as the period itself, however, a duel is by
far the most probable cause of his early death.

There are a number of reasons for this. One clue may lie in
his name – that long collection of syllables, 'de Sillègue d'Athos
d'Autevielle', has a boasting look to it: it is the name of a man, or
a family, that has only recently acquired noble status and is very
anxious that said status be recognised. It is reminiscent, indeed,
of one of Armand's literary associates, the Baron du Vallon de
Bracieux de Pierrefonds, as the social-climbing Porthos comes to

call himself. Dumas's picture of the older Porthos – wealthy, living in the lap of luxury, boasting, proud and self-satisfied, but perpetually yearning for the respect and welcome of his neighbours born of the 'old' nobility – forms a type of the new gentry which might well be a good guide to the aspirations and behaviour of a man who called himself by a similar triple-barrelled and conspicuously noble name.[21] It is entirely likely that Armand was – like Charles Castelmore d'Artagnan – proud, and touchy about his status.

Duelling occupied a particular place in the society of mid-seventeenth-century France. It was intimately tied in with ideas about honour, rank, status, courage and skill.[22] A gentleman was expected to fight to defend his honour, and slights to honour could be construed from almost anything. Men of the lower nobility, moreover, were trained from youth to martial pursuits and formed the core of royal armies: a sword was an essential part of the costume of the male nobility and gentry, and these were not worn simply as ornaments. V.G. Kiernan has argued that, by virtue of its close ties to ideas of honour, the duel in fact in some ways served as a badge of nobility, and willingness to engage in duels was a way in which a man might demonstrate his right to nobility in a very public way. It could be, therefore, that those whose claim to noble rank was recent or shaky might be especially keen to engage in duels, as a way of bolstering their position, while those of poor gentry backgrounds but long lines of descent might equally feel that duelling was a means by which they could make their mark against a rising tide of 'new' nobility.[23]

Duelling had been going on in France for well over a century, and kings and their ministers had made numerous, unsuccessful, attempts to curb it. It had become almost a popular aristocratic pastime: the last Valois King, Henri III, surrounded himself with a clique of attractive young men, popularly known as the *mignons*, the sweethearts, many of whom nevertheless had reputations as duellists, and several of whom met their deaths as a result of this. Henri III was unpopular and openly opposed by some of the nobility, notably the powerful Duke of Guise: the *mignons* became embroiled in several duels with supporters of Guise, most famously on 27 April 1578, when two of them, Quélus and Maugiron, met their deaths

— as did two of their opponents. Another *mignon*, Bussy d'Amboise, tried to arrange a duel of 300 men per side between the King's party and that of Guise in January of the same year.[24] The taste for duelling persisted through the reign of Henri IV – who is supposed once to have remarked rather wistfully that had he not been King, he would have acted as second for one of his courtiers.[25] Yet Henri, like his Valois predecessors, enacted laws to prevent duelling.

It is easy to see why kings were so ambivalent about duelling. On the one hand, it was wasteful of human life – under Henri IV alone, more than 4,000 men were killed in France in duels.[26] It was illegal, and all duellists were flouting royal authority, placing their honour above it. Duels were often engaged upon for frivolous reasons – a glance, an expression, an accidental collision. In the army, duels threatened discipline, while on the streets they threatened public order. On the other hand, the connection of the duel with ideas of honour and gentlemanly conduct appealed to royal pride and romanticism – one must suspect Henri III, at least, of taking vicarious pleasure in the martial exploits of the *mignons*. In *The Three Musketeers*, Dumas presents Louis XIII as similarly delighted by the duels of his musketeers. Kings, after all, were also gentlemen.

During the reign of Louis XIII, duelling was as popular as ever in France. Duels could and did occur anywhere, a fact vividly reflected in *The Three Musketeers*.[27] Under the code of practice of the time, they tended to involve fighting between more than two men; the seconds were also expected to fight, and there was no limit on the number of seconds that could be fielded. This was considered to be a matter of a man's bravery, but it tended to increase the death toll and contribute to the general lawlessness of the practice. Nor was the practice restricted to Paris: duels occurred throughout the kingdom, in towns and countryside. Duelling was first prohibited in France in 1560, during the reign of Charles IX, elder brother of Henri III. Further edicts outlawing duelling followed in 1566 and 1579. The Valois dynasty came to an end in 1589, and the first Bourbon King, Henri IV, likewise enacted anti-duelling laws in 1602 and 1609. Yet none of these measures seem to have had much effect, and alongside these laws, kings regularly pardoned nobles caught engaged in duels. The French nobility of Louis XIII were notorious around Europe for their duels. 'There is scarce a Frenchman worth looking on who has not killed his man in a duel' remarked Lord Herbert, the English ambassador.[28]

Cardinal Richelieu was greatly opposed to the practice. His elder brother Alphonse du Plessis, Marquis of Richelieu, was killed in a duel by the Marquis de Thémines at Angers on 8 July 1617, and this may well have influenced the cardinal's views. His desire to suppress duelling, however, was far more than a matter of personal preference: he was concerned with the establishment of royal rights and authority, and any activity which allowed the individual to take the law into his own hands was incompatible with this. Richelieu and Louis issued a stern prohibition against duelling in 1626. When the nobility continued to flout it, they took the unprecedented step of calling the combatants to account, in what was to become a famous incident.

The most noted duellist in France at this time was François de Montmorency, Comte de Bouteville, who had been involved in more than twenty duels, and was said to run a duelling school in his home. He had killed many men and took no notice of the edict. In May 1627, he was challenged by the Marquis de Beuvron and arranged to meet him at 2p.m. on 12 May. The duel took place right outside Richelieu's residence, the Palais Royal, and one of the seconds was killed. This was a clear challenge to the authority of King and cardinal. Richelieu was quick to take action: Bouteville and his second, des Chapelles (the latter was the actual killer on this occasion), were arrested, and beheaded on 22 June, despite appeals from leading members of the aristocracy. Beuvron fled abroad.[29] Such sanctions were unheard of, and made it plain that the King would not tolerate open flaunting of his laws. Yet even so, duels continued to occur.

This was the background against which Armand de Sillègue d'Athos d'Autevielle entered upon his fatal duel in December 1643. Perhaps he was a principal, perhaps a second; either way, he was engaged upon a dangerous and illegal activity, and no less than the Comte de Bouteville, he paid for it with his life.

Some attempt has been made to recover the circumstances of his death. Jean de Jaurgain turned to the pseudo-memoirs of d'Artagnan by Courtilz de Sandras for enlightenment. These relate an incident in which, having incurred the enmity of a certain English 'Milédi', d'Artagnan was set upon near Saint-Germain by a number of ruffians. His devoted comrades Athos, Porthos and Aramis came to his rescue and the four of them succeeded in putting the aggressors to flight, but at the cost of wounds to both Athos and d'Artagnan. Courtilz relates that Athos's wound was so severe that he believed himself dying, but with good care he eventually recovered.[30] Perhaps, Jaurgain suggested, this account represented a tradition regarding Charles Castelmore d'Artagnan and Armand de Sillègue d'Athos d'Autevielle having been friends in their youth and the latter having died from wounds received in some affair of honour involving the two of them.[31] Courtilz claimed he had served as a musketeer, and Jaurgain thought it possible he had known stories about Charles, even if he had not known Charles personally.

It is certainly tempting to think that some truth underlies the legend of friendship between Charles and Armand. But is it credible? A considerable period of time – around sixty years – separated Courtilz de Sandras from the event he described here, if it ever occurred at all, and the main aspect of it – Milédi and her spite – which Jaurgain accepts, is highly unlikely to be true. If Courtilz de Sandras served in the musketeers at all, it was in the second, not the first company. He was therefore unlikely to have been acquainted with Charles or any of his close associates. And then, Armand was an obscure man of an obscure family: unless he had died in a particularly noteworthy way (in which case other traces of it might be expected to survive) there is no reason to suppose it would be remembered for long. Courtilz had many reasons for concocting the memoirs, but historical accuracy was not one of them. We cannot accept his testimony regarding this duel and its consequences.

Did Armand know Charles? Certainly, they were both in Paris in the early 1640s, and both in the military. Both knew Tréville, both were Gascons, both came from the class of merchants–turned–gentry. They would have had a considerable amount in common. Contrary to Dumas's version, the historical Charles would probably have been older than Armand, perhaps by as much as ten years. Apart from his service in the musketeers, we know nothing of Armand's military career. Charles had been in the musketeers in the earlier 1630s, but he does not occur in the muster rolls of the company in 1640, suggesting that he had moved on to another regiment by that time. His brother Paul, however, was a member of that company at that time. We cannot say for sure whether or not Charles and Armand were ever friends. They may have met, perhaps through Paul, but the age difference between them and Charles's longer military experience may have been a barrier. By 1643, Charles was a seasoned veteran. What we know of his character – admittedly most of the evidence relates to him in late middle age – suggests a serious nature, and in an age when duels were common, he did not have the reputation of a duellist. Perhaps we malign Armand de Sillègue d'Athos d'Autevielle, judging his personality on a single, fatal act, but his youth and perhaps a tendency to engage in duels may have been a bar between him and any slight acquaintance with Charles Castelmore d'Artagnan.

PORTHOS

> At the centre of the liveliest group was a musketeer of a great height, a haughty countenance and a strangeness of dress which drew general attention to him. He was not wearing, on that occasion, the uniform cassock, which, anyhow, wasn't completely mandatory at that period of lesser liberty but greater independence, but a doublet of sky blue, albeit a little faded and worn, and over this garment a magnificent baldrick, with gold embroidery which gleamed like ripples in water in the sunlight. A long crimson velvet cloak fell gracefully over his shoulders, revealing only the front of the splendid baldrick, from which hung a huge rapier.[32]

From his very first appearance, Porthos leaps from the pages of *The Three Musketeers* and its sequels. Genial, loyal, vainglorious and expansive, he is larger than life, the most straightforward of the small band of men whom Dumas dubs The Inseparables. There is no mystery and no confusion about him – although he can be remarkably free with the truth on occasion. He was Dumas's favourite amongst the characters, the one whom he endowed with some of the more colourful characteristics of his own swashbuckling father, General Dumas. Through the sequence of the novels he rises from musketeer – of completely obscure origin – to wealthy landowner and peer. His ambitions are immediate: he wishes for admiration and for acceptance, and all his displays of splendour, from the baldrick mentioned above to the châteaux and riches he earns through marriage and adventure, are arranged to supply him with these commodities. He has no wish for power or influence, nor does he have any clear moral philosophy. He is above all else the loyal friend, the good companion, the brave adventurer who loves life for itself. Of all the musketeers, he changes the least and affects the movement of the plots of the books least. But the image of the musketeers is unthinkable without him, and he is perhaps the most memorable – because the most easily understood – of the four. He took his life from the bare record of Courtilz de Sandras and, through the latter, from a man named Isaac de Portau.

The de Portau family came from Pau, one of the three main towns of Gascony.[33] They seem to have begun their rise to prominence under Henri IV, who had close ties with Pau. In the late sixteenth century, one Abraham de Portau was part of his household, with the rank of *officier de cuisine*, some kind of steward. Abraham clearly served satisfactorily: in 1590 he received a monetary reward from the King, and his family continued to be in his service. By 1606, a kinsman, Isaac – not our musketeer – was secretary to the King. This was an influential position and potentially gave its holder access to the wider court world. This Isaac seems, however, to have retained strong ties to the region of his birth, and his rise to office was confined to it. On 23 May 1606, he became secretary to the estates of Béarn, the regional assembly. This role brought him into regular contact with the leading nobles, clergy and officials of Pau and its environs, and made him a man of considerable importance there. On 28 April 1612, he married. He was a widower (nothing is known of his first wife), but this new marriage was a step up. By this time, he was notary of Béarn, and his bride was drawn from the same administrative and official class. She was Anne d'Arrac, daughter of Bertrand d'Arrac de Gan, a Huguenot minister at the church of

Audaux. Was Isaac himself a Huguenot? Many Gascons were at this time, and Henri IV had been born into that faith. The King had no prejudices against Huguenots and neither disadvantaged them nor attempted to enforce their conversion. There would be nothing, therefore, in Protestantism to prevent Isaac from holding office or being close to the King in Béarn.

The Arrac family had useful connections. Anne was the protégé of Madame de la Force, the wife of Jacques de Caumont la Force, the governor and royal lieutenant of Béarn. After his marriage, Isaac became the governor's confidential man and made at least two trips to the royal court on his behalf, in July 1613 and October 1614. This was both an influential and a lucrative position, and in July 1619, Isaac bought the lordship of Campfort, together with valuable land at Turon.[34] At some time, he also acquired the château of Lanne-en-Baretous, which traditionally came to have the closest ties to 'Porthos'. He had acquired Campagne de Castetbon: in May 1621, it was raised to the status of a noble holding. Closeness to the King had clear advantages, and the descendant of the kitchen steward was now a lord.

He had several children. From his first marriage, he had a daughter, Sarah. She held in her own right the lay abbacy of Rivehaute, which she may have inherited from her mother.[35] She married Abraham de Bachoué d'Andrein on 16 October 1629. From his marriage to Anne d'Arrac, Isaac had three further children, Jean, Isaac (our musketeer) and Jeanne. The incidence in the Portau family of Old Testament names is another indication that they were Huguenot: such names were favoured by Protestants at this time in France. Another clue to their faith is provided by the marriage of Isaac's niece by marriage, another Anne d'Arrac. On 25 April 1632, she married one Gédéon de Rague. The de Ragues were related to the d'Aramitz family, and the latter were certainly Huguenot.

Isaac the younger was baptised on 17 February 1617, which may give us some hint as to his birth date. His godparents were drawn from the ranks of the influential people of Pau: a wealthy merchant, Isaac de Ségure, and his wife Jeanne d'Arrac. We know very little of either Isaac the younger or his father for some years hereafter. By 1642, however, Isaac the younger was in Paris, where he was serving

in the guard regiment of des Essarts, Tréville's brother-in-law. As far
as we know, Isaac was the first of his paternal family to embark on
a military career. His family, it would seem, had embarked upon
the familiar pattern of the minor nobility, sending the younger son
to pursue his fortune through arms. Isaac's elder brother apparently
remained in Béarn, where he followed his father into administration. By 1654, he was an advocate at the *parlement* of Navarre,
secretary of the estates of Navarre, and provincial controller of war
and artillery for Béarn, while his father had risen to be a royal
councillor. In passing, it should be noted that Jean de Portau's rank
of advocate suggests that he had enjoyed some formal legal training – and thus a level of education considerably higher than that
received by Charles Castelmore d'Artagnan and, probably, Armand
de Sillègue d'Athos d'Autevielle. This may well have been due to
the influence of Anne d'Arrac and her powerful patron, Madame de
la Force. The de Portau family was more successful both in acquisi-
tion of wealth and of status than the de Batz-Castelmores.

Was Isaac the younger ever a musketeer? We do not know. The
surviving muster rolls do not mention him. The connection to the
guards of Essarts and his very distant kinship to Jean-Arnaud de
Peyrer de Tréville (via the Aramitz family) might have brought him
into contact with Charles Castelmore d'Artagnan in the 1640s, if
the latter was in Paris. He and Charles would have been much of an
age, but Isaac was probably much better educated and accustomed
to moving in the circles of an urban elite, rather than belonging to
the rural gentry. As with Armand de Sillègue d'Athos d'Autevielle,
we cannot prove that there was any contact between the two, let
alone any friendship. Perhaps, however, Isaac knew Armand, even
though they were not in the same regiment, and as will be seen,
he must have known Henri d'Aramitz.

The de Portau family had built up a tight network of power
and influence at home in Gascony and the bulk of their interests
remained there. Isaac did not remain long away from his native
region. By around 1650, he had left Paris, and held the position of
subaltern of the guard of munitions in Navarrenx. Isaac doubtless
owed his post to the influence of his family. It has been suggested
that he had taken it up at least in part through necessity, as such

positions were often held by men who had received injuries such that they might no longer be in active military service.[36] However, it should be remembered that his brother Jean was controller of artillery for Béarn, and had also become controller of fortifications and repairs at Navarrenx. The family had a pattern of building up its power locally. It is not impossible that Isaac had never intended to serve away from home for long, and that his return may have been motivated by family politics. We do not know what became of him after 1650. Perhaps he died soon after his return, perhaps he retired to his family's holdings, lacking the administrative bent of his father and brother. If he married, we have no record of it. His brother Jean continued to serve in his various posts and was a frequent visitor to the royal court. At his death in 1670, he was an established man of substance. He passed the family holdings on to a son, Pierre, who was later ennobled: the family survived as lords of Lanne until shortly before the Second World War.

ARAMIS

This other musketeer made a perfect contrast to the one who was talking to him and who had just designated him by the name of Aramis: he was a young man of scarcely twenty two or twenty three years, with an artless and mild expression, soft dark eyes and with cheeks as pink and downy as an autumn peach; his neat moustache drew a perfectly straight line along his upper lip; his hands appeared to fear to lower themselves lest their veins become bloated, and from time to time he pinched himself on the lobes of his ears to keep them softly pink and translucent. Habitually he spoke little and slowly, bowed a great deal, laughed soundlessly while showing his teeth, which were beautiful and of which he appeared to take the greatest care, along with the rest of his person.[37]

Elegant, vain, watchful – and deceptive. The gentle exterior is misleading: reading *The Three Musketeers*, we soon learn that Aramis is clever, ambitious, intriguing, quick-tempered and proud. As a young man, he studied to enter the Church, before becoming a soldier 'for a short time', as he constantly reminds the reader, as a result of his quarrelsome nature. The older Aramis of *Twenty Years After* is a worldly priest who dreams of martial exploits; eventually, over the course of *The Vicomte de Bragelonne*, he rises to become bishop of Vannes, vicar-general of the Jesuit monastic order, Duke of Alméda and, finally, Spanish ambassador to France. He is the most difficult of Dumas's musketeers and the least clearly heroic – the final story arc of the sequence positions him as antagonist. And he is the only one of the four still standing as the novels draw to a close.

As with the other three, he has his roots in a real person: Henri d'Aramitz, squire and lay abbot of Espalungue and Aramitz in Béarn, only a few kilometres from Lanne-en-Baretous. It is unlikely that Dumas knew of this – he drew the religious tendencies of his Aramis from Courtilz de Sandras's portrait of Rotondis – but the lay abbacy is an entertaining coincidence. It does not mean that Henri was in religious orders: possession of a lay abbacy was a form of secular lordship, whereby a family had come to hold title not only to a particular noble land but with it the right to appoint the local priest and to receive the tithes raised by the local church. Far from being a priest, Henri was not even Catholic.

In Dumas's version, it is Athos who belonged to the old nobility: in reality, it was Henri d'Aramitz, something which Dumas's Aramis would doubtless have appreciated. Henri's family are recorded as lords of Aramitz at least as far back as the thirteenth century. In an account dated 13 August 1376 of the army of the famous Gaston Phébus, one Jean, lay abbot of Aramitz, nicknamed *Abadot d'Aramitz*, was serving in the companies brought by Menaud de Berger. This Jean was commander of 100 infantrymen. Jean served loyally and well, it seems, for, in June 1381, Gaston honoured him by raising the status of his domain.

During the second half of the sixteenth century, France was engulfed by religious warfare, the so-called Wars of Religion.[38] Gascony, which at the time belonged to the rulers of Navarre, was a Protestant stronghold. Protestantism had appeared in France by the 1550s and had affected all levels of society. There was considerable active proselytising, and a number of important figures had converted. There was often hostility between Catholics and Huguenots, and the rise of Huguenotism was of considerable concern to successive kings of France. In Gascony, this situation was made more complex in that the Queen of Navarre, Jeanne d'Albret, converted in 1560. She was married to a powerful noble-man, Antoine de Bourbon, Duke of Vendôme, who himself had a good claim on the French throne and was a political rival to the dominant Guise family. The future King Henri IV of France was their son. The French crown passed a number of repressive measures to curb the growth of the Huguenots, but failed to uproot it, and conflict continued. This often had a political dimension, as many Huguenots were perceived to be anti-government, and, conversely, those with quarrels with the politically dominant cliques, be it the Guises or the Queen-Mother, the infamous Catherine de Medicis, saw allies amongst the Protestants. Open warfare between the two religious parties continued intermittently right down to the end of the century. The Aramitz family had converted to Protestantism at some point in the mid-sixteenth century, perhaps following the example of Jeanne d'Albret. In 1569, we find Captain Pierre d'Aramitz commanding the defence of the strategically important castle of Mauléon. Overwhelmed by the royalist Catholic army, he was unable to hold it, but he continued to fight for the Protestant cause and for the royal house of Navarre. This Pierre was a descend-ent of the earlier Jean d'Aramitz and may have been the first member of the family to become Protestant.

Pierre was a significant man in his locality, more so than either the lords of Athos or those of Castelmore, and the family could be con-fident of their rank. Despite their later possession alongside Aramitz of the domain of Espalungue (which was to become their favourite residence), they did not find it necessary to add to their designation in order to identify themselves. The family married locally and made ties with people similar to themselves, rather than looking to wives for advancement and power. Nor did they seek civil office: they sought their careers in the military sphere, something which is probably linked to the age of their nobility – the old nobility simply did not think in terms of administrative offices in towns or regions, apart, of course, from such things as provincial governorships. Pierre operated typically for his class and rank, fighting for his lord and encouraging his sons into the army. He married Louise de Sanguis, whose father Louis de Tardets was from the same level of nobility as himself (Louis was squire and lay abbot of Sanguis), and had three children with her – Phébus (who died young), Marie and Charles. In October 1597, Marie married Jean de Peyrer, and with him had a son, the future captain de Tréville, whom she raised as a Catholic, despite her Huguenot background. Charles married Catherine de Rague, through whom he came into possession of the domain of Espalungue – her father was yet another squire and lay abbot, Jean de Rague, Lord of Laruns.

Like his father, Charles was a soldier. His father had followed the rulers of Navarre; in 1569, this was Jeanne d'Albret (her husband Antoine, who was King of Navarre through her, had died in 1562). Jeanne died in 1572 and Pierre then served her son Henri. In 1589, Henri became Henri IV of France. Charles d'Aramitz went not to Pau but to Paris to serve this King. Through his sister, Marie, he had a useful contact, Tréville, and he became a sergeant in the musketeers, serving under his nephew. This may suggest that he was considerably younger than Marie, although this should not be taken as certain. He fathered three children – Henri, Marie and Jeanne.

Henri was born around 1620, and was thus rather younger than Charles Castelmore d'Artagnan. We know nothing about his childhood or education, but, in around 1640, he was in Paris, where he followed his father's example and entered the musketeers under Tréville. Tradition in Aramitz says that he served alongside his father, who had continued in service. Certainly, the military bent of the family makes this plausible. Henri also served at exactly the same time as Armand de Sillègue d'Athos d'Autevielle. What did the Protestant scion of the comfortably established old family of Aramitz make of the *parvenu* with no tradition of soldiering? We do not know. Was Armand also Huguenot? It is possible, but it cannot be proved either way. The presence of Tréville ensured that there were a lot of Gascons from both the old and the new nobility amongst the musketeers. Certainly, Henri and Armand were comrades-at-arms. It is nice to think that perhaps they were also friends. And they may have known Isaac de Portau, serving under Tréville's brother-in-law Essarts. As far as Charles Castelmore d'Artagnan is concerned, similar problems arise with Henri as with Armand. There was an age gap; and also a religious difference. Charles may not have been in Paris regularly during the 1640s, but away on various campaigns. On the other hand, Henri seems to have remained with the company of musketeers until it was disbanded in 1646. But perhaps he and Charles were at least acquainted.

After the breaking of the musketeer company, Henri does not seem to have sought entrance to any other regiment. Certainly, he spent at least part of his time thereafter in his native Béarn, but he retained interests in Paris. On 16 February 1650, he entered into a contract of marriage with Jeanne de Béarn-Bonasse, a local heiress. It was another marriage of like with like, akin to those of his father and grandfather. We hear of him again in 1652, again at home in Béarn, when he was a witness at the marriage of his sister Jeanne to Arnaud de Casamayor, Huguenot pastor of the church of Oloron-Sainte-Marie, 15 kilometres from Aramitz. The family had ties at least one generation deep with that town, as we have seen in the marriage of Henri's aunt Marie. Marie's husband was Catholic, or became so, but Jeanne's marriage suggests strongly that the Aramitz family were tightly bound into the religious network of the beleaguered Huguenots, whose freedom of religion was increasingly under threat during the seventeenth century.

Religion must have presented a considerable problem for Henri. The musketeers were technically a Catholic regiment, but Henri was a close kinsman of Tréville, which may have eased his admission.[39] It would thus have been possible for him to have remained Huguenot and to have served in the regiment. If so, then it may have been religious interests that led to Henri's travels during the 1650s. We know that he at least intended to go to Paris in 1654 and that he expected either that his absence might be prolonged or that he might not live to return home. On 22 April 1654, he drew up his will. He left his goods and the guardianship of their three children to his wife Jeanne, with his eldest son Armand named as his heir. A fourth child was born a few months later, perhaps during his absence. Why was he so cautious? It is possible, of course, that he was in poor health, but we know he survived at least another three years. More significantly, the Fronde was just drawing to a close in 1654, and, in distant Béarn, Henri could not have been certain that the disturbances were over for good. Perhaps he was a *Frondeur* himself in some small way: if so, he would have found himself on the opposite side to Charles Castelmore d'Artagnan. Periods of civil disruption provide valuable opportunities for individuals and interest groups who are not directly involved in the conflict to expand their own influence or seek to establish wider influence and rights for themselves. He may have been involved in seeking to safeguard Huguenot interests.[40]

In the event, Henri returned safely from Paris to his family. We last hear of him on 10 February 1657, when he and Jeanne witnessed the marriage contract between her sister Anne and Arnaud de Juncas, advocate to the *parlement*.

Henri and Jeanne had four children – Armand, Clément, Louise and Madeleine. Armand inherited Aramitz and Espalungue from his father, but died himself without issue. His brother Clément had succeeded him by 1681, and in September of that year he is recorded presenting a request to the estates of Béarn. He was seeking access to the local registry to prove his noble birth, as he had recently married in the town of Montbrison, where it seems he was not well known, and needed to demonstrate his birth. His mother Jeanne, who was still alive, had refused to send the relevant papers to him, hence his appeal. Perhaps she disapproved of the marriage?

Clément was the last Aramitz to live at Aramitz. In December 1690, he sold the abbey to Jean de Casamayor, his first cousin. This Jean did not keep it long, however, as the property soon came into the hands of Antoine de Laure, the husband of Clément's sister Louise. This may have been some sort of family property shuffle to ensure land was settled on Louise, as she is found exercising lordship over it in 1702.[41]

The abbey at Aramitz no longer stands: its remains were demolished in 1980 to make way for a new police station. All that remains is a gateway, which leads into the village church, and a section of wall. Henri d'Aramitz is not forgotten, however: his history and arms are detailed on two plaques in the arch of the gate, while over the pelota court is the picture of a musketeer's plumed hat and two crossed swords.

Three families risen from the ranks of the merchant *bourgeoisie*, one long established amongst the minor nobility, all raised in properties of similar size and wealth, and amongst similar people. The historical Charles, Armand, Isaac and Henri were closer in origin than their literary echoes. And yet they were four different men, whose families moved on different paths. Armand and his kin formed almost the type of aspiring middle-class men who, having achieved sufficient funds, sought status through buying land and claiming lordship over it. Armand went to Paris as a soldier, as was appropriate for a younger son of the minor gentry, but fell victim to the violent fashions of the day. His family, lacking success at court and access to power through administrative office, fades from history without leaving much mark. Isaac came from a family which sought and gained success through the route of administrative offices and local patronage, who used lands and titles for position but remained essentially urban in their sphere of activity, and whose concerns focused upon building up a solid base of power within their native region. Comfortable, respectable, influential, their line survived down into the twentieth century. Henri's family had no need of new lands or offices to bolster their rank, as they could safely claim to belong to the old aristocracy. They followed a military tradition of service to the King, be it of Navarre or of France, but they did not seek to advance beyond their existing status. They were content to marry at their own level; if the family had a cause it was that of religion, not of ambition. Charles's family shared the ambitions seen in Isaac's, but looked to a wider stage: they married for advancement and for contacts at court; they sent their young men to operate where they might draw the attention of ministers and kings. A duellist, a younger son who was perhaps a bit of a disappointment to his family, a solid man of the lower gentry, and a glorious captain of the King's guards: these were the real four musketeers.

3

The Musketeer Companies

What was a musketeer, and what was the position of the musketeer companies within the army of France? Like d'Artagnan and his three companions, the idea of the musketeers has become mythologised over time into an image of brave, brash, flamboyant, swashbuckling swordsmen, engaged perpetually in duels, love affairs, heroic stands and desperate missions. The reality, as with Charles Castelmore d'Artagnan, was perhaps less flamboyant, but no less interesting.

The origins of the musketeer companies lie in the reign of Henri IV, who, in 1600, issued lightweight arquebuses to a company of light cavalry known as the *Carabins*, who became renowned for their accurate shooting. From 1615, they were dispersed amongst other light cavalry, for whom they carried out reconnaissance missions. Their skills as marksmen, as well as their lightness and manoeuvrability, made them especially suited to this task and drew upon them favourable attention. In 1622, at the time of his first expedition against the French Protestants of La Rochelle,

Henri's son Louis XIII recombined the unit. He replaced the arquebuses with the heavier and more effective muskets, and renamed the unit the King's Musketeers – the famous company of which Jean-Arnaud de Peyrer de Tréville was to become captain in 1634.

This new musketeer company became one of a number of guard companies which formed part of the King's household. The King's musketeers were trained to fight both on foot and on horseback, and were considered a light cavalry unit, even though, at that period, most musket-armed troops were infantry. This was due both to their origins in the *Carabins*, a cavalry unit, and to the fact that nearly all musketeers were members of the gentry. The martial traditions of the gentry emphasised riding skills as well as swordsmanship, and while infantry officers were gentry, cavalry carried higher prestige. Gentlemen very rarely found themselves fighting as common infantrymen.

The musketeers were an elite unit. In peacetime, their primary duty was to act as the King's escort when he travelled, whether between the various royal residences, or on progress. They always formed the van of the royal cortège, a jealously guarded privilege, but one which required mobility and stamina. They also took part in regular military reviews and in the mock battles that formed part of the entertainment of the royal court. In times of war, they would accompany the King when he was with an army, but were also frequently entrusted with particularly hazardous operations. With their speed and manoeuvrability, they could reach any part of the front where they were needed. They rapidly gained a reputation for acts of conspicuous, if sometimes foolhardy bravery, a status they worked hard at maintaining, from the captain down to the newest recruit. At sieges, they often led the assault, the position of greatest danger, and seem to have made a point of being the first into any fortress or city.

In 1671, Louis XIV formed the disparate military companies of his household into a separate army corps, the *Maison Militaire du Roi*.[1] This consisted of the four companies of the *Gardes du Corps*,[2] the two companies of the gendarmes and the *Chevaux-Leger*[3] (both of which dated from the reign of Henri IV), the *Cent-Suisse* and the two companies of musketeers. The *Gendarmes de la Garde* were added in 1676, resulting in a force of around 2,700 men. This corps held an unusual position within the French army, in that it was not subject to the jurisdiction of the Secretary of State for War, but rather of the Secretary of the Royal Household, who was responsible for providing provisions to these units. He also controlled the distribution of commissions in these prestigious and sought-after companies. While this arrangement worked smoothly in peacetime, it was capable of causing problems on campaign. Indeed, initially it was unclear as to whether or not units of the corps fell under the authority of the senior cavalry commander of the army to which they were attached, as technically they lay outside the jurisdiction of the Secretary of War.

Both Louis XIII and Louis XIV seem to have considered the musketeers as royal property and maintained a particular interest in them. While the majority of the French army worked on the purchase system, where commissions were bought and sold by the individuals concerned, the senior officers of the musketeer companies were appointed by the King.[4] Kings also paid, on occasion, for uniforms and equipment for the musketeer companies, which would normally have been their officers' responsibility.

The *Maison Militaire* as a whole, and the musketeers in particular, gained considerable status from their presence at court and their close association with the King, as well as from their martial prowess. The companies were highly privileged and positions in them were much sought after. A commission in the musketeers not only carried great cachet, but was a good route to gaining recognition and further promotion – in 1690, although the officers of the *Maison Militaire* accounted for about only five per cent of the army, it supplied a sixth of the lieutenants-general and a quarter of the marshals.

The company initially consisted of 100 musketeers, commanded by a captain, a cornet and a *maréchal des logis*. This last rank was peculiar to the cavalry. While a commissioned rank, its duties and responsibilities corresponded most closely to those of an infantry sergeant. When re-formed under Louis XIV, the company consisted of 150 men; this increased to 300 in 1663, decreased to 250 in 1668 and finally stabilised at a strength of 305 officers and men in 1693. Once the second company had been formed, it followed the same pattern as the first.

In 1693, the company contained 250 musketeers, commanded by a captain-lieutenant, two sub-lieutenants, two ensigns, two cornets and ten *maréchal des logis*. In addition, there were twenty non-commissioned officers, four brigadiers and sixteen sub-brigadiers. There were also some support troops attached to the unit: a chaplain, a surgeon, an apothecary, a quartermaster, a saddle-maker and a blacksmith. Added to these were a flag-bearer, a standard-bearer and ten musicians, six playing the tambour and four the hautbois. This small military band would perform when the unit was on parade, or escorting the King on public occasions. The detachment of musketeers escorting the King always retained the company flag, while those on active campaign carried the standard.

The musketeers were comparatively well paid. The rank and file received forty *sols* a day, which was about four times the rate for normal cavalry. In comparison, a skilled craftsman would earn around twenty *sols* a day. The musketeers also received an allowance towards their board and lodging, which varied according to the length of their service. The captain received a salary of 900 *livres* a month and an allowance of 6,000 *livres* for living expenses.[5] The lieutenants received a salary of 200 *livres* and an allowance of 3,000 *livres*. These were again around four times the rates of pay for a standard regiment.

The officers were expected not only to maintain their own household out of their allowances, but also to make good any deficiencies in their troops' supplies and equipment. For most officers in the regular army, this could easily result in them spending more than they were being paid, as was often the case for Charles Castelmore d'Artagnan. When pay was delayed, due either to transport difficulties or to the government's sometimes cavalier approach to such matters, some officers found themselves in severe financial difficulties. The close attention paid to the musketeer companies by the King caused great expense in terms of the high standards of appearance required of them, but this was cushioned by intermittent royal generosity.

EQUIPMENT OF THE MUSKETEERS

Uniform

The musketeers did not wear armour for military service, and the unit did not have an official uniform until 1673. Prior to that, they were identified by their cassocks. These were essentially a sort of sleeved tabard, which fastened down the back. Under Louis XIII, these cassocks were blue with a cross in white on the front, back and each sleeve. Initially, they were relatively short, but over time they lengthened to around knee-length. Underneath these cassocks, musketeers could and did wear what they chose – an element used for satirical purposes by Courtilz de Sandras in his depiction of Besmaux, and taken over by Alexandre Dumas for his characterisations both of Porthos and of Aramis. In the 1660s, after the creation of the second company, some distinctions were made in the cassocks: those of the first company were decorated with gold braid, while, for the second company, the braid was silver. In 1673, Louis XIV introduced a standard outfit for the company: thereafter their uniform consisted of a coat with large double pockets, which was lined and decorated in scarlet, with fringing, buttons and buttonholes in gold; breeches and stockings in red; and a hat edged with gold and adorned with a white plume. Their horse trappings were once again scarlet with gold trimmings.[6]

The use of the distinctive cassock continued, but its increased length had proved impractical in warfare, as it impeded movement. It was replaced in 1683 by the famous blue tabard. This retained the colour and emblem of the cassock (although the latter in a more elaborate form), but, being looser and shorter, was far more practical. The cross device was still white, and the arms of the cross ended in fleurs de lys, with flames in the corner angles. The two companies were distinguished by the form and colour of these flames. For the first company, the flames were red and ended in three points; those of the second company were dark orange and ended in five points. The tabards were lined in red and trimmed with silver braid.[7]

Military Equipment

The musketeers were equipped with the muskets from which they took their name, but they also carried rapiers, which were probably used at least as much as the firearms in war (and more in peacetime, if their reputation for duelling can be believed).

The Rapier
The rapier is a sword which is wielded with one hand, and is designed primarily for thrusting at an opponent rather than slashing or cutting. It has a long, thin blade, around a metre in length and less than 3cm wide. The blade is usually a diamond shape in cross-section, though this is often flattened slightly to produce a slightly hexagonal shape. As the rapier is a thrusting weapon, commonly only the last 15cms or so are sharpened to any great degree. The length of the blade means that it can be used effectively from horseback, acting almost as a lance. The blade is normally edged to within a few inches of the hilt, where there is a flat area, the ricasso. This can be used as an extension of the hilt, to give the swordsman greater control. The hilt consists of the grip, guard and pommel. The grip is shaped slightly to fit the hand and would have been wrapped in wire or fish skin (normally ray or shark) to reduce the chance of it slipping in the hand. The pommel is a metal ball at the end of the grip, which adds some extra weight to the hilt, thereby improving the balance of the sword. A thin extension of the blade, known as the tang, passes through the grip and pommel and is secured by a nut. The guard protects the hand from the opponent's sword. There are two main forms: the swept hilt, which consists of a series of thick wire rings, which curve up round the hand towards the pommel, or the cup hilt, where a metal cup covers the hand entirely from the front.

The rapier is normally seen as a gentleman's weapon, to be worn as a badge of honour and used in duels, while the sabre, a curved sword more suited to slashing from horseback, takes the military role. However, this distinction between military and civilian swords was not complete in the seventeenth century, and thus the musketeers would have used the same sorts of blades in both contexts. When Charles Castelmore d'Artagnan died in 1673, he had two swords – one with a gold-adorned guard and a brass grip, the other of blackened steel. One sword was for court and dress occasions, the other, very probably, for battle. The details are preserved in the inventory of his possessions made after his death, and the only distinctions drawn between the two swords relates to this decorative aspect, not to form.[8]

In 1680 the sabre replaced the rapier as the official sword of the French cavalry. Once the rapier had lost its military use, its form started to change. It became steadily shorter and lighter until it had been transformed into the gentleman's small sword of the eighteenth century – a delicate weapon, often highly ornamented, which was utterly unsuited for battlefield use.

Firearms

Nowadays, the term musket has come to be used for virtually any muzzle-loading, smoothbore firearm. In the sixteenth and early seventeenth century, however, the term was used to refer to a particular class of firearm. This originated in Spain in the early sixteenth century and was much heavier then the arquebus, which had first appeared around 1450. An arquebus weighed around 5 kilos, while a musket normally weighed around 7 to 9 kilos. This made it sufficiently heavy for the user to have to support the muzzle on a forked rest in order to fire it. While this meant it was substantially more awkward than the arquebus, it fired a much heavier ball, and so was considerably more effective both in penetrating armour and in causing damage. Both musket and arquebus had a matchlock firing mechanism, where pulling the trigger caused a piece of smouldering cord (the match) to be snapped forward to light the powder. It was this cumbersome weapon that was initially provided to the musketeers. Using a musket from horseback must have been particularly challenging. While musket rests, which were attached to a horse's bridle and would enable a musket to be supported between its ears, did exist, making effective use of them must have required an exceptionally skilful rider or an extraordinarily calm horse. Fortunately, over the course of the seventeenth century, the French army musket grew steadily lighter, until it had almost returned to the weight of the arquebus it replaced.

The use of a matchlock musket was remarkably complicated. The basic process was reasonably straightforward. The musketeer added some priming powder to the pan, then held the musket vertically, and poured a charge of powder down the muzzle; then he rammed the ball and wad down on top of it, returned it to the firing position, aimed and fired. However, a musketeer not only had to carry his sword, his musket and its rest: he also carried his lengths of match, a bandolier of cartridges containing the powder charges for each shot, a bag containing the balls, and another containing wads of cloth to separate the ball from the powder. Juggling this collection made reloading considerably more awkward. In particular, all actions had to be performed without letting the burning match either go out or, worse, come into contact with any of the powder that the mus-keteer, or his neighbours in the firing line, was carrying. As a result, rigorous drills were introduced, breaking the operation down into thirty or more stages.[9] The loading and firing process took between thirty seconds to a minute for a practised marksman, but, for anyone less experienced, could take considerably longer. Going through this procedure while on horseback must have been truly complicated. Mounted arquebusiers would only fire once in battle, either stand-ing in the stirrups or dismounting in order to do so. Thereafter they would fight with swords. It is likely that the musketeers operated in the same manner, and that loading would have been performed while dismounted and before any charge or advance.

Towards the end of the seventeenth century the matchlock was replaced by the flintlock, which was significantly easier to use. In the flintlock, the mechanism holding a match is replaced by an arm holding a flint. When the trigger is pulled, this snaps forward, striking sparks off a steel plate above the pan, which then ignites the powder.

Officers, and possibly some of the men, might on occasion also carry pistols. Indeed, under Louis XIV, a pair of pistols became part of their regular equipment. The pistol was favoured by the cavalry because it could be fired with one hand, making it significantly easier to use while mounted. In addition, in the seventeenth century, most pistols had a firing mechanism much more suited to cavalry use than the matchlock – the wheel-lock. This acted in a manner similar to a modern cigarette lighter. When the trigger was pulled, a wound spring would spin a toothed wheel against a piece of iron pyrites, generating sparks to ignite the powder. The spring would then be rewound with a key prior to the next shot. Also, unlike a matchlock, a wheel-lock pistol could be carried about safely when primed and ready to fire. Unlike the matchlock, the mechanism could be used sensibly on weapons with two barrels or more. This, combined with the gun's small size, led many cavalrymen to carry two or three pistols, and gave a huge advantage over the arque-bus or musket, which could only be fired once before retiring. A wheel-lock was however much more complex than a matchlock, and had to be constructed to much tighter tolerances in order to prevent powder from jamming the mechanism. This meant that a wheel-lock pistol was significantly more expensive than a musket, and hence remained a weapon of the rich. Many pistols were also ornately decorated, further to display their owners' prestige.

The main drawback of the pistol was its range. They were fre-quently considered only to be accurate at ranges of up to five metres. An infantry unit armed with them would have found itself at a considerable disadvantage if faced with opponents bearing muskets, which had a much longer range. When cavalry fought each other, however, the pistol was used in place of a lance. It had a longer range than the latter, and so had the advantage in the first shock of contact. Once mêlée was joined, a cavalryman would have to discard a lance, as its length made it impractical at close quarters. However, if he still had a loaded pistol, it could be used extremely effectively at such distances.

Pistols were considered a weapon far better suited than a musket to a nobleman. There were two reasons for this: as has been said, a set of pistols was expensive, putting them out of the reach of many rank-and-file soldiers. Secondly, their association with the cavalry – who retained a prestige inherited from the medieval knight – ensured that they were seen as a high-status weapon.

THE HISTORY OF THE MUSKETEER COMPANIES

When Louis XIII formed the musketeers in 1622, it consisted of a single company of around 100 men. He selected these, as mentioned, from the *Carabins*, supplemented with men hand-picked from his guard. Thereafter, musketeers tended to join the company young, usually at sixteen or seventeen. While the musketeers were drawn from the gentry, military reputation was more important than noble birth in their selection, despite the high status of the company. However, their first captain, the Marquis de Montalet, appears to have had a noticeable bias in favour of men of Gascon, or particularly Béarnais origin, perhaps because of their reputation for bravery, perhaps because of their association with the memory of Louis's father, Henri IV. This created a tradition which was to continue for much of the history of the company, and several of the most celebrated captains of musketeers were themselves Gascons, including, of course, Charles Castelmore d'Artagnan.

The first few years of the company's existence were peaceful. The musketeers took up residence in the area around the Faubourg Saint-Germain, and whiled away the time between their guard duties in various pursuits. They became renowned for fighting duels, and it was probably this reputation that led to them being selected for the company's first notable appearance. Duelling was banned in 1626, and in June 1627, when the Comte de Bouteville, a noted duellist, was arrested after his very public duel with the Marquis de Beuvron, Louis decided to set an example, and sentenced him to death. A troop of musketeers was ordered to guard the execution and arrest anyone who called for mercy. Perhaps the duty was intended as an object lesson.

War broke out the following month, when a Huguenot rebellion started near La Rochelle. The perennial unrest among the Huguenots had long been a concern of Richelieu, and as France had recently concluded a treaty with its old enemy, Spain, he decided to take the opportunity to resolve the situation by capturing La Rochelle, which was the last Huguenot stronghold. A large army was dispatched to put down the rebellion and lay siege to the town. When an English fleet arrived to assist the Huguenots, Louis decided to journey to the front himself, and the musketeers escorted him to Aytre, where he set up his headquarters. The rebellion was suppressed and the English were driven off in October. However, a second English fleet was dispatched in May 1628 to try to lift the siege. Louis sent the musketeers with orders to embark on French ships, so they could form boarding parties when they engaged the English. The English fleet retreated before combat could be joined, but the musketeers' enthusiasm made an impression on Richelieu, who decided they could be used as shock troops in his upcoming campaigns. The campaign was also to impress Alexandre Dumas, who used it as part of the plot of *The Three Musketeers*, introducing his heroes to a war fought while they were, in fact, still children. La Rochelle finally fell to the King's forces on 1 November 1628.[10]

Richelieu had the opportunity to test out the abilities of the musketeers the following year, when war broke out with Spain and Savoy. This was triggered by a succession crisis in the Italian duchies of Mantua and Montferrato.[11] There was no direct heir to either and when, despite a tradition of partible inheritance,[12] Charles de Gonzague claimed both duchies, the Duke of Savoy, who also had a claim, formed an alliance with Spain in order to enforce it. While the French were not initially involved, the risk that the Spanish would gain control of the strategic alpine castle of Casale-Montferrato was too great to be ignored. Once Spain held this, they would be able to limit any future French intervention in Italy, a prospect which appealed neither to Louis nor to Richelieu. The decision was taken, therefore, to offer French support to Charles de Gonzague.

Gonzague was also Duke of Nevers and governor of Champagne, and Louis initially limited French involvement to letting him raise an expeditionary force from these territories. When this failed, Louis himself led an army to Savoy, where his passage was blocked by the formidable fortifications of the Pas-de-Suse. The King decided to attempt a surprise attack on these on 5 March, and entrusted the musketeers with the task of identifying a weak spot in the defences. Having succeeded in this task, the musketeers were placed at the head of the assault. They stormed the ramparts with great élan and routed the Savoyards. Jean-Arnaud de Tréville, then a cornet, nearly

captured the Duke of Savoy, but was prevented by the intervention of the Spanish general, Cerbellon. So he captured the latter
instead. The victory was complete and the way forward was clear.
The Spanish abandoned their siege of Casale a week later. Tréville
was promoted to sub-lieutenant of the musketeers as a reward for
his bravery.

In 1632, the musketeers were again sent off on campaign, under
a new captain, Jean de Vieilchatel, Seigneur de Montalan-Savigny.
The leading nobility of Alsace, then outside France, were facing
a serious threat from Swedish armies campaigning in Germany.
Louis offered his support, and a French army was dispatched. As
they marched east, they found themselves opposed by a Spanish
force, seeking to prevent French interference in their sphere of
influence. It soon became clear that Charles, Duke of Lorraine, a
key figure in the politics of this region, was siding with the Spanish,
and Richelieu decided to launch an additional attack on Lorraine.
The musketeers formed part of the latter force. They distinguished
themselves storming the fortified village of Rouvroi, which was
strongly garrisoned. Once again, Tréville led an impetuous charge.
The musketeers overwhelmed the defenders with a ferocious assault,
killing around 200 and routing the rest.

In 1634, Louis XIII decided that he would take the rank of
captain of the King's Musketeers for himself. He therefore created
a new role, that of captain-lieutenant, who would be responsible for
the day-to-day running of the company. Jean de Vieilchatel stepped
down and was recompensed with the governorship of the duchy of
Bar, and Tréville was appointed as the first captain-lieutenant of the
musketeers, a post he was to hold until 1646. For the next ten years,
the musketeers saw regular duty on the frontiers of Picardy, Flanders
and Lorraine, but were not involved in any of the major battles or
sieges. During this period, the tendency for the musketeers to be
recruited from Gascony increased. Amongst the recruits welcomed
were Armand d'Athos, Henri d'Aramitz and Charles Castelmore
d'Artagnan.

In 1643, Louis died. His interest and patronage had protected
the musketeers from the ill effects of court intrigues, but with his
departure, they were more vulnerable. Tréville had long been an

opponent of Richelieu, and he transferred his enmity to Mazarin
when the latter became first minister. In Mazarin's eyes, he was
a relic of the old régime, a potential conspirator, and, above all, a
man of minor rank occupying a valuable position. When Tréville
refused to surrender his appointment, Mazarin decided to have
the company disbanded. A royal ordinance was enacted in 1646,
announcing that there was no longer a need for the musketeer
company. Louis XIV was only a child, he would not be going on
campaign: thus he did not require the musketeers' particular skills.
The musketeers were dispersed among the other guard regiments
and Tréville retired.[13]

Ten years later, Louis XIV, now adult, decided to expand his
guards. He was already starting to demonstrate the keen and detailed
interest in the military that would characterise his reign. Mazarin
suggested that Louis re-form the musketeers, and become their
captain, like his father. Louis was delighted by the idea and so a new
company was formed. He also accepted Mazarin's suggestion for
their new captain-lieutenant, Philippe Mancini, Mazarin's nephew.
Concerned at his nephew's lack of military experience and preference for more pacific pursuits, Mazarin also recommended the
appointment of a seasoned officer as sub-lieutenant. After a brief
false start, the choice fell on Charles Castelmore d'Artagnan.[14]

In 1658, the new company had an opportunity to demonstrate
that they were worthy of their name. France had formed an alliance with England against the old enemy, Spain. In May, Marshal
Turenne, supported by an English fleet, laid siege to Dunkirk, then
in Spanish hands. Accompanied by his new musketeers, Louis travelled to the front and set up headquarters at Calais. In June, a relief
force of Spanish troops arrived and attempted to lift the siege. Louis
was determined that his musketeers take part in any action and
sent a detachment to join Turenne. On 14 May, the two armies
clashed in the battle of the Dunes.[15] On arriving at the battlefield,
the musketeers, under the command of their sergeant, Lauroïde,
dismounted and promptly placed themselves right at the front of the
French army. The enemy general, on seeing their advance, ordered a
cavalry unit to drive them back. The musketeers repulsed this, and
what remained was routed by the French cavalry. Throughout the

battle, the Spanish repeatedly attacked the musketeers' positions, but were unable to dislodge them, and the French forces won the day. Louis was delighted by the musketeers' performance, and Turenne was sufficiently impressed to entrust them with leading the assault on the Dunkirk counterscarp. The musketeers attacked on 20 June and successfully stormed the defences. Dunkirk surrendered three days later and Louis made a triumphal entry, preceded by his escort of musketeers. Dunkirk was then, under the terms of the alliance, handed over to the English.[16]

The following year, the long-running war between France and Spain ended with the signing of the Peace of the Pyrenees, and the musketeers returned to their peacetime duties. In 1660, Mazarin presented the King with a second company of musketeers, commanded by Monsieur de Marsac. These became known as the Black Musketeers, while the first company was referred to as the Grey Musketeers; the distinction was based on the colours of the horses ridden by each company. A considerable rivalry soon developed between the two companies and in particular their officers. The same year, the musketeers formed Louis's escort on his journey to the south of France to collect his bride, Maria-Theresa, daughter of Philip IV of Spain, as has been described in Chapter 1.

On 4 September 1661, Charles Castelmore d'Artagnan arrested the finance minister, Fouquet,[17] and was entrusted with the task of guarding him. For the next four years, a large detachment of the Grey Musketeers accompanied them as they moved from prison to prison. The entire first company of 300 men was deployed on these escort duties. In the meantime, the second company shouldered most of the regular responsibilities of the musketeers. In 1663, they had an opportunity to show that they could live up to the military reputation of the first company. Louis had decided to seize Marsal from the Duke of Lorraine and sent the second company to assist in the siege. The second company did not perform well under fire. Monsieur de Marsac could not, in honour, retain his position and so sold his commission to the Comte de Maulévrier. The latter may well have felt that he had made a poor purchase, as Louis was so displeased with the musketeers' performance that he disbanded

the second company. A year later however, possibly at the instiga-
tion of Colbert, Maulévrier's brother, he relented and re-established
the second company. This interlude did nothing to diminish the
rivalries between the companies.

In 1665, Philip of Spain died, and Maria-Theresa's younger
half-brother Carlos II inherited the throne. Louis re-embarked
on his campaign to expand his lands to the east, this time using
Maria-Theresa's supposed rights of inheritance as a pretext. The
musketeers, commanded by Charles Castelmore d'Artagnan, accompanied the King to the front, but did not play an active part in the
fighting until the siege of Lille in August 1667. There they led their
famous midnight assault on the *demi-lune* which protected the gate
of Fives. Led by a lieutenant of the second company, they stormed
the ramparts and seized the defences in short order. Disheartened
by this setback, the governor of Lille surrendered the next day.
D'Artagnan took no part in this assault. He was acting as a brigadier
in the cavalry, which was patrolling in front of the army. Four days
later, however, he saw action against a force of 10,000 cavalry, which
had been sent to relieve Lille.

The assault on Lille followed a standard pattern. The besiegers
prepared gun emplacements from which they bombarded the walls.
Under cover of this fire, and working mainly at night, they exca-
vated zigzag trenches – 'saps' – forward towards the wall. They then
used these to develop another, closer, set of gun positions, and the
guns were moved forward to where they could do more damage. If
necessary, this process would be repeated until the guns had done
enough damage and the saps were close enough for an assault to
be mounted. The process was labour-intensive but, once started, the
town or fortress was normally doomed unless a relief army arrived.
Lille fell in less than three weeks.

When Dôle, in the independent province of Franche-Comté,
was besieged the following February, a detachment of musketeers
decided to circumvent this entire laborious procedure. The French
had barely started digging the trenches when this group, acting
completely without orders, decided to storm the covered way. They
took the enemy by surprise and gained a foothold on the counterscarp. The French general seized the opportunity and sent forward

troops to assist them, before they could be driven back. In the ensu-
ing struggle, the French gained control of all the outer works of the
town's defences, and Dôle capitulated after a siege of only four days.
In May 1668, Louis was forced to make peace when England, Spain
and the Dutch formed an alliance against him. While he retained
Lille, and several other towns in the Netherlands, Dôle was returned
to Franche-Comté.

The peace lasted four years and was marked by one of the most
curious events in the musketeers' history, when, in 1669, they took
part in a crusade. The Turks had been besieging the town of Candia,
on the island of Crete, for twenty-five years, and it was finally on the
point of falling. Pope Clement IX called on the princes of Europe
to send help. As one of the greatest Christian monarchs, Louis felt
obliged to respond and, in June 1669, he sent a force of 7,000 men
to assist in the defence of Candia. This force included 200 musketeers, drawn from both companies and under the command of
Maulévrier. When they arrived at Candia, the French decided to
dislodge a force of 10,000 Turks which had occupied one quarter of
the town. The musketeers were placed in reserve, ready to be flung
in wherever assistance was needed. At first, the assault went well
and the French soon drove back the Turks. Unfortunately, at that
point, a powder magazine exploded among the advancing French,
throwing them back in confusion. The Turks seized the opportunity
and counterattacked in force. The musketeers, and the rest of the
reserve, were sent forward to oppose them. They were outnumbered
ten to one, and, despite fighting ferociously, were driven back within
the walls of Candia. They left thirty men dead on the field and
a third of the remainder had been seriously wounded. The relief
force had failed to improve the situation significantly and it now
seemed inevitable that Candia would fall. The Turks launched a
frontal assault on 26 June, which was barely repulsed, and the French
decided to evacuate. This took three days, during which Maulévrier
led the musketeers in a final sortie to distract the Turks.

In 1672, Louis declared war on Holland. He had not forgiven the
Dutch for allying with the Spanish against him in the previous war
and wished to ensure they would not do so again. This was the first
war in which the musketeers acted as part of the *Maison Militaire*

du Roi. Half of the musketeers had wintered with an army based in Cologne: with the arrival of the King, they were reunited with their comrades. D'Artagnan was not with them, as he was acting as governor of Lille, and his place was taken by his sub-lieutenant. The French armies advanced from Cologne, and took the Dutch by surprise. They bypassed Maastricht and pushed on towards the Rhine, where a Dutch army opposed their crossing. The French cavalry led the assault, with the *Maison* attacking a separate unit on the flank. They drove back the Dutch and took many prisoners. The infantry could then cross on a pontoon bridge. This manoeuvre had outflanked the main Dutch army and the French quickly captured Utrecht. The musketeers, along with the rest of the cavalry, were sent out towards Amsterdam to ravage the territory. Alarmed at the speed of the French advance, the Dutch opened their dykes and flooded the land around Amsterdam. This effectively stopped the French, who withdrew. When the King returned to Paris, the musketeers remained with an army near Maastricht.

The following year, Louis decided to capture Maastricht. By now, d'Artagnan had rejoined his men. They were attached to a force headed by the Marquis of Rochefort,[18] which advanced towards the River Senne and forced a crossing at Capelbruge. This helped persuade the Spanish, who were now assisting the Dutch, that the French were planning to attack Brussels. In response, the Spanish forces were moved in that direction and away from Maastricht. The musketeers rejoined the main army, which invested Maastricht on 10 June. On 24 June, the musketeers headed the assault on the *demi-lune* protecting the Tongres Gate. They returned to defend it the following day when the Dutch tried to recapture it. The subsequent fighting was extremely bloody, and 100 musketeers were killed, Charles Castelmore d'Artagnan among them. The second company led an assault on a horn-work the following day and also took heavy casualties. But despite the heavy toll of men, Maastricht fell to the French on 3 June. The King was well aware of the contribution to this of the musketeers; indeed, their role in the siege is remembered in Maastricht to this day. Later in this campaign, the musketeers were sent into Franche-Comté, where they assisted in the taking of Besançon and once again took part in an attack on Dôle.

They took part in further campaigns over the next two years, and continued to lead assaults in the numerous sieges. As the war progressed, the musketeer companies developed a new technique for such attacks. Rather than focusing on a specific objective, they advanced in a loose formation over a wide front, and took advantage of whatever weaknesses they discovered. This proved particularly suited to night attacks. The most notable use of this approach, however, was a daylight attack during the siege of Valenciennes in 1677. Valenciennes lay in a very strong position: the approaches were flooded on three sides, it was heavily fortified, and well garrisoned. When the saps were close enough to the defences, Vauban proposed a daylight assault. He argued that this would be unexpected, as the French nearly always attacked at night, and that the troops would be inspired to further efforts by knowing that the King was watching. The King agreed and two columns were formed, with one company of musketeers at the head of each. When the assault commenced, the musketeers soon cleared the *demi-lune* they were attacking, driving back the Spanish and leaving most of the other French troops behind. The Spanish were forced back across a drawbridge leading to a much larger defensive work which defended the main bridge across the river. A group of musketeers pressed them so hard that they were unable to raise the drawbridge behind them. The far end of this bridge was protected by a barricade, in which the sole passage was only wide enough for one man to pass at a time. While some musketeers cut down the Spaniards defending the gap, others climbed the barricade and leapt down among the defenders beyond. This ferocious assault quickly broke the defenders, who fled across the main bridge and raised it behind them. At this point, the group, having advanced so far into the enemy defences and finding their way blocked, could have stopped and prepared to defend the works they had captured. The musketeers, however, found a stair in the wall that led to a gallery which crossed the river. They promptly headed off down this and found themselves on the town ramparts, from which they descended into the town itself. At this point, discretion finally got the better part of valour, and they prepared to defend their position. They built some barricades and awaited attack. The Spanish cavalry launched several cavalry charges but these were beaten off, and by the time some Spanish attacked along the ramparts in order to cut them off, the rest of the musketeers had arrived. Further French troops followed and quickly exploited this opening. The garrison soon realised their position was hopeless and surrendered. Quarré d'Aligny, who was amongst the first into the town, described the action of the first company of musketeers as 'an undertaking so daring, that one might without unfairness consider it reckless'.[19] Nevertheless, a delighted Louis gave the musketeers all the garrison's horses as thanks for this remarkable achievement.

The musketeers also distinguished themselves in open battle, whether fighting on horse or as infantry. They took part in the battle of Mont Cassel as cavalry and fought as infantry in the battle of Seneffe, where, charging on foot, they routed a regiment of pikemen.

During the Nine Years War (1688–97) and the War of the Spanish Succession (1701–14), the musketeers continued to distinguish themselves, not only in victory, but also in defeat. They were present at the battles of Ramillies and Malplaquet, and on both occasions their bravery and discipline helped the French army retire in good order. One wonders if Marlborough remembered them from his service alongside them thirty years earlier at Lille.

When Louis XV took the throne in 1723 the musketeers ceased to be a front-line unit, and thereafter they were restricted to ceremonial duties. The unit also took on the function of a cavalry school. They were rarely to see action again.

Their final engagement was at the battle of Fontenoy in 1745. During the battle, the English infantry advanced steadily, routing any cavalry sent against them and driving the French infantry back out of their defensive positions. At this point, when the battle seemed lost, the Duc de Richelieu led the *Maison* in a desperate charge which broke the English line, turning defeat into victory. The musketeers had lived up to their reputation one last time.

The musketeers were finally disbanded in 1776. Though the companies spent the latter half of their existence as ceremonial troops, their actions during the reign of Louis XIV and their association with the d'Artagnan legend ensured their name would live on.

4

Gatien de Courtilz de Sandras and the *Mémoirs de M. d'Artagnan*

Without Gatien de Courtilz de Sandras, it is likely that we would not have *The Three Musketeers*. Charles de Batz-Castelmore d'Artagnan would be a footnote in historical accounts of seventeenth-century France, and the names Athos, Porthos and Aramis would be unremarked and unknown. The popular image of Gascony – land of romantic martial heroes – might have been reduced. Even tourist guides might have been written somewhat differently. Yet it is unlikely that Courtilz set out to have any of these effects, or ever dreamt of them. He wrote for one major reason: money.

Like d'Artagnan and the three musketeers, Courtilz came from the ranks of the minor nobility. He was born sometime between 1644 and 1647, either in Paris or Montargis, the son of Jean de

Courtilz, Lord of Tourly and Marie de Sandras. His father's family
had lands in the Beauvais area, but were originally from Liège. His
branch of the family had moved to the Beauvais in the course
of the fifteenth century, and could prove a more than respectable
pedigree going back to the thirteenth century. They were neither
wealthy nor politically influential, and he could expect little by
right of birth beyond the usual career options of Church or army.
He is likely to have received the standard level of education for a
boy of his class – nothing in his later literary career suggests any
unusual early training.

Supposedly around 1660, his family arranged for him to enter
the musketeers – or perhaps the cadet training school attached to
that company. It seems that a military career was to be his destiny.
This connection to d'Artagnan might be seen as suggesting that the
two were acquainted and that Courtilz had heard something of the
former's life directly, but it must be borne in mind that very little
regarding Courtilz is certain, and the date of 1660 may be wrong.
There is a supposed portrait of him in musketeer dress: the tabard
he wears is that not of d'Artagnan's first company of musketeers,
but of the rival second company. That would suggest that he would
have been unlikely to have known d'Artagnan save at a distance.
However, it is not certain that the picture is genuine; the question
must to some extent remain open. The evidence for Courtilz's presence in the musketeers rests largely on his own statements: he does
not appear in surviving muster rolls.[1] Scholarly opinion on his connection to the musketeers is varied: Jean Lombard thinks it is likely
he served in the first company.[2] Jean-Christian Petitfils argues for
the second company.[3] Odile Bordaz suggests that he never served
in either regiment, and that the claim he made in around 1693,
on being imprisoned in the Bastille, that he had served with the
regiment 1660–66 was pure self-aggrandisement: this seems the
best explanation.[4] The obscurity of his family could be further
evidence for this view, as there is nothing to suggest that they had
any influence, and entry into the musketeers was highly sought after
and much prized. It might be argued that his use of the names of
obscure musketeers like Athos, Porthos and Aramis suggests he had
some tie to the musketeers, but, as will be seen, he may have had

other reasons for using these names, and his knowledge of them did not extend beyond their names.

Although Courtilz may not have been a musketeer, he was a soldier. In early 1667, he was made a cornet in the Royal-Étranger regiment. He saw service in the Low Countries under Marshal Turenne: his earliest literary works were histories concerned with the French wars in this area and show eyewitness knowledge. He fought in the sieges of Lille, Douai, Tournai, Ath and Charleroi. In 1668, he and his regiment served under the Prince de Condé in the latter's victorious campaign in Franche-Comté. In the second part of that year, after peace had been signed, he was garrisoned at Oudenarde. When hostilities resumed in 1673, he became captain of a cavalry regiment, that of Beaupré-Choiseul. It was a promotion, but not a particularly prestigious one, as this regiment was not part of the Royal Household and he was not well positioned to draw the attention of the King and the higher courtiers. We have no secure details of his actions during the Dutch War, although he claimed he fought in the battle of Salzbach in 1675. Peace was signed anew in 1678, and, shortly afterwards, he resigned his commission and left the army. He seems to have gained little or nothing in terms of monetary wealth or powerful contacts throughout his years of service, but he had acquired a wealth of information about the conduct of the wars, the events leading up to peace, and the gossip surrounding King, marshals and court. It was with this capital that he was to embark on a new career, that of writer.

He had had periods of leave during his military years, and in 1664 he had married Marie Despieds, with whom he had two children, a boy born sometime between 1665 and 1667 and a daughter born by January 1668. Marie died in July 1671. We know nothing more about her, and there is now no way of knowing how her husband felt about her or the circumstances of their marriage. He had been quite a young man – somewhere between seventeen and twenty; perhaps there was an element of romance to the match. In May 1678, however, he remarried, and this time advantage seems to have entered his thinking. His new bride was Louise Panetier, a girl of some fortune. Perhaps he sought to gain through marriage what he had failed to find through warfare. But he still needed to make a living.

Louis XIV's régime maintained tight controls over what was printed and sold, and any work which was deemed to be religiously, politically or morally objectionable would be suppressed. Authors of such works faced severe penalties, as did printers and booksellers who were found to be trading in banned works. It was also a crime to bring any banned books into France. Despite the law, however, such clandestine works were highly sought after, and a lively black-market trade existed.[5]

At first, Courtilz may have hoped to be able to build a reputation as a legitimate writer, drawing on his military experience. He may have begun writing before he left the army: his first two books appeared in 1678, with a third following in 1679, and a fourth in 1680.[6] All were published in Paris, having received official approval. Two were accounts of recent military campaigns, the other two dealt with the fashionable world of gallantry. It seems that no one particular field, passion or idea had drawn him to become a writer; he was commercial in his approach, seeking to provide simply what would sell. And he rapidly realised that legitimate works would not provide him with the scale of sales and success that he desired. He turned his attention, therefore, to the more lucrative – if much riskier – field of clandestine literature. While serving in the army, he had had opportunities to hear court gossip; moreover, family neighbours at Tourly were close acquaintances of Madame de Maintenon, who, in 1680, was governess to the King's children by his senior mistress, Madame de Montespan. It was known that the King's eyes had begun to wander, and Madame de Montespan had become embroiled with a famous scandal.[7] All this was ripe for exploitation, but any attempt to publish a work touching on it would be impossible in France. There was, however, likely to be a ready market. The lure of money outweighed any caution Courtilz might have felt, and sometime in 1680 he began writing *Le passe-temps royal ou les Amours de Mademoiselle de Fontanges* (*Royal Leisure, or The Loves of Mademoiselle de Fontanges*). This dealt with the King's liaison with Angelique de Fontanges, a court beauty who had seemed likely to supplant Madame de Montespan. When Angelique died late in 1680 after a pregnancy, gossip pointed a finger at the senior mistress. It was a very hot topic, but Courtilz had to travel outside France to

1 The château at Castelmore, birthplace of Charles Castelmore d'Artagnan.

2 Lupiac as it is today.

3 The castle at Bouillon, where Mazarin spent his second exile.

4 Fortified gate built by Vauban, citadel of Lille.

5 Anne of Austria, painted by Nicolas Mignard.

6 Statue commemorating
d'Artagnan at Maastricht.

7 Memorial stone to
d'Artagnan, near the place
where he was killed.

8 The château at Troisvilles, built by Jean-Arnaud de Peyrer de Tréville.

9 The château at Lanne, property of the de Portau family.

10 Cardinal Richelieu, painted by Philippe de Champaigne.

Above: 11 A *demi-lune.*
This example is from
the seventeenth-century
fortifications at Rocroi.

Right: 12 Statue of
d'Artagnan at Auch,
near Tarbes.

13 Louis XIV as a young man, studio of Mignard.

find a publisher. It marked the beginning of his new career as a specialist in the clandestine.

Courtilz was no stranger to risk, after his time in the army. From the early 1680s, he found it necessary to spend much of his time outside France, to avoid prosecution and imprisonment. The main centre for illicit printing was the Low Countries, and it was to Holland that he now went to pursue his new career. He made regular returns to France to see his family and oversee his business affairs. And he continued to produce a steady stream of works, which were all published outside France. The focus was still military matters and scandal. His lack of political allegiance was made clear when, in 1683, he published both an attack on French policy since the peace of Nijmegen and a refutation of his own attack.[8] He was safe from the charge of hypocrisy, if not that of illegality, as his works were all anonymous. In 1685, he added biography to his repertoire, producing a *Life* of the celebrated Marshal de Turenne, under whom he had served. He was not, however, yet satisfied with the level of his income, and in the following year he founded a monthly journal, the *Mercure historique et politique* (*The Historical and Political Mercury*). Like books and pamphlets, newspapers and journals were subjected to official regulation and censorship, and the information published was very carefully selected to show King, court and royal policy in the best light. Courtilz supplied the other news: scandals, mistakes and criticisms. In 1687, he produced the first of what would become perhaps his most effective type of work: memoirs, or, more correctly, pseudo-memoirs. This genre allowed him to produce critical and satirical accounts of aristocratic and royal behaviour under cover of being an eyewitness testimony. His first such was entitled *Memoirs of M.L.C.D.R.* and was to become one of his best-known works. The anonymous 'author' was supposedly one Charles-César, Comte de Rochefort, but the purpose of the book was less to provide a life-story of any real person than an exciting and racy read set against the background of high politics. It is, indeed, unclear who exactly Courtilz meant as his subject: there were several Comtes de Rochefort over the course of the seventeenth century, and it seems likely that Courtilz made a composite figure from several of them.[9] A century and a half later, Alexandre Dumas read these

Memoirs and drew from them not only one of the villains for *The Three Musketeers*, but also the idea of a woman with a deadly secret – that she has been branded – which produced one of the high points in the novel.

Pseudo-memoirs became Courtilz's favoured form of writing: they provided a means of blending historical events with interesting scandalous details, and of presenting major court or government figures in a satirical or critical light, while simultaneously having a an air of authenticity and an immediacy, provided by the use of the first-person narrator. He was able also to use parts of his own experience, notably his past as a soldier, but also his brushes with the law, his relations with women, and his background as a member of the lower nobility. This helped lend an air of truthfulness to the books.

His activities had not made him spectacularly rich, but his income level seems to have improved. He already had some property at Sandras, inherited from his mother; in 1689 he purchased the estate of Le Verger, near Montargis. His wife and children took up residence there: he had thus provided them both with a home and with a source of revenue which was less vulnerable to the raids of Louis's police (who had on several occasions seized and destroyed copies of his books, and who regularly disrupted the transport of clandestine literature into France). He himself was also vulnerable: although his books were anonymous, he was known to be writing illegal works and having them printed, and he had also involved himself in smuggling letters into France. His regular travels between Paris, the Low Countries and Sedan (which lay on one of the routes into France) were in themselves suspicious. In 1693, the authorities finally caught up with him. On 20 April, he was arrested in Paris and taken to the Bastille. He stayed there at least six years without trial. This imprisonment can be seen clearly reflected in the *Memoirs* of d'Artagnan.

If one had money, or contacts, or both, being in the Bastille was not necessarily too uncomfortable. Courtilz was probably able to ensure he was fed and clothed adequately, and reasonably housed, by paying bribes to his gaolers. The governor of the time was Besmaux, who had formerly been a colleague of Charles

Castelmore d'Artagnan in the service of Cardinal Mazarin. One might think that he might have provided Courtilz with information about the late captain-lieutenant of musketeers, but this was probably not so. Courtilz rapidly formed a loathing for Besmaux, whom he considered corrupt and grasping. He turned this to good use, and painted a very unflattering portrait of Besmaux in his writings. The level of corruption in the prison had its advantages for him: he was able to ensure a regular supply of writing materials, and continued to work. He even succeeded in having his manuscripts smuggled out and transmitted to his publishers – clearly imprisonment was no solution to the problem of clandestine books! During his stay, Courtilz wrote and published two books and founded a new journal.[10] The creation of the latter suggests that interesting news continued to reach him.

Courtilz was released in March 1699 and ordered to leave Paris. He went to Le Verger. If the imprisonment had been meant as a warning, he had learnt nothing from it. Rather, he simply published the works he had written while in prison. No fewer than five appeared during 1700–01. One of these was the *Mémoires de M. d'Artagnan Capitaine Lieutenant de la première Compagnie des Mousquetaires du Roi contenant quantité des choses particulières et secrettes qui se sont passées sous le Regne de Louis le Grand*, in three volumes.[11] The book rapidly went through two editions, the first published in 1700, probably in the Netherlands, although the title page bore a claim that it was the product of an imaginary printing house, Pierre Marteau, at Cologne. The second edition followed rapidly, the first volume being dated 1700, with volumes two and three appearing in 1702. Like all but his first four works, it was anonymous, but there was little doubt in the public mind that Courtilz was its author. It was no more or less controversial than his other anonymous works, but it was to become the book for which he would be remembered, and is the only one which is still in print in French today.

Throughout his life, Courtilz had had a complicated relationship with the authorities. After his release from prison, he did not find it necessary to retreat back into the Low Countries, and even his banishment from Paris was short-lived. In January 1700, he obtained permission to return to the capital for health reasons (one assumes he made a case for the need to visit a specific medical practitioner). Thereafter, he alternated between Paris and Le Verger. It is probable that the main focus of the Paris trips was more to do with the clandestine book trade than his health, although the volume of his writing began to decline. He was no longer a young man. In 1706, his second wife, Louise, died. She seems to have been complicit in his writing activities and may have encouraged him in them; it is unlikely he would have been able to transmit new material to publishers during his time in the Bastille without her help. Perhaps he experienced this as a pressure, for, after her death, he made a new attempt to secure legitimate means of publication. In 1711, he produced a book on the nature and practice of warfare, *Le Conduite de Mars* (*The Conduct of Mars* [War]). It was published with official sanction at Rouen. It seemed that Courtilz hoped for some formal recognition from his homeland. He had not abandoned the lucrative illegal book trade, however: in the same year yet another clandestine work of his was published outside France.[12] In the same year, he made an interesting third marriage. His bride was a widow, Madame Auroy, who had inherited from her husband a book-dealing business. This lady had not always been a friend to Courtilz – indeed, on one occasion she had informed against him to the police, but now, it appears, he hoped through her to continue his connection to the trade in literature and perhaps even secure an outlet for his own works. If so, he had only a short while in which to benefit: he died eighteen months after the marriage, on 8 May 1712.

Like Charles Castelmore d'Artagnan, Courtilz de Sandras owes much of his later renown to Alexandre Dumas père. He was only one of a number of writers who specialised in clandestine works, but none of his books ever achieved major success. He had no particular political, religious or social theory which he wished to expound: he was a commercial writer, supplying the market with whatever would sell. He was not particularly well regarded in his own lifetime: not simply because of the illegal nature of his activities, but because the product was not always considered of especial value or reliability. His contemporary, the writer and literary critic Pierre Bayle, wrote of his '…impudence to produce as the memoirs of Monsieur d'Artagnan three volumes of which not one line was written by Monsieur d'Artagnan'.[13]

The value of Courtilz's various books and pamphlets as sources for history remains under debate. The books can tell us a fair amount about the interests, tastes and habits of the book-buying public in the later seventeenth century. They also give an impression of the sorts of gossip that circulated about various public figures and the light in which they and their actions were regarded. Courtilz brought his own experience to bear upon his writing: as such, his books provide useful detail about such things as the conduct of siege warfare, the nature of the education of young male gentry, the lives of prisoners in the Bastille and so forth. They certainly provide us with some of the flavour of gentry life under Louis XIV. When it comes to the events and details of the lives of specific individuals, he is far less trustworthy. Courtilz was neither a historian nor a biographer as we would understand these terms today: he was perhaps more akin to a gossip-columnist, or a journalist writing for a wide popular audience. It is unlikely he felt much responsibility to be accurate in all details, or to undertake much by way of research into his subjects. His readers wanted to know about the feet of clay hidden under the splendid garb of their leaders, not about the strict truth (except, of course, where it was sufficiently exciting or scandalous). Where he lacked information, he was not afraid to invent it, or to fill in details by recycling events from his own life. When it comes to the lives of those whose memoirs he produced, therefore, he is a very unreliable witness.

What, then, of the *Memoirs of Monsieur d'Artagnan*? Over time, the degree to which they have been accepted as evidence for the life and career of the real Charles Castelmore d'Artagnan has declined. The first modern biographer of our musketeer, Eugène d'Auriac, who wrote in the mid-nineteenth century, accepted them in their entirety, using them as a means of 'correcting' the version of Dumas, with the result that his book is little more than a rewriting of Courtilz.[14] Charles Samaran, whose biography of Charles laid the foundation for scholarly investigation, was far more cautious in his approach. He based his work on records and letters surviving from the court of Louis XIV, and made recourse to Courtilz only for outline, and, to a degree, for the lives of Charles's famous colleagues, Athos, Porthos and Aramis.[15] Subsequent biographers have followed his lead. But what do the *Memoirs* say, and how do they fit into the growth of the legend of d'Artagnan and the three musketeers?

It has been mentioned above that Courtilz claimed to have served in the musketeers and that there is a purported picture of him in their uniform. It has been claimed in the past that his connection to the company would have given him access to Charles himself, and to stories about him current amongst the men. However, it is possible that this service was a product of his imagination: Courtilz seems to have been trying to enhance his own status when he was imprisoned, and there are no good grounds for believing the claim. He did not himself serve in any regiment attached to the royal military household, so is unlikely ever to have had any close contact with Charles. He may well have seen him, on parade or in camp, but it is highly unlikely that the two knew each other, or that the captain of musketeers, who was in his fifties or sixties when a teenage or early-twenty-something Courtilz began his military career, would have noticed the young man. On Charles's death, no papers of any kind useful to a biographer were found amongst his possessions, nor, even if such things had existed, does it seem probable that they would have come into Courtilz's hands. Courtilz thus had no privileged access to information about Charles, and would have been reliant upon public knowledge, derived from the *Gazette de France* and similar sources, along with some army anecdotes. Nor was he concerned to paint an accurate picture of the musketeer. For Courtilz, Charles Castelmore d'Artagnan was a conveniently placed figure about whom he might spin a tale of court intrigues, political manoeuvrings and amorous stories. As a known intimate first of Cardinal Mazarin and later of Louis XIV, Charles was a useful focus and a plausible witness to interesting events. He was a known participant at a number of famous happenings. A narrative written in his name would give an illusion of truthfulness to scandalous details about the highborn and powerful. As a soldier, his life could be expected to have been colourful. Moreover, Charles's heirs were of little account, and his family had only limited influence at court. The likelihood of problems or legal action from them was remote.

The *Memoirs* purport to present a first-person narrative of the life and times of Charles, from his departure from Gascony down to the siege of Maastricht. He lived through colourful times, and Courtilz makes the most of this, although it must be said that the overall tone is neither engaging nor intriguing. On a first reading, the narrative appears to provide considerable information about its supposed subject and author, but closer consideration reveals that this is an illusion, and one that is rather carelessly constructed. Rather more than half of the text has little directly to do with Charles Castelmore d'Artagnan. Instead, it narrates the progress and planning of different military campaigns, anecdotes of varying scurrility about officials, courtiers and army officers, and long excursions about general events. Such information as is presented about Charles himself is often very vague in nature: there are accounts of his intrigues with a succession of unidentified and unidentifiable women, occasional duels and colourful but fantastical stories about his activities as a spy for Cardinal Mazarin. It should be borne in mind, of course, that Courtilz was in the business of selling books, not recording precise truths – this kind of narrative is what his readers were expecting, and their interest was probably less in Charles himself (although the amorous exploits would have been considered pleasantly spicy) than in gossip, scandal and court intrigue. So in some senses, it is unfair to judge Courtilz on the grounds of his historicity, or lack thereof. The claim he makes in his preface to have used certain documents written by Charles and found after his death is almost certainly there simply for the sake of form.

There is more supposed personal detail about Charles in the earlier than the later parts of the book, suggesting perhaps that Courtilz was wanting in more general information and thus obliged to be more creative in his approach. The story begins in a fashion which will be familiar to readers of *The Three Musketeers,* with the young Charles leaving his home in Gascony with little money, a comical horse and a letter to Monsieur de Tréville. On his way to Paris, in the town of St Dié, he is mocked for his poverty by one Rosnai, who proceeds to have him beaten and robbed. As a result he finds himself imprisoned and judged to owe reparation for damage, a situation from which he is rescued after several days by a kind benefactor, Monsieur de Montigré. The outlines of Dumas's famous story can be discerned here, but Courtilz's account is far less dashing – and Milady is wanting. Charles then continues on to Paris, determined to repay Montigré (which he does in due course), and there seeks out Tréville. In the latter's antechamber, he makes the acquaintance of a musketeer named Porthos, one of three brothers who serve in the musketeers, who involves him in a duel against the musketeers of Cardinal Richelieu.[16] The account is admixed with details about Tréville and his brother-in-law des Essarts, and about the opponents – Bernajoux, Jussac, Biscarrat, Cahusac and Rotondis – whom Porthos has arranged for Charles, Athos, Aramis and himself. As Dumas was to do, Courtilz worked to blend his hero into the known events of the period, but with far less success. Much of his account of the early part of Charles's life consists of the rather tedious ramifications of the quarrel with Rosnai – which has none of the panache or intrigue of Dumas's version – and of equally drawn-out romantic adventures, the details of which are often more sordid than engaging, and which do not necessarily show Charles in a likeable light. The most interesting episode, from the point of view of a reader of Dumas, is the intrigue with an English woman, maid of honour to the exiled Queen of England, Henrietta Maria.[17] This woman – identified as 'Milédi' – is prejudiced against the French and unwilling to receive Charles's attentions. He nevertheless manages to intercept her correspondence with the man she loves, Comte de Wardes, and to substitute himself for the latter. He then becomes entangled by her plots for revenge, first upon the fake de Wardes, and then upon himself: it is Dumas's famous Milady, but without the details of political intrigue, bigamy and sinister genius.[18] There is no way to identify the woman concerned – Courtilz is always careful to avoid naming any of Charles's mistresses, and the only safe conclusion is that she is fictional, a way of tying Charles plausibly to the wider intrigues that occupied the court at that time. Indeed, such individuals as he does name are either well-known figures whose deeds and exploits were already renowned, such as Tréville, or the Prince of Condé, or else obscure individuals – such as Athos, Porthos and Aramis – whose families were of little account and unlikely to cause trouble. Courtilz's profession was inherently risky: he was expected to include calumnies and slanders, but at least as far as the pseudo-memoirs of d'Artagnan were concerned, he seems to have wished to avoid accidental trouble.

Courtilz made considerable use of his own experience in writing the book. The most interesting sections are those which deal with military matters. These have a more sober tone than much of the rest, often closer in style to narrative history than to memoir. In writing these, Courtilz drew not only upon his own career as a soldier but upon the works he had already written concerning various of the wars in which France had become involved over the course of the seventeenth century. He also gave rein to his own prejudices, notably his intense dislike for Besmaux. The famous incident of the half-decorated baldrick, which Dumas used to help paint the character of Porthos, is, in the *Memoirs*, related of Besmaux, and in a far less affectionate fashion.[19] Attacks on the governor continue intermittently throughout the whole book. The descriptions of Charles's two periods in prison probably also derive from Courtilz's own life – there is no reason to suppose that such a fate ever befell the historical Charles.

He was not entirely ignorant about Charles, but the information he seems to have possessed was thin and not always accurate. He knew, for instance, of the rivalry between the first and second companies of musketeers and the expense this put Charles to, but has his hero resort to a rich mistress for help.[20] The historical Charles seems to have been bailed out from time to time by the King. Courtilz knew that Charles had married, but had no details and includes the information rather late in the narrative, almost as an afterthought.[21] He knew that Charles had been detailed by Louis XIV to act as jailer to the fallen minister Fouquet, though again he provided little detail.[22] He did not seem to know anything about Charles's service to Mazarin, other than the bare fact that Charles had served the cardinal. Some of what he thought he knew about Charles was, moreover, wrong.

Courtilz seems to have known that Charles's actual surname was de Batz-Castelmore, and not d'Artagnan.[23] This may have led him

to recount two stories of espionage and exploits in disguise, one set
in Bordeaux and the other in London, both supposedly undertaken
at the behest of Cardinal Mazarin. The first adventure is said to have
occurred in 1653, towards the end of the Fronde. Mazarin was in the
process of reinstating himself definitively in power, having won over
or defeated much of the opposition to him, and was determined
to extinguish the last embers. The city of Bordeaux, a strategically
important sea port, had close ties to the Prince of Condé, who
remained in rebellion against King and cardinal. During 1652, a
rebel movement known as the *Ormée* had set up a local political
council, and the city continued to hold out against royal government.[24] According to Courtilz, Mazarin ordered Charles to disguise
himself and gain entrance to the city, pretending sympathy with the
rebels. He was then to endeavour to detach from the movement
the Prince of Conti, brother of Condé, who was closely associated
with the *Ormistes*, by bribing him with a lure of marriage to one
of Mazarin's nieces. Charles eventually succeeded in his mission
through a mixture of derring-do, subterfuge and the seduction of
Conti's mistress.[25] The second adventure is set in London, probably
around 1654 or 1655. Courtilz attributes several trips to England to
his Charles, but this is the most complicated. Once again in disguise,
Charles supposedly travelled to London to draw up a report for
Mazarin on the political situation there, and on the popular view of
Cromwell, in order that the cardinal might decide whether it would
be better to offer another niece as a bride to a son of Cromwell
or to the exiled Charles II. He was ordered not to identify himself to the French ambassador in London, Monsieur de Bordeaux,
whom Mazarin did not trust, but rapidly became embroiled with
Bordeaux's mistress, whom he met accidentally and as a result found
himself masquerading as her cook, while gathering the information
he sought. Attracting the attention of Bordeaux, he was mistaken
for a spy sent by Condé, still a rebel, to negotiate separately with
Cromwell. This error led to his arrest and removal into France, where
he found himself in the Bastille, from which he was eventually freed
by Mazarin, but not after some uncomfortable moments.[26]

These two escapades provide some of the livelier episodes in the
Memoirs, although the conduct of the hero is more reminiscent of

the plots of the Count of Monte Cristo or of the devious Joseph Balsamo than of Dumas's dashing version of d'Artagnan.[27] They were accepted at face value by Eugène d'Auriac,[28] but rejected by Charles Samaran and all subsequent biographers.[29] Yet, curiously, these events may not derive simply from the imagination of Courtilz. In the case of the London adventure, Courtilz may have confounded our Charles with a near homonym, one Isaac de Baas, who had been at one time an agent of the Prince de Condé, and subsequently one of Mazarin. This de Baas was no relation of Charles de Batz-Castelmore d'Artagnan, came from Nay in Béarn, and is noted in French diplomatic archives as having made a succession of trips to Monsieur de Bordeaux in London between 1654 and 1658 as part of the negotiations of the French government with Cromwell.[30] It may well be that Courtilz knew of these missions and attributed them – perhaps in genuine error – to Charles de Batz. The story of Charles and the *Ormée,* however, probably derives mainly from the imagination of Courtilz. There are no certain grounds to suppose that the historical Charles had any involvement in the defeat of the rebellion at Bordeaux, although Courtilz may have taken the idea for the secret mission from the activities of another of Mazarin's agents, a Franciscan monk, Father Berthod.[31]

From the point of view of those interested in Charles de Batz-Castelmore d'Artagnan and his comrades in the musketeers, what has made the *Memoirs* notable is the role they played in the creation and writing of *The Three Musketeers*. In his introduction to that novel, Dumas tells us:

> About a year ago, while carrying out research for my history of Louis XIV in the royal library, I came across by chance the *Memoirs of Monsieur d'Artagnan*, printed – like most of the works of that period in which the authors sought to tell the truth without going to spend a longish period in the Bastille – at Amsterdam by Pierre Rouge. The title attracted me: I took them home with me, with the permission of Monsieur the Archivist, naturally, and I devoured them.[32]

He was being disingenuous – he never published a thorough history of Louis XIV – but we do know that in 1842 he borrowed a

copy of the *Memoirs* from the national library at Marseilles: he never
returned it. We do not know if he read the book in its entirety: certainly, he made little or no use of the events described by Courtilz
relating to the later part of Charles's life, but he was to make considerable use of the earlier parts.

The influence of Courtilz's work is most clear in the first chapters of *The Three Musketeers*, although Dumas recast and reworked
much of it. He wished, first of all, to provide what he considered
a more fruitful background, and thus he put his d'Artagnan back
in time by some ten to fifteen years, having him come to Paris in
1625, and not 1635 x 1640. It was from the *Memoirs* that he drew
the image of the young Gascon setting forth to seek his fortune
mounted on a remarkably poor horse and, through this, becoming
embroiled in a quarrel which was to have long-reaching consequences. However, where Courtilz related a sordid tale of beatings,
imprisonment and debt, Dumas replaced this with the panache of
d'Artagnan's first encounter with Rochefort, his glimpse of Milady,
and his involvement through this with the intrigues of cardinal and
Queen. Courtilz's shadowy Rosnai, a coward who mainly pursues
Charles via ambushes and false legal proceedings, was replaced by the
sinister but honourable Rochefort (a figure derived from another of
Courtilz's works, the *Memoirs of M.L.C.D.R.*). In Courtilz's work,
Charles's first days in Paris are a rather rambling and confused succession of skirmishes, names and diversions about entirely other
people. Dumas extracted the bones – a sequence of fights with
members of the Cardinal's Guards – and recreated around them a
far more satisfactory and logical narrative which serves to heighten
the impression of tension between cardinal and King, the existence
of dangerous factions, and to establish the personalities of his heroes.
Athos, Porthos and Aramis are little more than names in Courtilz,
brought out to support Charles in fights or to supply him with
plausible allies in schemes against the husbands of his mistresses.
Their characters, as we now know them, are entirely the work of
Dumas. He took over the incident of Besmaux's part-embroidered
baldrick, and gave it a far less spiteful character to help establish
his big, boastful, loyal and loving Porthos. Courtilz mentions that
one of Mazarin's soldiers, Rotondis (a character who occurs once),

intended to become a priest. Dumas again borrowed this detail
and reworked it into his devious, secretive, seductive Aramis. For
Athos, he looked outside Courtilz, drawing instead upon a literary
tradition of nobility and its duties. Athos is part tragic Shakespearian
protagonist (Dumas admired Shakespeare greatly), part idealised
version of Dumas's own humane and high-minded father, General
Dumas.[33] As has been seen, he took over the English 'milédi',
with whom Courtilz's Charles had a brief affair, and transformed
her into the dangerous Milady, pivot of the plot of the novel,
arch-conspirator, *femme fatale*. Perhaps his greatest conjuring trick,
however, lies in the character of Constance Bonacieux, d'Artagnan's
first love. Courtilz relates a long story of an intrigue between
Charles and the wife of the tavern keeper who is his landlord. The
woman is clearly no lady and it is implied that Charles is far from
her first lover: their relationship is one of blackmail and trickery,
and it has no connection to any of the political events of its time,
ending eventually in separation and the marriage of the woman,
by then widowed, to a Swiss guardsman.[34] Dumas transformed
this woman into Constance, who, through her involvement in the
Queen's romance with Buckingham, draws Charles further into
conflict with the cardinal, and whose death becomes Milady's final
and perhaps greatest crime. From another section of the *Memoirs*,
Dumas took the story of abduction and imprisonment in a convent,
and by applying them to Constance, provided his hero with motiva-
tion for much of the second part of the novel. In the original, this
element related to a later mistress of Charles's, a widow in whom
he was interested solely for her money. The abduction is simply a
move in a struggle between Charles and the lady's son over access
to her fortune.

Gatien de Courtilz de Sandras and his *Memoirs of Monsieur
d'Artagnan* occupy only a minor place in history, and have little or
no literary merit in their own right. But they were the first step in
the development of the stories of Charles d'Artagnan and the three
musketeers: without them, we would be one legend the poorer.

5

Alexandre Dumas and the Musketeers

When, in March 1844, the newspaper *Le Siècle* published the first instalment of a new serial – *The Three Musketeers* – its author was forty-one years old, and already his life had been almost as colourful as that of one of his heroes. He lived in a world of courtesans and actresses, louche playwrights and impoverished but ambitious young novelists. His friends included Victor Hugo and Eugène Delacroix. He was an established playwright, a renowned *raconteur* and a *bon viveur*. He had dined with members of the French imperial family, yet considered himself a republican. His name was Alexandre Dumas.

He had been born on 24 July 1802 at Villers-Cotterêts, near Soissons. His father was Thomas-Alexandre Dumas-Davy de la Pailleterie, known usually as General Dumas, and himself a remarkable man. Thomas-Alexandre was the illegitimate son of a minor nobleman, Antoine-Alexandre Davy, Marquis de la Pailleterie, by

his mistress, a black slave named Marie-Cessette Dumas. The future
general was born in the French colony of San Domingo, to which
Antoine-Alexandre had retreated, having failed to make a success of
a military career in France. Thomas-Alexandre was born into slavery, according to the law at the time, and when his father decided,
in 1772, to return to France, he abandoned most of his illegitimate
family on the island to continue to live in slavery. Marie-Cessette
had died that year, but of their four children, only one accompanied
Antoine-Alexandre to France: this was Thomas-Alexandre, then
ten years old.[1]

Antoine-Alexandre was fond of this son, but he did not intend
either to legitimise him or to support him throughout his adult
life, and in 1786, Thomas-Alexandre enlisted as a private soldier in
the Queen's Dragoons. He was twenty-four, and already known
in Paris society, where he had lived for the last several years. He
had moved in aristocratic circles, attending *soirées*, theatres and
parties with a succession of beautiful mistresses. His illegitimacy
and his mixed blood, however, were a bar to advancement in that
world, and his decision to join the army may have been motivated
as much by the wish for a secure career as by his father's lack of
support.

It was the very dawn of the French Revolution, and Thomas-
Alexandre, now using his mother's surname of Dumas, was to find
his army career advancing higher than he might have dreamed. By
January 1793, he was a regimental commander, and in the summer
of that same year, he became a brigadier-general. He came close to
achieving even higher rank when in 1795 the ruling body of France,
the Convention, summoned him urgently to protect them against
restless elements in Paris. He was away: the summons therefore
passed to another general, Napoléon Bonaparte, thus initiating the
latter's rise to status of emperor. Thomas-Alexandre was at first on
good terms with Bonaparte, but the two men were very different,
and their friendship did not last. Bonaparte neither valued nor
trusted General Dumas. He was to die in obscurity in February
1806, his health broken by a long spell in prison in Sicily (which
had declared itself at war with France). He left neither fortune
nor influence to his wife, Marie-Louise-Elisabeth Labouret, whom

Left: 14 D'Artagnan
arrives in Paris.

Below: 15 Cardinal
Mazarin.

16 Fortifications at Navarenx, where Paul Castelmore d'Artagnan served as governor.

17 The flight of Mazarin from the Fronde in Paris.

Above left: 18 Nicolas Fouquet.

Above right: 19 Jean-Baptiste Colbert.

20 Fouquet's grand residence at Vaux-le-Vicomte.

21 Louvois, Minister of War under Louis XIV.

22 The Palais de Rihour, Lille: a welcome banquet was held here for d'Artagnan.

23 Apartment behind La Botte Chantilly, Lille, said to have been d'Artagnan's lodgings.

24 Fortified sluice at Maastricht.

25 Musketeers at the Hôtel de Tréville.

26 Remains of the
château at Athos.

27 The powder store, Navarrenx, where Isaac de Portau ended his career.

Above left: 28 Athos on horseback.

Above right: 29 Porthos.

30 Seventeenth–century wing of the Louvre.

31 Louis XIII.

Above left: 32 Musketeers in action.

Above right: 33 Gateway, all that remains of the abbey of Aramitz.

34 D'Artagnan
in his musketeer
uniform.

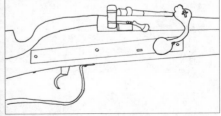

Left: 35 Seventeenth-century rapier, of the
type used by the musketeers.

Above: 36 Seventeenth-century matchlock
musket.

37 Musketeers storming a bastion.

38 The wedding procession of Louis XIV and Maria-Theresa entering Paris.

39 Versailles in 1667.

40 The Comte de
Rochefort, nemesis
of the literary
d'Artagnan.

41 D'Artagnan, from the
frontispiece to Courtilz de
Sandras, *Mémoirs de M. d'Artagnan*.

42 Duelling under Louis
XIII.

43 Milady reveals her brand.

44 Alexandre Dumas père.

Above left: 45 Statue of d'Artagnan, Place Général Catroux, Paris, where he sits on the plinth of a statue of Dumas.

Above right: 46 Statue of Dumas, Place Général Catroux, Paris. His readers sit at his feet.

47 The immortal musketeers.

48 Musketeers in action.

49 Musketeers on parade.

50 Musketeers triumphant.

51 Musketeers off duty.

52 The new d'Artagnan museum
at Lupiac.

he had married in November 1793, and two children – Marie-Alexandrine-Aimée, born 1793, and Alexandre.[2]

Alexandre Dumas was intensely proud of his father and of his ancestry, and although only four years old when Thomas-Alexandre died, he had strong memories of him. His mother passed on to him his father's humanitarian and republican beliefs, and while Alexandre harboured a fascination for the trappings of royalty and aristocracy, he liked to consider himself a revolutionary at heart.[3] Much of his writing was to be informed by the sense of humanity and moral courage which had characterised his father. His mother had little money, and received no help from Bonaparte's government to keep herself and her children, but she ensured that Alexandre was properly educated. He was not naturally scholarly, and on his own testimony preferred hunting and poaching to studying, but when he set out for Paris in 1823, he had already formed the ambition to become a writer. He found work as a clerk to the Duc d'Orléans, but his intention was to become a playwright, and, after several attempts, in 1828 he had a play accepted by the Comédie-Française. Entitled *Henri III et sa cour* (*Henry III and his Court*), it debuted on 11 February 1829 and was a huge hit.

It marked a new departure in French theatre: the dawn of the Romantic movement. Up to this time, French theatre had been dominated by a severe classical tradition whose strict rules stultified realism and emphasised stagy, wooden acting. The Romantics sought to liberate themselves from these conventions and to introduce a world of emotion and melodrama to the stage. Dumas was by no means the greatest exponent of this movement on the stage, nor the first to write plays in this style, nor the most original, but he was the first to have one of his plays produced by a major company, and this by itself would secure him at least a minor place in literary history. He was part of a literary movement which included Victor Hugo and Alfred de Vigny.[4] He was to continue to write plays throughout his literary life, but the main period of his success in this form was between 1829 and 1840. Alexandre was a writer in the most catholic sense: he did not confine himself by genre or subject or scope, producing fiction and non-fiction, autobiography and romance, short stories, journal articles, a little poetry and even a cookbook.[5]

Alexandre turned to novels in around 1840. This was partly through necessity: the first flush of the Romantic movement was spent, and the theatre was moving on to new forms. He had already written a travel book, which had been partly published as a newspaper serial. This latter form was also highly suited to fiction: in 1838 an editor from *Le Siècle* approached him to write a serial novel for that paper. Alexandre accepted and produced *Le capitaine Paul* (*Paul Jones*) based on the life of the American revolutionary hero John-Paul Jones and inspired by a novel by James Fennimore Cooper (*The Pilot*).

Alexandre admired both Fennimore Cooper and Sir Walter Scott, and was very drawn to the idea of fictionalising history. Many of his most successful plays had been inspired by historical events, and he carried this over into his novel-writing. Another practice which he carried over from playwriting to novel-writing was the use of collaborators. This was not unique to him – other writers both before and contemporary with him worked in a similar way, and literary collaboration still occurs today. Alexandre – and a whole range of other writers including Shakespeare – borrowed ideas from each other, reworked or remodelled material they had found in earlier works, and wrote in tandem with a partner.[6] At the beginning of his playwriting career, Alexandre wrote a number of plays with partners, although none of these proved successful.[7] He also borrowed ideas – and sometimes lines – from other writers in writing his solo plays, but this was not a case of simple plagiarism. Rather, it would be more accurate to say that he derived inspiration from things he had seen and read, but in reworking or echoing these he brought to it his own particular voice and interpretation. As a playwright, his importance lies more in the serendipity of timing than in the quality of his writing, and of his plays, only two – *Le Tour de Nesle* and *Kean* – are still performed (the latter in a revised version by Jean-Paul Sartre). As a novelist, however, his work is altogether more significant.

Le Capitaine Paul had been inspired by Fennimore Cooper, but Alexandre had not stopped with that source: he had found the time to visit Lorient on the south-west coast of Brittany, with which John-Paul Jones had had connections, and had gathered additional information from local folk memories. Published in serial form, the novel increased the circulation of *Le Siècle* by 5,000 readers.[8] It was clear both to Alexandre and to the publishers of Paris that the novel presented an exciting and potentially lucrative new route for the popular writer. Newspapers were anxious to secure works of this type, and Alexandre was only one of several writers who were published in this form. He rapidly proved to be one of the most successful. Honoré de Balzac, a contemporary of Alexandre, also published some of his books as serials in the newspapers, but his novels of social commentary were less attractive to readers, and in 1844 he suffered the indignity of having one of his books (*Les Paysans — The Peasants*) cancelled by the paper *La Presse* and replaced by Alexandre's novel *La Reine Margot* (*Marguerite de Valois*).[9] Balzac today far outweighs Alexandre in terms of critical appreciation, but in his lifetime he felt overshadowed and never really forgave Alexandre for his success.[10]

Alexandre was quick to see the advantages of this form, and from 1838 turned his hand more and more to the writing of novels. At first, he was paid by the line, and this led him to initiate a form of writing which is still in use today: quick-fire dialogue, like this sample from Chapter 11 of *The Three Musketeers*, in which d'Artagnan questions his beloved Constance about her nocturnal ramblings.

'Come on, now! Are you going to tell me you don't know Aramis?'
'This is the first time I've heard this name.'
'Therefore, this is the first time you've come to this house?'
'Undoubtedly.'
'And you didn't know that a young man lives here?'
'No.'
'A musketeer?'
'Not at all.'
'So it wasn't him that you came to find?'
'Not in the slightest. Besides, you saw very well that the person I spoke to was a woman.'[11]

To Alexandre, this was simply a device to increase his income, but it was to become one of the trademarks of his work, making a great contribution to their sparkling pace and liveliness. Newspaper editors soon came to understand the trick, and changed his basis of payment, but Alexandre continued to write in this fashion when events in a story required.

Dumas carried over the use of collaborators into his novel-writing. At the dawn of his novel-writing career, Alexandre was a literary lion, much in demand by publishers and journals. His works sold well and there was thus pressure on him to produce in quantity and at speed. Temperamentally, also, he thrived on hard work, and always seems to have had several projects on the go at any one time. Already, as a playwright, he had been presented with work by unknown writers – often via a theatrical producer or manager – with the request that he adapt or improve these.[12] Money was also an issue: Alexandre enjoyed an extravagant lifestyle, and he was also generous to a fault, with the result that he was often short of cash. He needed to be productive in order to support himself and his ever-growing entourage of mistresses, friends, staff and hangers-on. As a result, his collaborators were of considerable importance to him, both to maintain the desired output and financially. It was not that he simply put his name to work that was not his. Rather, his collaborators acted more as assistants or amanuenses. He was always on the look-out for new materials and ideas, but he did not have time to read through every possible source that he came across. Collaborators – notably Auguste Maquet and Paul Meurice – found new documents and histories and researched topics on his behalf. They would also work up outlines of plots and rough drafts, having first discussed with him what elements were to be included. Alexandre would then work from these, adding muscle, flesh and blood to the bare bones. In general, his collaborators were well rewarded financially, and happy with the arrangement. It should be borne in mind, as well, that the publication of books solely under Alexandre's name was imposed not by him but by publishers. The Dumas name was worth more solo.

His best-known collaborator was Auguste Maquet. In 1838, Auguste, then a twenty-five-year-old aspiring writer, contacted

Alexandre. Auguste had written a play, which he had called *Soir de Carnaval* (*Carnival Evening*), which he had been unable to place with a theatre. On the suggestion of a mutual friend, he sent the play to Alexandre, to solicit his help in revising it. Alexandre willingly did so and the play was eventually produced as *Bathilde* under Auguste's name alone. The play was insignificant, but the meeting of Alexandre and Auguste was not. Auguste subsequently wrote a novel, *Le Bonhomme Buvat* (*Good Mr Buvat*), and again, he brought his first draft to Alexandre, after having failed to find a publisher. It was to be the beginning of a long-running and mutually beneficial partnership.[13] Alexandre read Auguste's draft, and saw clear potential in it. But Auguste, while an admirable researcher, lacked the ability to tell a story engagingly. Alexandre took the outline, and, from an account of a conspiracy told through the eyes of a worthy but uninvolved third party, created an exciting swashbuckler. He was happy to see the book published as by Dumas and Maquet, but the publisher objected and the book – retitled *Le Chevalier d'Harmental* – went out under Alexandre's name alone.[14] It proved a success. Auguste was happy with the arrangement, and received payment for his part which far outweighed any amount he might have expected to receive as an unknown first novelist. The two were to continue to collaborate on novels for over a decade.

What exactly was Auguste's role, and to what extent did he write the novels? In later years, after the two men had become estranged, he was to lay claim to a number of Alexandre's novels, including both *The Count of Monte Cristo* and *The Three Musketeers*. However, where Auguste's drafts survive, they differ from the published versions of the books. Certainly, Auguste acted as Alexandre's researcher, seeking out interesting historical memoirs, chronicles, legal reports and other materials which might provide ideas for novels. He also produced first outlines of chapters, having discussed what was to go in them with Alexandre beforehand. The two men often worked alongside each other in Alexandre's writing-room, exchanging ideas and papers. Alexandre would recast and rewrite Auguste's outlines, adding colour, style and depth: it should be noted in passing that every one of the extant manuscripts of Alexandre's books are entirely in his hand.

This method of working had its problems, and, even during his lifetime, Alexandre was attacked for it. One of his early collaborators, Frédéric Gaillardet, was highly dissatisfied by his relationship with Alexandre, even though he was at first acclaimed as sole author of the play he co-wrote with Alexandre (*Le Tour de Nesle*), and the two even apparently fought a duel, although in the end Gaillardet seems to have regretted his behaviour.[15] In 1845, Alexandre was attacked by one Eugène de Mirecourt. Mirecourt wrote a pamphlet entitled *A Factory of Novels: the House of Alexandre Dumas and Company*, in which he alleged that Alexandre's books were wholly the work of his collaborators and compared Alexandre to the overseer of a slave gang. The attack was based at least in part on envy,[16] but it also had disturbing racist overtones. Alexandre was proud of his ancestry, but some of his enemies and critics held it against him, and were shamefully ready to abuse him for it.[17] The greater part of literary Paris was outraged, however, and supported him when he sued de Mirecourt for libel and won.[18]

Auguste Maquet was by and large content with his relationship with Alexandre. Mirecourt named him as one of the 'slaves': Auguste responded by writing Alexandre a letter in which he reaffirmed his satisfaction with his role and his rewards and renounced any claim he might have over those works on which he had collaborated.[19] It was only in 1858 that the two fell out, and the cause was neither authorship nor reputation, but simply money. The chaos into which Alexandre's finances had descended by that time had resulted in disruption of payments due to Auguste. The latter came from a wealthy background, but he was not financially independent, and he needed this income. As a way of trying to secure it, he sued Alexandre for part-authorship of a number of books, including *The Three Musketeers*. He received some sympathy, but he was unable to provide secure proof for his claim, and in the end he lost the case. Legal opinion in the mid-nineteenth century held that Alexandre's books were essentially his own work.[20] Alexandre could be disingenuous about his collaborators, perhaps through sheer bravado. In 1843, he told a meeting of the Society of Men of Letters that Maquet was his sole collaborator, even though there had been others where plays were concerned. Perhaps he meant it to be understood that he was referring to that specific time. On another occasion, he joked to an archivist in Bourg-en-Bresse who had taxed him with the question that he had had his last book written by his valet – but that he'd been obliged to dismiss the man as he had then demanded a rise in wages. He seems to have found the interest in the subject a little odd.[21] He did not always use collaborators, and was capable of maintaining a formidable output both in quantity and in quality all on his own. One of his most critically admired books is *La San Felice* (*The Neapolitan Lovers*), which he wrote on his own and while also writing a memoir and an eight-volume history (the latter in Italian).[22]

The problem of collaboration has continued to pursue Alexandre's reputation, and to complicate literary criticism of his work, nevertheless. What conclusions can be drawn? Where Alexandre's writing is compared side by side with the work on the same material of a collaborator, the difference is immediately clear. Alexandre's versions have a life and a style which are wanting in the draft versions. Henri d'Alméras has printed part of Chapter 66 of *The Three Musketeers* in the draft by Auguste Maquet and the final version by Alexandre in parallel columns (text in French).[23] The two samples make interesting reading: the outline of events is there in the work of Auguste, but all the atmosphere, tension and style is wanting. These elements, together with tightening and refining of dialogue to allow for character and tone, were all created by Alexandre when he wrote his final version. On the other hand, financial pressure occasionally led Alexandre to put his name to – or allow his name to be put to – several books in which he had had little part. A comparison of the opening chapter of *Cécile* (1844; *The Wedding Dress*) with the rest of that book again reveals a marked difference between the writing of Alexandre and that of a collaborator. Alexandre wrote the former, but seems only to have outlined the rest, and it is very flat. Both *Les Deux Dianes* (1846; *The Two Dianas*) and *Le Fils de Porthos* (*Son of Porthos*) are now accepted as wholly the work of collaborators, and do not appear in lists of Alexandre's authentic works, although old translations of them under his name are still to be found in second-hand bookshops. Reading either of them, again, will reveal a considerable gap in style, ability and talent between Alexandre and the ghost-writer. In both cases, the books were the product of demands from publishers for the Dumas name: there is no evidence that Alexandre deliberately had them written.[24] Indeed, anecdote relates that he allowed his name to be put to *The Two Dianas* in order to help Paul Meurice out of a cash-flow problem. André Maurois has printed a selection of the letters and notes between Alexandre and Auguste, along with extracts from Alexandre's *Memoirs* which provide a fascinating insight into how the two men collaborated on *The Three Musketeers*.[25] None of his collaborators enjoyed any success as solo writers: the talent and the distinctive voice of *The Three Musketeers*, *The Count of Monte Cristo*, *Marguerite de Valois* and so forth belong to Alexandre.

One of the sources that came into the hands of Alexandre and Auguste was Courtilz de Sandras's *Memoirs of Monsieur d'Artagnan*. Did they know that these were fake? Probably not, but it does not matter: the *Memoirs* were no more that a kernel of inspiration for the book which was to become *The Three Musketeers*. Alexandre rapidly recognised in them the potential for an exciting story, and in their supposed narrator a vivid hero. He took certain elements from the *Memoirs*, but chose not to follow them exactly in either chronology or detail. His d'Artagnan was to be bolder, more honourable, and more closely tied to the intrigues of court and King. He moved d'Artagnan back in time, also, considering that the central years of Louis XIII would make a more appealing background. His reading for earlier works, along with Auguste's researches, had revealed a wealth of exciting material in histories and authentic memoirs from Louis's reign. In writing *The Three Musketeers*, Alexandre made use of a number of these, including the *Memoirs* of Madame de Motteville, lady-in-waiting to Anne of Austria, of La Porte, her cloak-bearer, of the Duke de la Rochefoucauld and the Comte de Brienne, who had direct and indirect experience of the court, and the *Historiettes* of Tallemant de Reaux.[26] To these, he added an imaginary source, the *Memoirs of the Comte de la Fère,* a playful idea which lent the books a spurious air of historicity.[27] These provided him less with accurate detail than with colourful incidents and scandals, out of which he fashioned his plot, blending it with material from the d'Artagnan pseudo-memoirs.

What of his methods of writing? The character of Milady provides a useful illustration. He had derived the basic character from
the pseudo-memoirs, in which a nameless English *milédi*, a lady-in-
waiting to the exiled Queen of England, conceives a violent hatred
of d'Artagnan.[28] From Brienne and La Rochefoucauld he took the
story of Anne of Austria's diamond studs, substituting Milady for
the Cardinalist agent of the two memorialists.[29] The idea of the
woman who has been branded – a deadly secret – he took from
another of Courtilz's works, the *Memoirs of M.L.C.D.R.*, which
also provided him with the character of Rochefort, with whom he
replaced Courtilz's far less interesting Rosnai. But her relationship
with Athos, and her involvement in the assassination of the Duke
of Buckingham, were his own invention. He performed similar
transformations with the characters of the musketeers themselves,
bringing them to the foreground of the events of the 1620s, such
that it seems that certain historical events might not have happened
– or would have occurred – without them. It is history as imagination would have it, not history as it really was, and it has a romance
and verve to it that cold fact frequently lacks.

The Three Musketeers was a huge success, first as a newspaper serial
and subsequently in book form. It ran as a serial from mid-March
1844 until mid-July, and then appeared in eight volumes from the
Paris publisher Baudry. It was to set the seal on Alexandre's renown
as a novelist. All levels of society read and enjoyed it and each new
episode was eagerly awaited. The minister of Foreign Affairs, Guizot,
took *Le Siècle*, a consistent critic of his policies, solely to follow the
story.[30] Young women wrote fan mail to d'Artagnan and Porthos.[31]
To use the words of Henri d'Alméras, 'All France was musketeer-
ised'.[32] The serial rapidly became successful outside France also, to
the extent that the Marseille-based writer Joseph Méry commented
'If there is, anywhere, another Robinson Crusoe on a desert island,
it can be certain that at this very moment this hermit is busy reading *The Three Musketeers*, in the shade of his umbrella made of
parrot feathers.'[33] The success of the novel was repeated when it
appeared in book form, and it was rapidly translated into various
other European languages. A full English translation appeared in
1844, and is still available today, although for some reason in the

United States only abridged versions were published until early in the twentieth century.

How was the book received by the literary establishment? Critics had – and still have – an ambivalent attitude. Alexandre's popularity told against him. The annual French literary review, the *Annual historique universal,* ignored *The Three Musketeers* in its volume for 1844, considering it not worth comment. Alexandre never achieved membership of the Académie Française, a great literary accolade, and this rankled.[34] On the other hand, Alexandre's friend, the writer and critic Jules Janin, described the book as a wonder. Modern literary scholarship continues to find him an uncomfortable subject.[35] But he has found a number of distinguished defenders, including André Maurois and Robert Louis Stevenson, and *The Three Musketeers* continues to be read – and to be filmed, and to be referenced and echoed and pastiched – almost worldwide. Alexandre himself was certain of the book's merit – he rated it as his best work.

He was quick to capitalise upon its success, following it with *Twenty Years After* in 1845, and *The Vicomte de Bragelonne* in 1848–50. Both works appeared first as serials in *Le Siècle* and subsequently in book form. Both were, once again, well received by the reading public. The musketeer books belong to the zenith of Alexandre's career, when he was one of the great figures of Paris, sought out by visitors and widely fêted. Alongside the musketeer novels, he produced *The Corsican Brothers* (1844), *The Count of Monte Cristo* (1844–45), *Marguerite de Valois* (1845), *Chicot the Jester* (1846) and *The Black Tulip* (1850) amongst others. His primary focus was now the novel, but he did not abandon the theatre: indeed, he soon sought to transfer the success of his musketeers to the stage. In October 1845, a play entitled *The Musketeers* was presented at the Ambigu Theatre, written by Alexandre in collaboration with Auguste Maquet, based on *Twenty Years After*. It was a long piece – five acts plus twelve tableaux, lasting six hours – yet it represented only part of the novel (it covered the attempt by d'Artagnan and his friends to save Charles I of England from the block). Like the novels, the play was a success: audiences flocked to see their heroes made flesh. Alexandre insisted that Auguste share the credit for this play: his name was on the playbills, and, at the premier on 27 October, Alexandre presented him to the audience as co-writer. It was to be followed by a second play – *The Youth of the Musketeers*, based on *The Three Musketeers*. Again, it was a collaboration with Auguste, and again it was very long – five acts and twelve tableaux once again. It premiered at the Théâtre Historique on 17 February 1849.

The Historique was Alexandre's own project: the Duc de Montpensier had granted him permission to build it in 1846, and it was completed by early 1847. It was to see the premieres of a number of plays written by him and based on his novels, and owed its initial success to his fame.[36] It was not solely a vanity project, however: alongside Alexandre's works, it presented plays by Victor Hugo, Balzac, Alfred de Musset and Jules Verne, as well as by Alexandre's son, Alexandre Dumas the younger, who had followed his father into the profession of writer.[37] By 1848, the Historique had gone into a decline, partly as a result of the political upheavals in France the year before when the reigning King, Louis Philippe, was deposed, and a new republic proclaimed. *The Youth of the Musketeers* was an attempt to revive the theatre's fortunes, but it did not enjoy the success of the first play, and the Historique eventually closed on 16 October 1850.

By this time, Alexandre's fortunes were in decline. A number of expensive projects – not only the Historique, but the building of a fantastic house, known as Monte-Cristo, at Marly-le-Roi near Paris – had brought him into debt. Alexandre had never been good with money, and he could not check his own extravagance. His generosity was legendary, but one result was that people took advantage of him, and he collected a circle of hangers-on who did little save drain his resources. In addition, he had made a bad marriage to the actress Ida Ferrier, which ended in an expensive divorce, and to this he had added a succession of more or less demanding mistresses. The revolution of 1848 led him to involve himself in politics, and he made an attempt to have himself elected as a deputy to the new provisional government. This interrupted his writing and damaged his reputation, and, by the end of 1848, he lost Monte-Cristo. In 1850, Alexandre fled France, ostensibly for political reasons, but in fact to escape his creditors. He settled in Brussels, where he continued to write. He was fortunate to find a good business manager during his exile, and was able to return to France in 1853, having settled with those to whom he owed money. However, his fortunes were never to recover fully, despite his various schemes. He began by founding a new newspaper, *The Musketeer,* in which he intended to publish his newest writings: the first issue appeared on 30 November 1853. At first, the paper was a success: the name Dumas still held appeal for the public, while the name of the paper recalled one of his best-loved works. But the venture was ultimately to fail, and for much the same reasons as had undone Alexandre in the later 1840s – mismanagement of money, extravagance and hangers-on – and the paper ceased publication in February 1857.[38] The truth was that literary fashion was changing. Romanticism was losing its appeal and being replaced by a more realistic movement, led by Gustave Flaubert, who had published the ground-breaking *Madame Bovary* earlier in that year.[39] Alexandre had continued to write novels, but he seems to have realised that his market was shrinking. From 1857, he increasingly turned his attention to travel-writing and to memoirs.[40] He visited England, Russia and Italy, and hoped to visit Syria and Palestine. The Russian voyage resulted in two more successful books.[41] In Italy, he involved himself in Garibaldi's political movement and with the excavations at Pompeii, and produced several books based on these experiences.[42] This brought him sufficient income to return to Paris in April 1864. He was no longer a literary lion, but he had friends and colleagues, and his books were still popular in the provinces. Throughout the 1860s, he wrote, published, went on lecture tours, and conceived various new schemes for renewed success (none of these latter came to anything). One of the most unusual of his books was written in this period – his *Grand Dictionnaire de la Cuisine* (*Dictionary of Cuisine*) – which was to be published posthumously in 1873.[43] But by the end of the 1860s, his health was failing. He had always worked at a furious pace, often on two or three works at a time. He would work in a plainly furnished room, starting at dawn and continuing through the day with few breaks, before going out in the evening to the theatre, and then returning for several hours' more writing before sleep. In 1845, he had entered into a wager that he could complete the first volume of a novel within seventy-two hours, which he won with six hours to spare.[44] In his last years, however, he found himself no longer able to maintain his old habits. His working hours shrank as his energy declined.

Alexandre Dumas died at ten o'clock in the evening on 5 December 1870, at Puys, near Le Havre, where he was staying with his son and daughter. A stroke earlier in the same year had left him partially paralysed, and his optimism had finally begun to desert him. He had not published anything since 1868 (*The Prussian Terror, Souvenirs of the Theatre, Parisians and Provincials* and *Caroline of Brunswick*),[45] although he had continued to work on the *Dictionary* and other things. Several works were to be published between 1871 and 1873, after his death, including the *Dictionary, Creation and Redemption, The Prince of Thieves* and *Robin Hood the Outlaw*.[46]

Alexandre had lived his life to the full, like one of his own heroes – exploiting every opportunity that came his way, always full of confidence and optimism, defying convention and never questioning his own ability. His output is undoubtedly patchy: his plays are seldom performed or even remembered, many of his novels and memoirs are out of print and rarely read. Critically, he remains something of an outsider, although this is beginning to change. Throughout his life, he yearned for – but never received – formal recognition by the literary establishment and by his country. He finally achieved it when, on 29 November 2002, as part of a celebration of the bicentenary of his birth, his body was disinterred from its grave at his birthplace, Villers-Cotterêts, and reburied with great ceremony in the Panthéon in Paris, alongside many other French people of renown.

Above all, certain of his books have become classics, read and reread over generations, always in print, something achieved by only a handful of writers. His most famous heroes have become legends: the Count of Monte Cristo, d'Artagnan, and the Three Musketeers.

6

After *The Three Musketeers*

Few novels have had the kind of afterlife enjoyed by Dumas's *The Three Musketeers*.[1] There have been something of the order of eighty-two novels, plays, pastiches and homages published, plus more than thirty film, television and animated versions. The three musketeers and d'Artagnan seem to have entered the literary consciousness and remained there at a profound level. The books have inspired literary fiction, thrillers, science fiction, fantasy, comic novels, pulp romance and vampire stories. Many writers write sequels or prequels to their own books, but elaboration and embellishment of Dumas's tale by other writers began in Dumas's lifetime, and, indeed, before he himself had embarked upon sequels. In June 1845, a one-act play opened at the Vaudeville Theatre in Paris. Written by a trio of playwrights, and entitled *Porthos in Search of His Equipment*,[2] it was based upon Chapter 32 of *The Three Musketeers*, in which Porthos endeavours to persuade his miserly mistress to equip him for war to his and not her standards of luxury. It is a comic incident in the book – the playwrights embroidered upon it by adding in a rival mistress and creating a sort of bidding-war between them. The play is minor, but it demonstrates clearly just how the characters of d'Artagnan and his three friends had seized upon the popular imagination in France and created an appetite for more about them. The name 'Porthos' would have been instantly recognisable to an audience, and a reliable draw. What Dumas thought about it is unknown: he was himself a playwright, and no stranger to the idea of adapting the work of others. He was well aware of the dramatic potential of his novels: with Auguste Maquet he adapted for the stage both part of *Twenty Years After* (as *The Musketeers*) and *The Three Musketeers* (as *The Youth of the Musketeers*), the former in 1845, the latter in 1849. Moreover, in *The Man in the Iron Mask*, there is a comic incident in which Porthos is observed buying a highly decorated suit of clothes for court by a young playwright who turns out to be Molière. The chapter is entitled 'Where, probably, Molière formed his first idea of *The Bourgeois Gentilhomme*'.[3] As a playwright, Molière is far superior to Anicet and his friends, but perhaps Dumas was flattered by the early Porthos play, and here embroidered upon it. When it was first performed, he was himself more than halfway through the first 'official' sequel – *Twenty Years After* – which was in the process of appearing in serial form in *Le Siècle*. It is likely he was amused and flattered by the short vaudeville, reflecting as it did the popularity of his creations.

Three more short comic plays, plus a comic recitation, followed within five years of *Porthos in Search of His Equipment*.[4] But Dumas's novels had also inspired interest in the historical musketeers, and particularly d'Artagnan. The first attempt at a biography of him appeared in 1847. Written by Eugène d'Auriac, it was based heavily upon the pseudo-memoirs written by Courtilz de Sandras, and has little or no independent value.[5] But in context, it appeared to offer more information about a new folk-hero and his associates, and, indeed, to provide an historical corrective to the novels. Its introduction assures the reader that it is by no means written as an attack on Dumas – who is spoken of with reverence – but to correct those critics who have assumed that Dumas simply copied his story from an earlier memoir and to provide a more 'historical' account of Charles Castelmore d'Artagnan. Still in print today, it provides a condensed version of the narrative of Courtilz, omitting the long digressions which do not deal with d'Artagnan. Its sales, however, depend not on its own merits, but on the continued fame of *The Three Musketeers*.

The first wave of interest in the musketeers peaked by 1850. The novels by Dumas continued to be available, and his name was closely associated with them, but once the first fervour had passed, the number of imitations and homages dropped off. It was only after his death in December 1870 that interest seems to have re-awoken. At least eight continuations and variations on his theme appeared between 1874 and 1900.[6]

Some of the continuations take Dumas's story beyond the end of *The Vicomte de Bragelonne*, thus dealing mainly with heirs and descendants of his heroes; some attempt to fill in the gaps left by him between his novels; some use his characters or their context as background, theme, or inspiration; some purport to provide a more historically accurate account than that of Dumas. It is a pattern which has continued down to this day, with most of the continuations falling into one of more of these types, along with a number dealing with individuals peripheral to either Dumas's novels or the true history of the musketeers. Some of them are good, some are not; some vanished soon after publication, others continue to be readily available. There are too many to cover in detail here.[7] But this chapter will look at some of the better known, more readily available and most notable ones, with an emphasis on those written in English. Many, sadly, are no longer in print.

The earliest sequels were all in French: the first English continuation known to the present writers appeared in 1901: Henry L. Williams's novel *D'Artagnan the kingmaker,* which sends D'Artagnan and Porthos into Spain on a secret mission for Cardinal Richelieu. The novel was first published under the name of Dumas, without the permission of his estate, but the true authorship was easily established from its preface. Williams was to go on to publish three more d'Artagnan romances, but his books are neither easily found nor remembered. This was not the case with the next English-language continuator of Dumas, H. Bedford-Jones.

Bedford-Jones produced two novels on the musketeer theme. The first was *D'Artagnan: the sequel to The Three Musketeers.*[8] Bedford-Jones had come into possession of a fragment of a manuscript of *The Three Musketeers*, and he used this as his inspiration. In fact, this was a piece of Chapter 26 of *The Three Musketeers*, in which Aramis discusses his thesis with two clergymen. Dumas had pretended to have found Athos's memoirs; Bedford-Jones in his preface pretends that the fragment was from an unpublished work by Dumas, presenting his playful sequel therefore as a work merely co-authored by himself. It was, of course, entirely his own work, but it is none the worse for that. In it, d'Artagnan finds himself drawn into an intrigue involving Anne of Austria, Madame de Chevreuse and a young child who may be the son of the Queen. Assisted by Athos and Porthos, he must save the honour of both ladies, protect the child from the enmity of King and cardinal and save the life of Aramis, who lies dangerously ill. The book sets the scene for *Twenty Years After*, providing an alternative origin for Raoul de Bragelonne. It is not Dumas, but the story proceeds with pace and verve, and the characters are well drawn; currently out of print, it remains sought after today. His second musketeer novel, *The King's Passport*, mines a different seam, that of the historical d'Artagnan.[9] Set late in the reign of Louis XIII, it pits d'Artagnan against another legendary soldier-hero, Cyrano de Bergerac, once again against a background of court intrigue. It is not history, any more than *The Three Musketeers*, but once again it is an exciting read, and a worthy homage to the original.

Perhaps the best-known continuator of Dumas was Paul Féval the younger, who wrote four sequels to the musketeers romances (sometimes published over eight volumes). Himself the son of a successful historical novelist,[10] Féval the younger made a career out of writing sequels to famous books. His first two musketeer books follow the career of a purported son of d'Artagnan, Georges, a ward of Athos, and are now hard to find.[11] He followed these, however, with a sequence of novels which, like Bedford-Jones's *The King's Passport*, brought together d'Artagnan and Cyrano.[12] The d'Artagnan of Féval is Dumas's d'Artagnan in the years after *The Three Musketeers*, but seemingly before the events of *Twenty Years After*. Athos and Porthos are referred to; Aramis plays a larger part, particularly in the middle section of the sequence. The story centres upon a young man, known as the Mysterious Cavalier, who is in France seeking to discover the secret of his birth. He soon becomes embroiled in a variety of court intrigues, and falls foul of Mazarin. D'Artagnan, employed by Mazarin, finds himself unwittingly pitted against both the hero and Cyrano, who has befriended the youth. The tone is both breathless and imitative: as many famous incidents as possible are shoehorned into the plot to lend excitement, including the Iron Mask legend, a story about Madame de Chevreuse fleeing in male disguise, and various famous incidents of seventeenth-century French court gossip. Ideas and incidents are also freely borrowed from Dumas, so that the adventures and villains encountered by the hero are all too similar to those met by d'Artagnan in *The Three Musketeers*, while the original characters are flat and lifeless. Wherever convenient, the books ignore the life stories of the musketeers as according to Dumas. The last part of the sequence is impossible to reconcile with *Twenty Years After* and *The Vicomte de Bragelonne*, and it is hard, now, to account for their relative success. It is true that they were first published at the height of popularity of the pulp adventure novel, and that they provide more of the same formula which had already received an enthusiastic response. They remain relatively easy to find, and recently have been reprinted in French. But Bedford-Jones used some of the same ideas – hidden heirs, royal secrets, and the meeting with Cyrano – to better effect and with more respect for Dumas's originals.

Perhaps the most entertaining of all the novels that attempt to account for the years between the novels of Dumas is *D'Artagnan Amoureux (D'Artagnan in Love)* by Roger Nimier.[13] Nimier, a gifted writer and humorist, admired Dumas, and had already written a short story, 'Frédéric, d'Artagnan and la petite Chinoise' ('Frederic, d'Artagnan and the little Chinese girl'), in which d'Artagnan escapes from Dumas's novel to come to the aid of a young boy who seeks to woo his Chinese neighbour.[14] *D'Artagnan Amoureux* is set some fifteen years after *The Three Musketeers*, and finds d'Artagnan embroiled in the turbulent events of the last months of Louis XIII. Sent on a secret mission by Richelieu, he rapidly becomes entangled with a succession of plots, counter-plots, and, above all,

romantic problems. As with Dumas, Nimier skilfully blends original
and historical characters: d'Artagnan falls in love with the charming
Marie – better known to history as Madame de Sévigny – but she
hesitates in the face of his swashbuckling behaviour. Her friend
Julie loves him, but he is afraid of her obsessiveness. He repeatedly
encounters, and comes to blows with, Marie's cousin, one Bussy-
Rabutin,[15] and he meets future leaders of the Fronde. Throughout
his adventures, he is accompanied by the faithful Planchet, who
himself has problems with his wife and brothers-in-law. The story
moves along with pace, humour, verve and charm, very much in the
style of Dumas himself, and shows close knowledge of the original
novels: the third candidate for d'Artagnan's affection is his landlady
Madeleine, whom he barely notices. She is a character we meet in
Twenty Years After, where she is established as his mistress: Nimier
provides us with their history. The story of the obsessed Julie is
inspired in part by the pseudo-memoirs of d'Artagnan by Courtilz
de Sandras. The story climaxes with the famous battle of Rocroi, at
which Athos, Aramis and Porthos make an appearance, just in time
to rescue d'Artagnan from his confusion. This is a book written
with attention, respect and love, and it is well written: Dumas would
surely have approved. An English translation is long overdue.

The vast majority of the novels seeking to infill Dumas's story
are inferior to the work of Bedford-Jones and Nimier: few repay
reading for any reason other than completism.[16] Novels which continue the story of the musketeers beyond the end of *The Vicomte de
Bragelonne* are generally similarly poor. Heirs have been invented for
the musketeers – sons, nephews, daughters and godchildren,[17] who
have adventures very similar to those of their eminent precursors,
sometimes under the guidance of the latter. Most have never been
translated into English and most make dull reading: the opportunity
remains for someone to write a sequel of this kind which is worthy
of Dumas's originals.

Novels based on the 'historical' d'Artagnan are also generally
minor and of little interest. Many are based on Courtilz's pseudo-
memoirs and show little originality.[18] A few make use of the modern
research into d'Artagnan, usually using him as a supporting or
background character. Chelsea Quinn Yarbro, *A Candle for d'Artagnan*

(1989), shows care for the historical facts, while weaving a tale of vampires and romance. The book is one of a series concerned with Olivia Atta Clemens, a vampire born in the Roman empire: here, Olivia finds herself in the suite of Cardinal Mazarin, and falls in love with the young soldier Charles Castelmore d'Artagnan. Isaac de Portau plays a minor role; Henri d'Aramitz makes a cameo appearance. As a romance, the book is enjoyable, but the tone is far removed from the swashbuckling of Dumas – and d'Artagnan's real-life exploits are largely glossed over in favour of court politics and the minutiae of Olivia's estate. It is certainly one of the most original sequels, but its d'Artagnan seems only peripherally related to both his fictional and his historical self.

Et Charlotte Épousa d'Artagnan (*And Charlotte Married d'Artagnan*) provides another twist on the usual narrative.[19] It is the story of d'Artagnan's wife, Charlotte de Chanlecy, who has generally received a bad press in biographies. Here, she is presented in a more sympathetic light, as a woman caught up by social convention, and married to a man who places duty far ahead of marital affection. As an attempt to make sense of her recorded actions, the novel is a success, and, while d'Artagnan is shown in a harsh light, this is certainly one of the most interesting variations on Dumas's original theme.

The Three Musketeers has also attracted a number of reinterpretations and rewritings, often – though not always – humorous. *Tiffany Thayer's Three Musketeers* (1939) purports to be the story of Milady, although it also delves into the back stories of Athos, Aramis, Madame de Chevreuse, Lord de Winter and Buckingham. The emphasis is on farce: duels and dangerous missions give way to amorous misadventure, slapstick and improbable coincidences. A prolific writer over a number of genres, and a founder of the Fortean society, Thayer was largely concerned with making a living by his writing, but his musketeer novel shows not only a thorough knowledge of Dumas's book, but also familiarity with some of the more scurrilous accounts of seventeenth-century France. This is a good example of the pulp novel, and a quirky homage to the original. It is regretable that Thayer did not go on to turn his irreverent eye on the later novels in the musketeer sequence

– Raoul de Bragelonne in particular might have benefited from some gentle pastiche.

Another notable pastiche is Tim Scott and William Vandyck, *The Musketeers' Adventure Agency* (1990). Paris is overrun by a plague of cardinals; the King's life is in danger and there have been a rash of burglaries. Meanwhile, the King is concerned with how to explain philosophical complexities in everyday language… Enter the staff of the Musketeers' Adventure Agency – super-cool Aramis, beautiful (female) Athos, bungling Porthos and their pushy new friend d'Artagnan – to save the day, protect the King, and resolve their personal problems, which they do more by luck than intent, and with much wrangling along the way. Part parody – the narrative is supplemented by quizzes, games, faked newspaper articles and advertisements, and 'public service' announcements – part homage, the tone is more *1066 and All That* than *The Three Musketeers*, but it is none the worse for it. This is one of the most unusual – and certainly the funniest – of all the books written after Dumas.

Other reinterpretations are more serious, notably Yak Rivais, *Milady Mon Amour* (1986), which presents the story from Milady's point of view, and completely reworks Dumas's characterisation. Here, Milady is not villain but tragic heroine, exploited and betrayed by a world set up to benefit men and the well-born. It is a startling and thoughtful book, informed by modern sensibilities about female oppression and stereotyping. Like *D'Artagnan Amoureux*, it is yet to find an English edition.[20]

Perhaps the largest group of novels written in the shadow of *The Three Musketeers* is that of homages, which are shaped to echo plot, character and style of the original. The range of these is considerable – from paperback romance novels[21] to serious literary fiction. Arturo Perez-Reverte took some of the structure of *The Three Musketeers* to create *The Dumas Club*, in which the protagonist must trace fragments of a Dumas manuscript as well as pictures from a legendary occult text, lured on by a mysterious, Milady-like figure.[22] Pierre Nord and Voldemar Lestienne both relocated Dumas's musketeers to the Second World War, as heroes in the French struggle.[23] Joel Rosenberg took the theme, if not the personalities, of *The Three*

Musketeers as the framework for a sword-and-sorcery adventure.[24] The most complex of the homages is *The Phoenix Guards* and its sequels, by American writer Stephen Brust.[25] Four young soldiers – Khaavren, Aerich, Tazendra and Pel – form an unshakeable friendship against a background of intrigue, duels, magic and romance, and succeed in saving the day, however the odds are stacked against them. Brust is one of very few writers to tackle the entire arc of Dumas's musketeer novels, and he does so with great deftness and skill. A long-time fan of Dumas, he has also chosen to write this sequence in a voice deliberately echoing the style both of Dumas himself and of his early English translators. His books are amongst the most accomplished of all those written in the shadow of the musketeers, and probably come closest of all to finding the same flavour and atmosphere as the originals.

Musketeer pastiches and homages range from the ridiculous to the sublime, taking in comic books, children's fiction and adult works. Most of them fall into the category of genre fiction of some kind or another, and, like the novels by Dumas, have attracted little or no critical attention, with two exceptions. One is the excellent literary thriller by Arturo Perez-Reverte, the other is *Le Dernier Amour d'Aramis (Aramis's Last Love)* (1993), by Jean-Pierre Dufreigne. Like Mahalin's *Son of Porthos,* or Féval's *Le Fils de d'Artagnan,* Dufriegne's book is a sequel to *The Vicomte de Bragelonne.* At the end of the latter, Aramis has found a home in Spain, where he has risen to be Duke of Alméda and sometime ambassador to France. He is eighty, alone and blind; his former friends are all dead, but a young woman, his goddaughter Louise-Charlotte, comes to visit him. The book represents his memoirs, part dictated to her, part written by the blind man himself. Aramis is widely considered the least appealing of the musketeers, and certainly he is the most devious: he has seldom found much sympathy from the continuators of Dumas. Dufreigne's novel explores the psychology of a man who finds himself isolated by his intellect and his ambition, and endeavours to resolve the undoubtedly difficult question of his relations with the other three musketeers and his many mistresses. 'Naturally cold' was the verdict both of Athos and Dumas;[26] Dufreigne's Aramis is less cold than estranged. The book is undeniably modern in its psychological approach and its depictions of interpersonal relationships, but it stands as a very plausible account of a very complicated character. In style and tone, it has little in common with the works of Dumas: this is more reflective, darker territory – the borders of death, not of life. Critically acclaimed, it was awarded the French Prix Interallié for 1993.

In addition to the works mentioned above – and the others for which there was no space – the three musketeers and d'Artagnan have made cameo appearances in many, many other books, either as their historical selves, or as Dumas's characters. Their names have been applied to a range of cosmetics, a credit card, a chocolate bar and a wine. It is an extraordinary tribute to Dumas that he should have inspired such a range of books, from prize-winning to pulp. Yet alongside this afterlife in print and consumables, the musketeers have made themselves at home in yet another genre – film.

The musketeers took solid form almost as soon as the books appeared, in plays and revues. Their transition to film was to be almost as rapid. Late in the nineteenth century, an English director produced a short film entitled 'A Fencing Contest from the Three Musketeers'. The piece is long lost, and not even its exact date is known, but it is highly likely that it was the first film inspired by Dumas's novel. As technology improved, longer and more detailed versions began to appear. Two French films inspired by the novel appeared in 1903 and 1908, but it was to be an Italian director, Mario Caserini, who filmed the first full version.[27] The film was well received, and paved the way for several more adaptations, including the first American production, in 1911. A full-length French production followed in 1912.

It was not until after the First World War, however, that the novel was to meet with high-budget treatment, and when this happened, two productions appeared almost simultaneously. Perhaps the greatest star of the time, Douglas Fairbanks, had long identified the novel as a vehicle for himself, and had made a modern-dress film inspired by the book in 1918.[28] He could afford to spend serious money on his projects, and lavished great care and attention upon them. He assembled a cast drawn from both the US and France, had elaborate sets built, and imported a fencing champion to choreograph the duels and fights. Fairbanks was a handsome and physically gifted actor who performed his own stunts. To the role of d'Artagnan, he brought verve, daring and energy, but as star he also had the grace to allow his fellow cast-members to shine. Directed by Fred Niblo, his *The Three Musketeers* appeared in 1921, and was a huge hit.

It remains a very entertaining adaptation, and Fairbanks's central performance continues to impress. The stunt-work, in particular, is remarkable, and there is good chemistry between the leads. On the other hand, 1920s morality and the demands of the star system enforced some considerable revisions to Dumas's original. The adulterous nature of d'Artagnan's relationship with Constance was unacceptable in terms of Fairbanks's public image: she became Bonacieux's unmarried niece. The relationship of Anne of Austria with Buckingham was likewise downplayed. A happy ending was desired, so Constance survived, to be restored to d'Artagnan by Richelieu. To a modern eye, also, while the costumes are fairly good, the make-up, particularly of the female cast, is heavy-handed and anachronistic, while some of the performances now seem overstated.

While the Fairbanks version was in production, another production was underway in France, which was released in 1922. Directed by Henri Diamant-Berger, it was to be presented as a serial in twelve parts. Diamant-Berger was young and fairly inexperienced, but, like Fairbanks in the US, he paid the greatest care to every detail of his film. He hunted out appropriate locations, commissioned accurate costumes and props, and drew his actors from the French stage, avoiding star names. In the lead, he cast forty-two-year-old Aimé Simon-Girard, who was known for musical-comedy performances, and not considered an actor of quality. This risk, however, was more than justified. Simon-Girard responded to the challenge with a career-making performance, with all the physicality of Fairbanks, but without the constraints that stardom could place. This is a d'Artagnan without sentimentality or self-consciousness, but possessed of immense élan, charm and vulnerability. Despite the passage of more than eighty years, Simon-Girard remains probably the greatest screen d'Artagnan ever.

His performance is matched by the quality of the adaptation. Issues of modern morality and taste were not permitted to interfere with Dumas's text, and the story remains intact. It remains the sole version to include all the valets belonging to the musketeers, not just d'Artagnan's loyal Planchet. Constance remains the wife of Bonacieux. D'Artagnan's deception of Milady is presented unflinchingly. The cynicism of seventeenth-century politics is reflected without any softening sentimentality. Diamant-Berger remains the most faithful translator of *The Three Musketeers* to the screen, and his film is perhaps the finest of all the many versions. It broke all box-office records in its day and was loved by both audience and critics.

Diamant-Berger's adaptation was one of the many films that was destroyed during the Nazi occupation of France, and for years it was considered lost. In 1995, however, a copy turned up in the UK. Diamant-Berger's grandson has overseen a painstaking restoration, and the film has recently become available on DVD in France. The original captions have been replaced with subtitles, and a soundtrack giving sound effects added (with a music score and a small amount of voiceover). These make this silent classic easier in some ways to watch than the Fairbanks version. To date, there is no English-language version, but the French is easy to follow, and the film more than repays watching. Diamant-Berger went on to adapt *Twenty Years After* as a silent serial, and later on to make a talking version of *The Three Musketeers*. It is greatly to be hoped that these too will be recovered and once more made available.

It was not just *The Three Musketeers* that was translated onto the screen. While directors have tended to avoid *Twenty Years After*,[29] the last section of *The Vicomte de Bragelonne* (*The Man in the Iron Mask*) has proved to have enduring appeal. Indeed, thanks to Douglas Fairbanks, it was in the context of the latter that the musketeers first appeared with a voice soundtrack. Fairbanks's *Three Musketeers* had been well received (although for copyright reasons it was not screened in Europe until 1930), but he was not personally satisfied with it. With director Allan Dwan, he set about making *The Iron Mask* in 1929. He hired as artistic advisor French artist Maurice Leloir, famous for his illustrations of Dumas's novels, and reunited as many of his original cast as he could. The screenplay began shortly after the end of *The Three Musketeers*, allowing for the murder of Constance and for the introduction of the idea of the twin brother of Louis XIV. The film then jumps forward some fifteen to twenty years, at which point Rochefort is conspiring with Louis's twin – here an out-and-out villain – against the King. The film takes considerable liberties with the plot of the novel – there has yet to be a film version which has not done so – but it is well paced and has some good set pieces. It was released at the dawn of the age of talking pictures, and so Fairbanks provided a prologue in which he delivers a speech in character as d'Artagnan. He was thus the first d'Artagnan to talk, but the first fully talking film appeared in 1932 – this was Henri Diamant-Berger's remake of his own *Three Musketeers,* again starring Aimé Simon-Girard.

Several more versions of both *The Three Musketeers* and *The Man in the Iron Mask* appeared over the course of the 1930s, including a cartoon version from Russia, an Italian version and one from Argentina. The American director Rowland V. Lee made a twelve-part serial version in 1935, which received only a lukewarm reception. Two years earlier, another serial appeared under the title *The Three Musketeers.* Set in nineteenth-century North Africa, and starring John Wayne, it has more in common with *Beau Geste* than Dumas. Allan Dwan revisited the musketeers in 1939 with *The Singing Musketeer,* an uneven vehicle for the Ritz Brothers which is part musical, part parody.

The first serious Hollywood production since that of Fairbanks appeared in 1948, directed by George Sidney, and starring Gene Kelly. The film did well, and is still admired for its technical merits. It suffers, however, from the moral restrictions imposed upon it – not only the removal of the adultery elements, but the suppression of the religious character and responsibilities of Cardinal Richelieu. The costumes are anachronistic, and while Kelly's performance is energetic, he seems more aware of Fairbanks than of d'Artagnan. Its main redeeming feature is a strong and moving performance by Van Heflin as Athos. Perhaps as a result of the constraints under which it was made, however, it now seems more dated than many earlier film versions.

A number of mainly low-budget productions based on the musketeers books followed. These included one which seems to owe more to Paul Féval the younger than Dumas, *Sons of the*

Musketeers (1949), starring Maureen O'Hara as Claire, daughter of Athos, and centring on a plot by a fictitious Duc de Laval to murder the child Louis XIV and take his throne by marrying (an equally fictitious) princess.[30] The fifties saw the first television productions, also, in France, the US, and the UK. Another French film version directed by Bernard Borderie was released in 1961. It attracted little attention outside France, but, within that country, it made a considerable contribution to the rehabilitation of Dumas, and was followed by a prestigious production of *The Man in the Iron Mask* the following year. This took huge liberties with the book, but starred top actor Jean Marais as d'Artagnan. In the same year, Abel Gance began filming *D'Artagnan et Cyrano*. This was a production with an A-list cast, including Jean-Pierre Cassel and José Ferrer in the leading roles. Despite its title, it had no connection with any of the earlier novels which had brought these two heroes into contact. Rather, it centred on their fictitious amours with legendary courtesans Marion de Lorme and Ninon de L'Enclos. Despite its credentials, it disappointed the critics and failed at the box office.

Early in the 1970s, producer Ilya Salkind succeeded in putting together funding for a new, big-budget English-language film with an all-star cast. Directed by Richard Lester, with a script by George MacDonald Fraser and action choreography by William Hobbs, it soon became clear that there was more material than might be comfortably accommodated in one film, and as a result it was split into two halves, which were released under the titles *The Three Musketeers* (1973) and *The Four Musketeers* (1974). The script plays to the comic potential of the novel, but the plot has been transferred almost intact, and the films do not shy away from either the adultery or the violence of some of the encounters. As with all versions, there have been adaptations to modern taste – there has yet to be a film or television adaptation which takes over the romantic language in which the musketeers address each other in the book – but, as with the silent film of Diamant-Berger, the sheer verve, energy and charm of the films, combined with impeccable costuming, strong performances and fine locations, give them the genuine flavour of the original novel. Michael York's d'Artagnan is very nearly as fine as that of Aimé Simon-Girard, while Christopher Lee is surely the definitive Rochefort.

The Lester films marked a high point in the cinematographic history of *The Three Musketeers*. Regrettably, many of the films that have followed them have been disappointing. Both Stephen Herek's *The Three Musketeers* (1993) and Peter Hyams's *The Musketeer* (2001) have taken inexplicable liberties with the plot of the novel, rendering it all but unrecognisable. It appears to have become a necessity that the musketeers have been disbanded, and that d'Artagnan must save his dreams, not his Queen or country. Constance is radically altered in both plots, avoiding any danger of adultery, while Milady – who appears only in Herek's film – is misunderstood and innocent.[31] Richard Lester returned to the musketeers in 1989 with *The Return of the Musketeers*, based on *Twenty Years After*, and with the same strong cast. The film, however, fails to reach the heights of its two predecessors: the plot appears rushed, for one thing, and budget restrictions undermine the set pieces. Several versions of *The Man in the Iron Mask* have also appeared, all with the storyline adjusted to make Louis XIV a cruel fop, and his twin Philippe the hero, while Aramis's complicity in the plot to usurp the throne is completely removed. Mike Newell's 1976 version has a strong central performance by Richard Chamberlain, but is hampered by its low budget. Ken Annakin's *The Fifth Musketeer* (1979) met with universally poor reviews and has little to recommend it. *The Man in the Iron Mask* (1998) directed by Randall Wallace is uneven: there are some excellent performances. Gabriel Byrne captures the melancholy of the older d'Artagnan, Gerard Depardieu brings a genuine pathos to Porthos, and Jeremy Irons offers the finest Aramis to date, but some of the changes made in the plot are curious. Notably, the film makes both Louis and his twin, Philippe, children of d'Artagnan and the Queen, which raises uncomfortable and unaddressed questions about the nature of legitimate power, as well as compromising Dumas's conception of his hero. The script was intended to reflect on identity and democracy, but too often descends into cliché, while necessities in the storyline succeed in making the character of Athos almost incomprehensible.

By far the best of the recent musketeer films is one which is only peripherally related either to Dumas's books or to the historical musketeers. In *La Fille de d'Artagnan* (*D'Artagnan's Daughter,* 1994), director Bertrand Tavernier returns to the territory initially opened up by Paul Mahalin and Féval the younger – that of producing a sequel to the novels of Dumas. D'Artagnan's daughter, the spirited and headstrong Eloise, flees her convent school on discovering what she believes to be a plot against the King, and endeavours to enlist the help of her elderly father and his friends. Duels, chases, disguises, coded messages (which turn out to be faked), and bad poetry ensue as Eloise and her allies chase the evil Duc de Crassac. The film is engaging, funny and beautifully made: despite the liberties it takes, this is the only truly successful sequel to the full sequence of Dumas's works.

The Three Musketeers and its sequels have been turned into animations and into children's films. The blue tabards and rapiers have been picked up by Mickey Mouse[32] and Tom and Jerry;[33] turned into a musical;[34] and adapted as a serial as part of a magazine show.[35] *Dogtanian and the Three Muskehounds,* a television series produced in Spain and animated in Japan, has been dubbed into numerous languages and won a bronze medal at the International Film and Televisions Festival of New York in 1982. A Japanese version, *Anime San Jushi* (1987), which featured a female Aramis, was a huge hit in its country of origin. *Albert the Fifth Musketeer,* a British-French-Canadian co-production, was a charmingly quirky variation, in which Cardinal Richelieu wore bunny slippers, Milady's brand could talk, and the titular hero saved the day with ingenuity and spaghetti.

Over 300 years have passed since Charles Castelmore d'Artagnan, Armand de Sillègue d'Athos d'Autevielle, Isaac de Portau and Henri d'Aramitz served in the King's musketeers. Did they dream that their names would be remembered? We cannot know, at this remove. Alexandre Dumas, certainly, believed in his talent and in the quality of his work and would feel both proud and justified that his books are still read and loved today. But did even he imagine when he began writing *The Three Musketeers* that he was creating a legend? The musketeers have come a long way from their historical origins to become a part of our common western European heritage. To quote Dumas himself: 'Strange destiny of these men of brass!'[36]

Notes

CHAPTER ONE: THE HISTORICAL D'ARTAGNAN

1   For full details of Arnaud and his sons, see Odile Bordaz, *D'Artagnan* (Baixas 2001) pp.18–22; Jean-Christian Petitfils, *Le Véritable d'Artagnan* (new ed., Paris 2002), pp.20–21.

2   He had already inherited La Plagne. Arnaud de Batz had been succeeded by his son François. On the death of François, the family lands had been divided between his sons Bertrand I (who received Castelmore) and Pierre (who received La Plagne). Charles's father Bertrand II was the eldest son of Pierre: his uncle Bertrand I having no children made this nephew and namesake his heir. See Bordaz, *D'Artagnan*, pp.19–20.

3   As Bordaz has pointed out, the authenticity of this document and the existence of the persons named are questionable. Bordaz, *D'Artagnan*, p.19 and n.7.

4   Given the paucity of evidence, it is impossible to make any hard and fast judgement as to the personal relations between Bertrand and Françoise. At the period, noble marriage was largely a matter of economics and alliance. While the difference in rank makes it tempting to hypothesise a love-match, it is more likely to be a product of local circumstances which have gone unrecorded.

5   Quoted in Petitfils, *Le Véritable d'Artagnan*, p.27. The King by this time was Henri IV's son, Louis XIII. Translation by KM.

6   Bordaz, *D'Artagnan*, pp.33–34; Petitfils, *Le Véritable d'Artagnan*, pp.27–28.

7   For Paul's career, see Petitfils, *Le Véritable d'Artagnan,* pp.24–27; Bordaz, *D'Artagnan,* pp.36–38, 41, 139–140.

8   Petitfils, *Le Véritable d'Artagnan,* p.24. There is no reference to his death in battle in any extant source, so it may be that rather than being killed in battle, he may have contracted a fatal illness.

9   Petitfils, *Le Véritable d'Artagnan,* p.43.

10   Curiously, Charles was, on his mother's side, very distantly connected by marriage to Richelieu's family, the du Plessis. The relationship had no bearing upon his fortunes.

11   For these important individuals, see Wendy Gibson, *A Tragic Farce: The Fronde (1648–1653)* (Exeter 1998), pp.86–7, 96–9, 105–6.

12   A great deal has been written on the Thirty Years' War. However, for a clear and thoughtful introduction to a complex subject, see especially Richard Bonney, *The Thirty Years' War 1618–1648* (Oxford 2002).

13   See Gibson, *A Tragic Farce*; G.R.R. Treasure, *Seventeenth Century France* (2nd ed. London 1981), pp.215–227; Geoffrey Treasure, *Mazarin: the Crisis of Absolutism in France* (London 1995), pp.103–229.

14   Dumas, *Twenty years After*, Chapter 54; Geoffrey F. Hall and Joan Sanders, *D'Artagnan the Ultimate Musketeer* (Boston 1964), pp.56–7; Armand Praviel, *Histoire Vraie des Trois Mousquetaires* (Lagny 1933), p.37.

15   Recipients included the Queen of England, Henrietta, who had taken refuge in her native France from the English Civil War; Bordaz, *D'Artagnan,* p.53.

16   This letter, dated 23 April 1651, shortly after Mazarin arrived at Brühl, is quoted in Bordaz, *D'Artagnan,* p.54.

17   Bordaz, *D'Artagnan,* p.57. Petitfils has come to a similar conclusion: Petitfils, *Le Véritable d'Artagnan,* pp.59–60.

18   For the nature of this second exile, very different to the first, see Treasure, *Mazarin,* pp.199–201.

19   An *intendant* was a royal official whose job was to oversee fiscal, administrative and sometimes military matters in the provinces of France. Richard Bonney, *Political Change in France under Richelieu and Mazarin 1624–1661* (Oxford 1978) gives a full discussion of these officials.

20   The exception was the province of Guyenne, and particularly the port of Bordeaux. See Treasure, *Mazarin,* pp.203–205; Gibson, *A Tragic Farce,* pp.57–58.

21   The French Guards were part of the ceremonies also. Alongside the King's Swiss guard, they were arrayed in the square in front of Reims Cathedral, and fired off a gun salute. It is possible that Charles, in his capacity of lieutenant of the Vitermont company, may have been involved.

22   Cited in Bordaz, *D'Artagnan,* p.66. Translation by KM.

23   In addition to Spanish forces, the rebellious Condé was amongst those opposing the French army.

24   Bordaz, *D'Artagnan,* pp.68–9; Petitfils, *Le Véritable d'Artagnan,* pp.69–70. Stenay fell to the French on 5 August.

25   Petitfils, *Le véritable d'Artagnan,* pp.70–71.

26   Bordaz, *D'Artagnan,* pp.69–70; Petitfils, *Le Véritable d'Artagnan,* p.70.

27   Isaac de Baas, despite his surname, was no relation to Charles. Like Charles, he had served Mazarin during the Fronde. The similarity of the names de Baas and de Batz may have led Courtilz de Sandras, the author of the pseudo-memoirs of our d'Artagnan, to confuse the two, hence his attributing to our Charles a

mission to England which was in fact conferred on Isaac. This is discussed below, in Chapter 3.

28   This idea is most marked in the Douglas Fairbanks vehicle *The Iron Mask* (dir. Allan Dwan, 1929) and in *The Man in the Iron Mask* (dir. Randall Wallace, 1998).

29   Bordaz, *D'Artagnan*, pp.75–6.

30   The text of this contract may be found, in French, in Bordaz, *D'Artagnan*, appendix pp.363–366.

31   There is a lively and vivid account of the marriage of Louis and Maria-Theresa and the circumstances surrounding it in Philippe Erlanger, *Louis XIV* (Paris 1965; English translation by Stephen Cox, London 1970), pp.76–92.

32   Spanish protocol dictated that an Infanta could only leave Spain after marriage. As a result, a proxy marriage was held on 2 June 1660, at Fuentarabia. Louis XIV was represented by the Spanish minister Don Luis de Haro.

33   The peace included a formal pardon for the rebel Prince of Condé, who was reinstated to most of his former positions (his governorship of Guyenne was not returned).

34   Cited in Bordaz, *D'Artagnan*, p.156: 'toute à fait bien ajusté et sur un cheval de prix' Translation by KM.

35   It is not known if Charles ever saw his younger son.

36   For Louis's relations with Mazarin, see Treasure, *Louis XIV*, pp.13–16, 31–34; Bonney, *Political Change*, pp.419–420.

37   The *surintendant des finances* was in charge of the administration of public finances, a very powerful – and lucrative – position.

38   An *intendant des finances* also had responsibility for financial matters, and was frequently recruited from the ranks of wealthy financiers, who might be expected to possess special expertise in this area. Colbert was Mazarin's particular *intendant*, which gave him added influence. For a detailed discussion of the many and varied roles of *intendants* in seventeenth-century France, see Bonney, *Political Change, passim*.

39   The fullest account of his character and career is Jean-Christian Petitfils, *Fouquet* (Paris 1999). There is no recent English-language biography.

40   However, his former comrade and co-servitor, Besmaux, was close by when Mazarin died, and is said to have wept. See Bordaz, *D'Artagnan*, p.159.

41   Bordaz, *D'Artagnan*, appendix p.105. Translation by KM.

42   '...leur âge fort avancé leur ayant l'ouyë un peu difficile'. Cited in Bordaz, *D'Artagnan*, p.175. Translation by KM.

43   Some of these are printed in French in Bordaz, *D'Artagnan*, appendix pp.366–68.

44   This was to be Charles's sole experience of the Bastille.

45   Petitfils, *Le Véritable d'Artagnan*, pp.116–117; Bordaz, *D'Artagnan*, pp.176–177. Bordaz assumes a prior friendship between Charles and Besmaux, based on their joint service under Mazarin, and on Besmaux's presence at the marriage contract. However, it should be pointed out that this is not proof of warm relations: Charles's selection of witnesses looks to have been based mainly on a show of his connections and patrons, and Besmaux, who had profited well from working for Mazarin, may have been more a useful contact than a close friend.

46   'M. d'Artagnan était auprès de lui; cinquante mousquetaires derrière, à trente ou quarante pas. Il parassait assez rêveur. Pour moi, quand je l'ai aperçu, les jambes m'ont tremblé, et le coeur m'a battu si fort, que je n'en pouvois rien. En s'approchant de nous pour rentrer dans son trou, M. d'Artagnan l'a poussé, et

lui a fait remarquer que nous étions là.' Madame de Sévigny, *Lettres*, ed. Henri
Baudin (Paris 1968), pp.31–33. Translation by KM.

47   They included treason, for the fortification by Fouquet of his property at Belle-
Île-en-Mer, off the coast of Brittany, and attempting to usurp royal rights.

48   On this Saint-Mars, see Petitfils, *Fouquet*, pp.461–462; Bordaz, *D'Artagnan*,
pp.186–188.

49   'Il me parut chagrin du voyage qu'on luy faisoit faire à Pignerol, dont on le
pouvoit dispenser.' Olivier Lefèvre d'Ormesson, *Journal*, ed. M. Cheruel, 2 vols
(Paris 1860–61), 2, 286. Translation by KM.

50   One can only think that they had had news of his temper from Grenoble!

51   For most of this time he was alone and forbidden communication with the
outside world. His family were exiled to Montluçon, and were not allowed to
join him until 1679.

52   The colours were derived from the coats of the horses on which they were
mounted.

53   Bordaz, *D'Artagnan*, pp.197–199; Petitfils, *Le Véritable d'Artagnan*, pp.132–133.

54   Charles also received a pension of 6,000 *livres* per year.

55   Thus, in September 1662, he was godfather to the daughter of Louis de Laurens,
captain of the Piemont regiment. In October 1664, he was godfather to one of
his musketeers, Jules Arnolfini. Petitfils, *Le véritable d'Artagnan*, p.130.

56   This was not the full number of serving musketeers. Louis retained a certain
number of them as his personal guard. In addition to the musketeers, a number
of other companies belonging to the royal household were included in the
expedition.

57   A *fascine* was a bundle of long wooden stakes, which would be used to create a
rampart, line a trench, or fill up a ditch, thus allowing the passage of infantry.

58   The letter is quoted in Bordaz, *D'Artagnan*, p.214.

59   He received several letters of commendation for this. See Petitifils, *Le véritable
d'Artagnan*, pp.144–145.

60   'Monsieur d'Artagnan, sage et preux/Fut receu d'un air gracieux.' Cited in
Bordaz, *D'Artagnan*, p. 218; Petitfils, *Le Véritable d'Artagnan*, p.146. Translation by
KM.

61   Various of these are found quoted in Bordaz, *D'Artagan*, pp.233–234; Petitfils,
Le Véritable d'Artagnan, p.248. The most charming is that found in the rhyming
Gazette of Charles Robinet, the official poet of Henriette d'Angleterre, the
King's sister-in-law. Robinet wrote 'A la teste des Mouquetaires/Il a mis pour
leur Lieutenant/Un des Preux de maintenant,/Que le Sieur d'Artagnan l'on
nomme.' ('At the head of the musketeers he placed as their lieutenant one of the
most valiant men today, whom people call the Sieur d'Artagnan.' Translation by
KM.)

62   For a rather one-sided account of these two of Louis's mistresses, see Lisa Hilton,
Athénaïs: the Real Queen of France (London 2002). La Vallière has no modern
English-language biographer: for a French account see Jean-Christian Petitfils,
Louise de la Vallière (Paris 1990). She figures considerably in the later volumes of
Dumas's musketeer romances.

63   This appointment brought with it a salary of 500 *livres* a month, which Charles
doubtless found useful. Petitfils, *Le Véritable d'Artagnan*, p.156.

64   The fighting did not cease, however. While King and court were absent,
Marshal d'Aumont took the town of Courtrai, an encounter in which the

second company of musketeers saw action. Turenne, meanwhile received a check at Dendermonde, when the defenders opened the dykes and flooded the surrounding land, preventing the French advance.

65 Turenne was so distressed by this habit that he threatened to leave the army if the King did not take more precautions. The senior officers also remonstrated with Louis, but the King was not deterred. The rank and file of the army – and the ladies of the court – were impressed by this display of royal bravery, however.

66 'Ce malheureux général', Pierre Quarré d'Aligny, *Mémoire des Campagnes de M. le comte d'Aligny-Quarré sous le règne de Louis XIV jusqu'à la paix de* Riswich (Beaune 1886), p.66. Translation by KM.

67 This is not the Rochefort familiar to readers of *The Three Musketeers.*

68 Lauzun was captain of the King's dragoons, and had made sure that their costumes were as glorious as possible. This irritated Charles, who was very jealous of the position of his own men.

69 Anne-Marie-Louise de Montpensier, *Mémoires de Mademoiselle de Montpensier, petite-fille de Henri IV*, ed. A. Chéruel, 4 vols (Paris 1858–59), p.325. Translation by KM:

Je lui demandai les nouvelles de M. de Lauzun. Il me dit qu'il l'avait laissé en bonne santé, tout autant qu'il pouvait l'être ne voyant point le roi; qu'il dit des choses si touchant sur son respect et son amitié pour le roi, que rien n'était égal. Je lui dis
'L'avez-vous dit au roi?'
'Assurement; enfin tout ce que je puis dire, c'est qu'il aime tout ce qu'il doit aimer, and qu'il n'a la coeur plein d'autre chose, et qu'il en sent la privation bien sensiblement. Il ne m'a chargé de rien dire, et il ne me convient pas de prendre des commissions; mais il est tout comme il doit être et comme ceux qui l'aimetn peuvent souhaiter.'

I asked him for news of Monsieur de Lauzun. He told me that he had left him in good health, insofar as he might be, not being able to see the King; that he had said very touching things regarding his respect and friendship for the King, such that nothing was equal to it. I said to him
'Have you told this to the King?'
'Certainly: in the end, all that I can say is that he loves everything which he should love, and that he feels his deprivation keenly. He didn't give me anything to say, and it wasn't proper for me to undertake commissions for him; but he is just as he should be and as those who love him may hope.'

70 For a detailed account of the causes of this war, see Treasure, *Louis XIV*, pp.161–169. For the conduct of war and a clear overview of Louis's military activities, see John A. Lynn, *The French Wars 1667–1714* (Oxford 2002).

71 This was the key interest of the Duke de Saint-Simon, who documented the later years of Louis's court in his famous *Memoirs.*

72 Turenne had been a *Frondeur* for a time; he had also been a Huguenot, although he had converted to Catholicism by this time.

73 I would like to thank the staff of the La Botte Chantilly for their kindness in allowing me into their private courtyard to take photographs.

74 This child, the Duc d'Anjou, survived only a few months. However, he was

Louis's second legitimate son: the *Tè Deum* served to underline that this King, already victorious in war, was also blessed with heirs to inherit his kingdom.

75 '…commander dans nostre dicte ville et citadelle de Lille et dans les pays et la chatellenie de Lille, Orchies et pays de Lalloeue'. The commission is printed in full in Bordaz, *D'Artagnan*, appendix pp.368–369. Translation by KM.

76 'Depuis que je suis à Lisle, j'ai vécu avec le chevalier de Mongivrau le plus honnêtement du monde, et je crois même que j'en ai trop fait. Jamais depuis que j'y suis, il ne m'a parlé un mot de tout ce qu'il fait ici que pour me dire qu'il avoit ordre de vous de jamais rendre compte ni au gouverneur ni à l'intendant…' cited in Bordaz, *D'Artagnan*, appendix, pp.371–2. The spelling is Charles's. Translation by KM.

77 'Je suis persuadé, Monseigneur, que le roy serait faché contre moi si je souffrais qu'un petit ingénieur de deux jours méprisât le caractère que Sa Majesté m'a fait l'honneur de me donner ici…'. Bordaz, *D'Artagnan*, appendix p.372. Translation by KM.

78 'Si j'osais, Monseigneur, vous supplier de faire auprès du Roy qu'il voulut abréger ma commission et me retirer auprès de lui. Je vous serais bien obligé.' Cited in Bordaz, *D'Artagnan*, p.372. Translation by KM.

79 Bordaz, *D'Artagnan*, p.306.

80 'J'é cru et j'espère, Monseigneur, que vous n'aprouverès pas le procédé de monsieur de La Bergentière, et s'est ce quy fait, Monseigneur, que je vous en demande justice…'. Cited in Bordaz, *D'Artagnan*, appendix p.373. Translation by KM.

81 Le Peletier mentioned the incident in a letter to Louvois. Bordaz, *D'Artagnan*, pp.312–313.

82 Petitfils, *Le Véritable d'Artagnan*, p. 214.

83 Louis had sent part of the second company there to fight the Turks.

84 For an account of Vauban as an innovator in strategy, see John A. Lynn, *Giant of the Grand Siècle: The French Army, 1610–1715* (Cambridge 1997), pp.569–575.

85 The *glacis* is the sloping clear area situated just outside the main walls, often used as a killing ground,

86 'Je fus assez heureux pour n'être pas blessé, non plus que M. d'Artagnan, quoique nous ne nous fussions pas épargnés, dont le roi fut fort content.' Quarré d'Aligny, *Mémoire*, p.100.

87 I am grateful to the Maastricht tourist office for their kindness in supplying me with additional information to flesh out the bare bones of internet reporting of these finds.

88 '…il n'y a personne au monde quy est ressanty se malleur plus forteman que moy. Se n'et pas par se que j'an esperé pour ma fortune, mes par la perte d'eun pere que j'é perdu en le perdant.' The full text may be found in Bordaz, *D'Artagnan*, appendix p.375. It is notable that Joseph's spelling is as creative as Charles's had been: clearly education back home in Gascony continued to be a minor priority amongst young male gentry!

89 Most of this is printed in Bordaz, *D'Artagnan*, appendix pp.375–378.

90 Bordaz, *D'Artagnan*, p.120.

91 'D'Artagnan et la gloire ont le même cerceuil.' *La gloire* in French means rather more than 'glory', taking in also a sense of personal distinction and achievement. The poem on Charles is given in full in Bordaz, *D'Artagnan*, p.341.

CHAPTER TWO: ATHOS, PORTHOS, ARAMIS – AND MONSIEUR DE
TRÉVILLE

1   Jean-Henri Ducos, Préface to Véronique Larcade, *Les Cadets de Gascogne* (Portet-sur-Garonne 2000), p.2.

2   Armand de Sillègue d'Athos d'Autevielle, for example, or the Sieur de Carbon de Biron de Casteljaloux, the captain under whom Cyrano served.

3   Larcade, *Cadets*, pp.5–6. Cyrano was in fact born in Paris.

4   For a detailed discussion of this, see Larcade, *Cadets*, pp. 5–17.

5   The fullest account of Tréville remains Jean de Jaurgain, *Troisvilles, D'Artagnan et les Trois Mousquetaires études biographiques et heraldiques* (Paris 1910).

6   This is the des Essarts to whom, in *The Three Musketeers*, Tréville sent d'Artagnan to become a guard cadet. Dumas took this detail from Courtilz de Sandras, but the historical Charles Castelmore d'Artagnan did not serve under des Essarts, who did not become a guard captain until 1642, and who retained the post for only a short while, having compromised himself in the Cinq-Mars affair. Petitfils, *Le Véritable d'Artagnan*, pp.32–33.

7   On Louis and his favourites, see A. Lloyd Moote, *Louis XIII the Just* (London 1989).

8   For a rather romantic account of the career and character of Cinq-Mars see Philippe Erlanger, *The King's Minion: Richelieu, Louis XIII, and the Affair of Cinq-Mars*, trans. Gilles and Heather Cremonesi (1971). For a more sober discussion, see Lloyd Moote, *Louis XIII*, pp.286–289.

9   There remains some doubt that Louis may have allowed himself to become involved on some level with the plot: see Lloyd Moote, *Louis XIII*, pp.288–289.

10   For an excellent biography of Anne, see Ruth Klein, *Anne of Austria Queen of France* (Columbus 1985).

11   This abbey had family connections: Jean-Arnaud's brother-in-law was one of its former abbots, and he had stayed there during his brief exile in late 1642.

12   On the legend of the Gascon *cadets*, see above. Not only the famous four musketeers and their captain belonged to this group. At least one of the 'Cardinal's Guard' with whom Dumas has them fight in the early chapters of *The Three Musketeers* was also from Gascony. Bernajoux or Vernajoul (the Gascon spelling) was from the minor nobility of the area around Foix. The others were also historical people: Cahusac and Biscarrat were brothers, the family surname was de Rotondis, and Biscarrat – Jacques de Rotondis, Lord of Biscarrat – later became governor of Charleville, and had been a lieutenant in Richelieu's light horse. Claude, Comte de Jussac came from a slightly higher echelon of the nobility and thus enjoyed a slightly more elevated career: he was appointed governor of the young Duke of Vendôme and subsequently made first gentleman of the bedchamber of the Duke of Maine. (The latter was an illegitimate son of Louis XIV and Madame de Montespan, and a considerable figure at court in the later part of Louis's reign.) He continued his martial pursuits, however, being killed aged well over seventy at the battle of Fleurus on 8 July 1690. On these four, see Jaurgain, *Troisvilles*, pp.190–192. In 1677, a Madame de Jussac was junior governess to two others of Louis's illegitimate children with Madame de Montespan, the Comte de Toulouse and Mademoiselle de Blois; Hilton, *Athenaïs*, p.167. She could well have been married to our Jussac.

13   Jaurgain, *Troisvilles*; Charles Samaran, *D'Artagnan Capitaine des Mousquetaires du Roi* (Paris 1912).

14   Notably Chelsea Quinn Yarbro, *A Candle for d'Artagnan* (New York 1989). The book works hard to accommodate the facts, but succeeds in bringing three of the four into contact.

15   Alexandre Dumas, *Les Trois Mousquetaires* (Editions Flammarion, 1984), p.110. Translation by KM.

Depuis cinq ou six ans qu'il viviat dans la plus profonde intimité avec ses compagnons Porthos et Aramis, ceux-ci se rappelaient l'avoir vu sourire souvent, mais jamis ils ne l'avaient entendu rire. Ses paroles étaient brèves et expressives, disant toujours ce qu'elles voulaient dire, rien de plus: pas d'enjolivements, pas de broderies, pas d'arabesques. Sa conversation était un fait sans aucun épisode.

Quoique Athos eût à peine trente ans et fût d'une grande beauté de corps et d'esprit, personne ne lui connaissait de maîtresse. Jamais il ne parlait de femmes. Seulement, il n'empêcherait pas qu'on en parlât devant lui, quoiqu'il fût facile de voir que ce genre de conversation, auquel il ne se mêlait que par des mots amers et des aperçus misanthropiques, lui était parfaitement désagréable. Sa réserve, sa sauvagerie et son mutisme en faisaient presque un viellard…

16   The fullest account of him remains that of Jaurgain, *Troisvilles*, pp.230–238.

17   Dumas comments in the course of *Twenty Years After* that the French spoken in the Blois area is the purest in France – just what one would expect of his Athos! Dumas, *Twenty Years After* (Everyman Library, London 1907), p.117.

18   Photographs survive, and can be seen in Praviel, *Histoire Vraie*, opposite p.49, and in the booklet *Au Pays des Trois Mousquetaires*, published in the Promeneur des Lettres series, and available from the d'Artagnan museum at Lupiac. The château was a neat, three-storey square building with corner turrets, about the same size as that at Lupiac. A modern house now stands on the site.

19   For the details of this branch of the family, see Jaurgain, *Troisvilles*, pp.234–238.

20   'Conuoy, service at enterrement de deffunct Armand Athos Dautubiele mousquetaire de la garde du Roy, gentilhomme de Béarn, pris poche la halle du Pré-aux-Clercs.' Quoted in Jaurgain, *Troisvilles*, p. 234.

21   In passing, it is worth noting that the literary Porthos is the one of the musketeers about whose background we are told least – and, given his personality, had he had any claim to old nobility of high birth, one can be sure he would have mentioned it. Porthos as drawn by Dumas is almost certainly a son of the aspiring bourgeois, the same class which produced the historical d'Artagnan, Athos, and Isaac de Portau.

22   For a detailed discussion of the development of the duel and its social and political contexts, see V.G. Kiernan, *The Duel in European History* (Oxford 1989), especially Chapters 4 and 5.

23   Kiernan, *Duel*, pp.54–56, p.91.

24   On the *mignons*, see R.J. Knecht, *The Rise and Fall of Renaissance France 1483–1610* (London 1996) pp.485–6, 491–2, 501, 505. The turbulent reign of Henri III and the exploits of the *mignons* provided Dumas with yet another exciting canvas and some intriguing heroes – for fiction: the novels *La Dame de Monsoreau* (*Chicot the*

Jester, 1847) and *Les Quarante-cinq (The Forty Five,* 1848) as well as the play *Henri III et sa cour (Henry III and his Court,* 1829).

25 Richard Cohen, *By the Sword: Gladiators, Musketeers, Samurai Warriors, Swashbucklers and Olympians* (New York 2002), p.48.

26 Cohen, *Sword,* p 48.

27 Duelling fascinated Dumas, and plays a role in many of his novels. He liked to hint that he was himself a duellist, a character trait exploited admirably in Guy Endore, *King of Paris* (London 1965), a novel in which Dumas is himself the hero.

28 Quoted in Cohen, *Sword,* p.66.

29 Cohen, *Sword,* pp.77–8; Kiernan, *Duel,* p.76; G.R.R. Treasure, *Seventeenth Century France* (2nd ed. London 1981) pp.166–167.

30 Gatien de Courtilz de Sandras, *Mémoirs de Monsieur d'Artagnan,* ed. Gilbert Sigaux (Paris 1965, 1987), pp.118–120. This is the French text. For an English translation see Gatien de Courtilz de Sandras, *Memoirs of Monsieur d'Artagnan captain-lieutenant of the 1st company of the King's Musketeers* trans. Ralph Nevill, 3 vols (London 1898), I, 313–319. 'Milédi' is a phonetic French rendering of 'My lady'.

31 Jaurgain, *Troisvilles,* p.234.

32 Dumas, *Les Trois Mousquetaires,* p. 63. Translation by KM:

> Au centre du groupe le plus animé était un mousquetaire de grande taille, d'une figure hautaine et d'une bizarrerie de costume qui attirait sur lui l'attention générale. Il ne portait pas, pour le moment, la casaque d'uniforme, qui, au reste, n'était pas absolument obligatoire dans cette époque de liberté moindre mais d'indépendance plus grande, mais un justaucorps bleu de ciel, tant soit peu fané et râpé, et sur cet habit un baudrier magnifique, en broderies d'or, et qui reluisait comme les écailles dont l'eau se couvre au grand soleil. Un manteau long de velours cramoisi tombait avec grâce sur ses épaules, découvrant par-devant seulement la splendide baudrier, auquel pendait une gigantesque rapière.

33 When Athos is getting to know d'Artagnan in *The Three Musketeers,* he comments 'After all, as you come from Dax or Pau…' to which d'Artagnan replies 'From Tarbes'. ('Après cela, comme vous arrivez de Dax ou de Pau…' 'De Tarbes', Dumas, *Les Trois Mousquetaires,* p. 87.) Translation by KM.

34 This cost him 6,250 *livres,* a not inconsiderable sum. Jaurgain, *Troisvilles,* p.242.

35 On lay abbacies, see below, pp.98.

36 Petitfils, *Le Véritable d'Artagnan,* p.41; Bordaz, *D'Artagnan,* p.41.

37 Dumas, *Trois Mousquetaires,* p.64. The musketeer speaking to Aramis to whom he forms such a contrast here is Porthos.

> Cet autre mousquetaire formait un contraste parfait avec celui qui l'interrogeait et qui venait de la désigner sous le nom d'Aramis: c'était un jeune homme de vingt-deux à vingt trois ans à peine, à la figure naïve et doucereuse, à l'oeil noir et doux et aux joues roses et veloutées comme une pêche en automne; sa moustache fine dessinait sur sa lèvre supérieure une ligne d'une rectitude parfaite; ses mains semblaient craindre de s'abaisser, de peur que leurs veines ne se gonflassent, et de temps en temps il se pinçait le bout des oreilles pour les maintenir d'un incarnat tendre et transparent. D'habitude il parlait peu

et lentement, saluait beaucoup, riait sans bruit en montrant ses dents, ils avait belles, et dont, comme du reste de sa personne, il semblait prendre le plus grand soin.

38 For a good introduction to the Wars of Religion, see R.J. Knecht, *The French Wars of Religion 1559–1598* (2nd ed., Harlow 1996).

39 Henri d'Alméras, *Alexandre Dumas et Les Trois Mousquetaires* (Paris 1929), p.12.

40 The names given to children have sometimes been taken as an indication of religious inclination: it is certainly the case that none of Henri's bore strongly reformist names (often Old Testament). Two of his children had names which are more often found in Catholic families – Clément and Madeleine – so a conversion is possible. But we cannot know for certain. Nor can we know if both parents converted. By the end of the seventeenth century, remaining Huguenot had become a very uncomfortable choice. Tradition in Aramitz, however, views Henri as Huguenot.

41 For a detailed account of the family, see Jaurgain, *Troisvilles*, pp.218–230.

CHAPTER THREE: THE MUSKETEER COMPANIES

1 The military household of the King.

2 Bodyguards.

3 A company of light cavalry.

4 For fuller information on the venal system of appointments, see Lynn, *Giant of the Grand Siècle*, pp.228–231.

5 There were twenty *sols* to one *livre*.

6 Arnaud Jacomet, 'Les Mousquetaires', in *Les Corps d'Élite du Passé*, gen. ed. Dominique Venner (Paris 1972), 163–223 & 379–392, pp.387–88; Louis Susane, *Histoire de la Cavalerie Française* (1874), vol. 1, *Les Mousquetaires*, pp.232–233.

7 Jacomet, *Les Mousquetaires*, p.388.

8 Bordaz, *D'Artagnan*, appendix, p.377.

9 Jacob Van Gheyn, *The Exercise of Armes* (1607).

10 For a more detailed account of this siege, see Treasure, *Seventeenth Century France*, pp.147–152; David Parrott, *Richelieu's Army: War, Government and Society in France, 1624–1642* (Cambridge 2001), pp.87–91.

11 See Treasure, *Seventeenth Century France*, pp.156–8; Parrott, *Richelieu's Army*, pp.91–100.

12 Partible inheritance refers to the practice whereby a property, title or position would be divided between several heirs simultaneously.

13 For more detail on Mazarin, Richelieu and Tréville, see Chapter 2.

14 See Chapter 1.

15 The battle takes its name from the terrain on which it was fought.

16 However, upon taking the throne in 1660, Charles II promptly sold it back to the French.

17 See Chapter 1.

18 This is not the Rochefort of *The Three Musketeers*.

19 Quarré d'Aligny, *Mémoire*, p.148.

CHAPTER FOUR: GATIEN DE COURTILZ DE SANDRAS AND THE *MÉMOIRS DE M. D'ARTAGNAN*

1   The same is true, it must be noted, of Isaac de Portau – the real Porthos.

2   Jean Lombard, *Courtilz de Sandras et la crise de la roman à la fin du grand siècle* (Presses Universitaires de France 1980), pp. 58, 61–2.

3   Petifils, *Le Véritable d'Artagnan*, p. 15.

4   Bordaz, *D'Artagnan*, p. 10.

5   For clandestine literature, see Robert Darnton, *The Forbidden Best-Sellers of Pre-Revolutionary France* (London 1996).

6   They were *Relation de ce qui c'est passé en Catalogne* (1678), *Nouvelles amoreuses et galantes* (1678), *Relation de ce qui s'est passé en Flandre et en Allemagne* (1679) and *Nouveau receuil de lettres et de billets galands avec leurs responses* (1680).

7   This was the notorious affair of the poisons, which exposed a supposed network of poisoners, sorcerers and blasphemers: Madame de Montespan was popularly believed to have had recourse to some of these to attract and keep the King's love. For an account of this scandal, see Frances Mossiker, *The Affair of the Poisons* (London 1969); Anne Somerset, *The Affair of the Poisons* (London 2003); Hilton, *Athénäis* (London 2002), pp. 189–215.

8   The *Conduite de la France depuois la paix de Nimègue* and *Response au livre intitulé: Conduite de la France depuois la paix de Nimègue*, both published probably in The Hague. See Lombard, *Courtilz*, p. 84.

9   Lombard, *Courtilz*, p. 374.

10 The books are the *Vie de Jean-Baptiste Colbert* and the *Mémoires de Messire J-B de la Fontaine*; the journal was *L'Elite de nouvelles de tous les cours de l'Europe*. The latter was published only for a few months in 1698.

11 'Memoirs of Monsieur d'Artagnan, captain-lieutenant of the first company of the King's Musketeers, containing a number of particular and secret things which happened during the reign of Louis the Great [Louis XIV]'. For an English-language edition of these, see Courtilz de Sandras, *Memoirs of Monsieur d'Artagnan*, trans. Nevill. The other works which appeared in this short period were the *Annales de la Cour et de Paris, Entretiens de M. Colbert avec Bouin, Mémoires du Marquis de Montbrun,* and *Mémoires de Madame la Marquise du Fresne.*

12 This was the *Mémoires de M. de B., secrétaire de MLCDR*. It appears that in his last years, he sought to capitalise on the more successful of his earlier works.

13 '... quelle impudence de donner pour du mémoires de M. d'Artagnan trois volumes dont il n'y a pas une ligne faite par M. d'Artagnan,' Pierre Bayle to the Abbé Dubos, quoted by Lombard, *Courtilz*, p. 155.

14 Eugène d'Auriac, *D'Artagnan Capitaine-Lieutenant des Mousquetaires* (Paris 1847, reprinted 1993).

15 Samaran, *D'Artagnan*.

16 Courtilz, *Memoirs*, trans. Nevill, I, 1–23.

17 Henrietta Maria was the sister of Louis XIII and took refuge in France during the English Civil War.

18 Courtilz, *Memoirs*, trans. Nevill, I, 242–317.

19 Courtilz, *Memoirs*, trans. Nevill, I, 54–59.

20 Courtilz, *Memoirs*, trans. Nevill, III, 258–9, 270.

21   Courtilz, *Memoirs*, trans. Nevill, III, 260–2.
22   Courtilz, *Memoirs*, trans. Nevill, III, 151–58, 196–200. Most of the intervening
       pages are devoted to the account of an intrigue involving Fouquet's brother, the
       Abbé Fouquet.
23   Courtilz, *Memoirs*, trans. Nevill, III, pp.159–60. Courtilz uses this information,
       furthermore, to launch another attack on Besmaux, stating that the latter had no
       right to the title de Montlezun.
24   For the *Ormée*, see Gibson, *A Tragic Farce*, pp.57–8, 112–113; Treasure, *Mazarin*,
       pp.203–5.
25   For this episode, see Courtilz, *Memoirs*, trans. Nevill, II, 162–204.
26   Courtilz, *Memoirs*, trans. Nevill, II, 304–347.
27   Alexandre Dumas, *Le Comte de Monte Cristo* (1844–45; first translated into
       English as *The Count of Monte Cristo*, 1846); *Mémoires d'un Médecin* (1846–48; first
       completely translated into English as *Memoirs of a Physician*, 1847–48)
28   Auriac, *D'Artagnan*.
29   Samaran, *D'Artagnan*, pp.105–16.
30   Bordaz, *D'Artagnan*, p.64. Petitfils, *Le Véritable d'Artagnan*, pp.16–17. There seems
       to be some confusion over the forename: Isaac de Baas had a brother, Paul.
       Both served as agents to Condé and to Mazarin. Isaac de Baas was to precede
       Charles de Batz-Castelmore d'Artagnan as sub-lieutenant of musketeers. Bordaz,
       D'Artagnan, p.70.
31   On Berthod, see Gibson, *A Tragic Farce*, pp.58, 112–3.
32   Dumas, *Les Trois Mousquetaires* (Éditions Flammarion), p. 41. Translation by KM.

       Il y a un an à peu près, qu'en faisant à la Bibliothèque royale des recherches
       pour mon histoire de Louis XIV, je tombai par hasard sur les *Mémoires de M.
       d'Artagnan*, imprimés, – comme la plus grande partie des ouvrages de cette
       époque, où les auteurs tenaient à dire la vérité sans aller faire un tour plus
       ou moins long à la Bastille, – à Amsterdam, chez Pierre Rouge. Le titre me
       séduisait: je les emportai chez moi, avec le permission de M. le conservateur,
       bien entendu, et je les dévorai.

33   Dumas used his memories of his father also in his depiction of Porthos.
34   Dumas borrowed the incident of the Swiss suitor for another character, Charles's
       later mistress, Madeleine, in *Twenty Years After*. In that book, however, Charles
       dismisses the Swiss and reinstates himself in a comfortable, if unromantic,
       relationship with the lady.

CHAPTER FIVE: ALEXANDRE DUMAS AND THE MUSKETEERS

1   For a fuller account of Antoine-Alexandre, see F.W.J. Hemmings, *The King of
       Romance: A Portrait of Alexandre Dumas* (London 1979), pp.1–7.
2   On General Dumas, see Hemmings, *King*, pp.5–16; Michael Ross, *Alexandre
       Dumas* (Newton Abbot 1981), pp.11–27; André Maurois, *Three Musketeers: a study
       of the Dumas family*, trans. Gerard Hopkin (London 1957), pp.17–42. The latter
       study is rather old-fashioned in its approach to racial politics.
3   Thomas-Alexandre earned the nickname 'Monsieur l'Humanité' for his known
       dislike for the guillotine and the death penalty. Hemmings, *King*, p.9.

4 On this movement, see Hemmings, *King*, pp.48–55; D. Coward, 'Popular Fiction in the nineteenth century,' in T. Unwin, ed., *The Cambridge Companion to the French Novel* (Cambridge 1997).

5 Regrettably, there is not space for a detailed account of the life and works of Alexandre Dumas here. For a full account see Hemmings, *King*; Ross, *Dumas*. There are also two older, but still interesting, books – J. Lucas-Dubreton, *Alexandre Dumas The Fourth Musketeer*, trans. Maida Castelhun Darnton (London 1929); H.A. Spurr, *The Life and Writings of Alexandre Dumas* (London 1902). Guy Endore, *King of Paris* (London 1956) is a very enjoyable novel based on Alexandre's life.

6 See Ross, *Dumas*, pp.213–214.

7 For details, see Ross, *Dumas*, pp.50, 69–70, 73, 75-6, 80, 111–19.

8 Ross, *Dumas*, p.196.

9 Ross, *Dumas*, p.117.

10 Henri d'Alméras, *Alexandre Dumas et Les Trois Mousquetaires* (Paris 1929), pp.55–56.

11 Alexandre Dumas, *Les Trois Mousquetaires*, (Éditions Flammarion), p.147. The translation is by KM.

– D'un de vos amis? interrompit Mme Bonacieux.

– Sans doute; Aramis est de mes meilleurs amis.

– Aramis! qu'est-ce que cela?

– Allons donc? allez-vous me dire que vous ne connaissez pas Aramis?

– C'est la première fois que j'entends prononcer ce nom.

– C'est donc la première fois que vous venez à cette maison?

– Sans doute.

– Et vous ne saviez pas qu'elle fût habitée par un jeune homme?

– Non.

– Par un mousquetaire?

– Nullement.

– Ce n'est donc pas lui que vous veniez cherchez?

– Pas le moins du monde. D'ailleurs, vous l'avez bien vu, la personne à qui j'ai parlé est une femme.

12 Plays written in this way include *Richard Darlington* (1831), which was brought to him as no more than a sketch and a prologue by a minor writer, Félix Beudin, who had himself drawn the idea for the play from Walter Scott's novel *The Surgeon's Daughter* (1827); and *Teresa* (1832), offered to him by the actor Pierre Bocage in the form of a draft written by a lesser playwright, Anicet Bourgeois. In all cases, pressure was applied to Alexandre that the plays be presented under his name only, although there is evidence that he would have been happy to appear as a co-writer. There is at least one instance of him revising a play – *Bathilde* (1839) – for another writer, Auguste Maquet, and the play being presented under Maquet's name alone. See Hemmings, *King*, pp.79–81, 84–86, 120; Ross, *Dumas*, pp.147–149.

13 On Maquet, see Ross, *Dumas*, pp.194–5, 199–200, 205–206, 209–211, 214, 242, 244; Hemmings, *King*, pp.119–23, 162; Alméras, *Dumas*, pp.63–70, 77–81.

14 It goes under the same title in the English edition.

15 See Ross, *Dumas*, pp.160–64.

16   Alexandre had rejected de Mirecourt as a potential collaborator. Ross, *Dumas*, p.209.

17   On the question of Alexandre and race, see the fascinating and valuable analysis by Dorothy Trench-Bonett in her introduction to her translation of his play *Charles VII chez ses grands vassaux*: Alexandre Dumas, *Charles VII at the Homes of his Great Vassals*, trans. Dorothy Trench-Bonett (Chicago 1991), pp.1–35.

18   Ross, *Dumas*, pp.208–214; Hemmings, *King*, pp.137–38; Alméras, *Dumas*, pp.42–66; Maurois, *Musketeers*, pp.182–187.

19   A translation of this letter may be found in Ross, *Dumas*, p.211.

20   On this law suit, see Maurois, *Musketeers*, pp.315–17.

21   Ross, *Dumas*, p.209; Hemmings, *King*, p.136.

22   Maurois considered this book to be one of Alexandre's best. Maurois, *Musketeers*, p.352-3.

23   Alméras, *Dumas*, pp.81–89.

24   Hemmings, *King*, p.137.

25   Maurois, *Three Musketeers*, pp.177–181.

26   On Alexandre's sources, see Richard Parker, 'Some Additional Sources of Dumas's *Les Trois Mousquetaires*', *Modern Philology* 42 (1944–1945), pp.34–40; Jacques Suffel, 'Introduction' in Dumas, *Trois Mousquetaires* (Éditions Flammarion), pp.30–32; Alméras, *Dumas*, pp.67, 70–71; Lord Sudley, 'Introduction' in Dumas, *Three Musketeers*, trans. Sudley (Penguin Books, Harmondsworth 1952), pp.11–15

27   Dumas, *Three Musketeers*, author's preface.

28   Her desire for the Comte de Wardes, and d'Artagnan's seduction of her maid and clandestine substitution of himself for that gentleman are taken from Courtilz, as is her desire for revenge upon him. However, Alexandre changed the means of her revenge and the nature of her initial contact with d'Artagnan, along with a number of smaller details.

29   Lady Clarik in Brienne and the Countess of Carlisle in La Rochefoucauld. 'Milady Clarik' is one of the many names used by Milady in *The Three Musketeers*.

30   Alméras, *Dumas*, p.115.

31   Alméras, *Dumas*, p.114.

32   'La France entière était *mousquetarisée*', Alméras, *Dumas*, p.114. Translation by KM.

33   'S'il existe quelque part un autre Robinson Crusoe dans une île déserte, tenez pour certain que ce solitaire est occupé en ce moment à lire *Les Trois Mousquetaires* à l'ombre de son parasol fait de plumes de perroquet.' Cited in Alméras, *Dumas*, pp.115–116.

34   His son, Alexandre Dumas fils, was elected in February 1875. That he was chosen and his father ignored was down more to prejudice than merit. The elder Alexandre was too popular, lived in too irregular a fashion with his numerous mistresses, was too full of himself – and perhaps his mixed blood was too obvious. The younger Alexandre was an inferior writer, but by the 1860s, his life was well regulated and in accord with social principles, and his plays – now largely forgotten – were considered to have high moral tone. Maurois, *Musketeers*, pp.401–407.

35   To the extent that at least one paper has been written endeavouring to decide whether or not he is a worthy subject of study: Renee Wintergarten, 'Alexandre Dumas: fact and fiction', *The New Criterion* vol. 9 no. 9 (May 1991), pp.32–39. On

the other hand, Michel Guérin, *Les Quatres Mousquetaires: Essai sur la trilogie de Dumas* (Monaco 1995) makes an insightful and interesting case for the *Musketeers* sequence as a study of the development of the human character and of friendship over time.

36 On the Historique, see Ross, *Dumas*, pp.229–230; Hemmings, *King*, pp.151–152.

37 Alexandre Dumas fils is today remembered mainly for his novel *La Dame aux Camélias* (1847, *The Lady of the Camelias,* also known as *Camille*), but produced in addition a number of successful plays. His life is discussed in Maurois, *Three Musketeers*.

38 For more detail on this venture, see Ross, *Dumas*, pp.246–249; Hemmings, *King*, pp.166–169.

39 Alexandre did not like *Madame Bovary*. After reading it, he remarked 'If that is good, then everything we have written since 1830 is worthless'. Hemmings, *King*, p.169.

40 On this phase of his career, see Ross, *Dumas*, pp.250–262; Hemmings, *King*, pp.170–198.

41 *La Caucase* (1859, *Adventures in the Caucasus*), and *En Russie* (1860, *Adventures in Russia*).

42 *Memoires de Garibaldi,* a translation made by him from Italian (1860, *Memoirs of Garibaldi*); *Les Garibaldiens* (1861, *The Garibaldians in Sicily*); *Un nuit à Florence chez Alexandre de Medicis* (1861, *A Night in Florence under Alexander de Medici*); *I Borboni di Napoli,* an eight-volume history which he wrote in Italian (1861, *The Bourbons of Naples*); and *La San Felice* (1864, *The Neapolitan Lovers*). He wrote all of these without the use of collaborators. He also wrote a memoir of his voyages in the Mediterranean on his boat, the *Emma,* which is yet to be published in French. An English translation by R.S. Garnett was published as *On Board the Emma* in 1929.

43 Alexandre was a true *gourmet* and an accomplished cook, who took great interest in the new dishes he encountered on his travels. The *Dictionary*, which is available only in an abridged version in English (*Alexandre Dumas' Dictionary of Cuisine,* ed., trans. and abridged Louis Colman, New York 1958), is a fascinating mixture of recipes, anecdotes, memoirs and history.

44 On Alexandre's working habits, see Hemming, *King*, pp.117–119.

45 *La Terreur Prussienne; Souvenirs Dramatiques; Parisiens et Provinciaux; Caroline de Brunswick.*

46 *Le Grand Dictionnaire de la Cuisine* (1873); *Création et Rédemption* (1872); *Le Prince des Voleurs* (1872), *Robin Hood le Proscrit* (1872).

CHAPTER SIX: AFTER *THE THREE MUSKETEERS*

1 The Sherlock Holmes stories are probably the nearest parallel. For detailed discussion of the afterlife of *The Three Musketeers* and its sequels, see Daniel Compère, *D'Artagnan et Cie: Les Trois Mousquetaires, un roman a suivre* (Paris 2002); Stéphane Baumont, *D'Artagnan: des siècles d'aventures de cape et d'épée* (Toulouse 1999); and *Alexandre Dumas, suites, plagiats, pastiches et hommages,* the splendid on-line annotated bibliography by Patrick de Jacquelot at http://www.pastichesdumas.com/index.html.

2 *Porthos à la recherche d'un équipment,* by Anicet, Dumanoir and Brisebarre.

3   Dumas, *The Man in the Iron Mask*, Chapter 33.

4   Gabriel Richard and Charles Monselet, *Les Trois Gendarmes* (1846); Anonymous, *Fanfan le Batoniste à la Représentation des Mousquetaires* (1848); Paul de Kock and Guénée, *La Graine de Mousquetaires*; M Grafetot, *Porthos au Bal Besnard* (1850).

5   Auriac, *D'Artagnan*.

6   Albert Maurin, *Les véritables mémoires de d'Artagnan* (1874), a novelisation of Courtilz; Emile Desbeaux, *Les trois petits mousquetaires* (1992), a children's novel echoing the form of *The Three Musketeers*; Paul Mahalin, *Le Fils du Porthos* (1883), a sequel to *The Vicomte*, charting the adventures of Porthos's illegitimate son Joël, translated into English as *Son of Porthos* and marketed under the name of Dumas; Alexandre de Lamothe, *La fiancée de Vautour-Blanc* (1885); Frantz Beauvallet, *Mademoiselle d'Artagnan* (1887); Paul Mahalin, *D'Artagnan* (1890); Alphonse Brown, *Mademoiselle la Mousquetaire* (1896); Paul Mahalin, *Le filleul d'Aramis* (1896).

7   *Alexandre Dumas, suites, plagiats, pastiches et hommages* has the fullest coverage, summarising over eighty of the sequels. A shorter account of mostly French works can be found in Compère, *D'Artagnan*, pp.98–115.

8   H. Bedford-Jones, *D'Artagnan the sequel to The Three Musketeers* (New York 1928).

9   H. Bedford-Jones, *The King's Passport* (New York and London 1928).

10   Paul Féval the elder. His best known book is *Le Bossu* (1858), (*The Hunchback*). This is probably best known to British audiences through the 1997 film version by Philippe de Broca, and starring Daniel Auteuil and Vincent Perez.

11   Paul Féval, *Le fils de d'Artagnan* (1914); *Le vieillesse d'Athos* (1925).

12   In French, the novels are usually published as one or two volumes, under the titles *D'Artagnan contre Cyrano de Bergerac* (1925) and *D'Artagnan et Cyrano Réconciliés* (1928). The first is made up of four sections – *Le Chevalier Mystère*, *Martyre de Reine*, *Le secret de la Bastille*, *L'héritage de Buckingham* – and the second of three – *Secret d'Etat*, *L'évasion du Masque du fer*, *Les Noces de Cyrano*. The sequence was translated into English shortly after their first French publication, and published in six volumes: *The Mysterious Cavalier* (1928), *Martyr to the Queen* (1928), *The Secret of the Bastille* (1928), *The Heir of Buckingham* (1928), *Comrades at Arms* (1931) and *Salute to Cyrano* (1931).

13   Roger Nimier, *D'Artagnan Amoureux* (Paris 1962).

14   Roger Nimier, 'Frédéric, d'Artagnan and la petite chinoise', in his *Les Indes Galandes* (1952).

15   The author of the famous – and in its day scandalous – *Histoire Amoureuse des Gaules*, a *roman à clef* about the love affairs of senior members of the nobility under Louis XIV.

16   For details of these, Patrick de Jacquelot's website provides a comprehensive guide. See note 1.

17   These include Paul Mahalin, *Le Fils de Porthos* (1883) – which was translated into English as *Son of Porthos* and published under Dumas's name; Paul Mahalin, *Le Filleul d'Aramis* (1895); Féval fils, *Les Fils de d'Artagnan* (1914) and *Le Vieillesse d'Athos* (1925), which show his customary disregard for Dumas's narrative; Cami, 'Le fils des trois mousquetaires', in *Pour Lire Sous la Douche* (1912) – a short comic play which is perhaps the most entertaining of these sequels; Cami, *Le Fils des Trois Mousquetaires* (1919), which takes the idea from the play and expands it into a comic novel; Maxime La Tour, *L'Enfant des Mousquetaires* (1929); and Gabriel Fersen and Le Rallic, *Le Protégée de d'Artagnan* (1945). The best novel

of this type is probably Jean-Luc Dejean, *Le Cousin de Porthos* (1981), which concentrates on minor characters from Dumas's novel.

18 These include Adrien Guignery, *D'Artagnan* (1900); Charles Quinel and Adhémar de Montgon, *Le Beau d'Artagnan et son époque* (1933); and Lucien Pemjean, *Le jeunesse de d'Artagnan* (1930) and *Le capitaine d'Artagnan* (1931). The latter have been translated into English as *The New Adventures of D'Artagnan* (1932–33).

19 Henri Nicolas, *Et Charlotte Épousa d'Artagnan* (Précy-sous-Thil 2001).

20 Other reinterpretations include Jean Burnat, *C'est Dupont, Mon Éminence* (1955), a comedy; and Simon Hawke, *The Timekeeper Conspiracy* (1984), a science-fiction re-tread.

21 Donna Kauffman, *The Three Musketeers: Surrender the Dark* (1995), *The Three Musketeers: Born to Be Wild* (1996) and *The Three Musketeers: Midnight Heat* (1996). The trilogy recounts the romances of three women with three friends, nicknamed Athos, d'Artagnan and Aramis.

22 Arturo Perez-Reverte, *The Dumas Club,* trans. Sonia Soto (London 1996, original Spanish edition 1993). When the book was filmed as *The Ninth Gate*, the Dumas material was dropped from the plot.

23 Pierre Nord, *Vrai Secret d'Etat* (1959); Voldemar Lestienne, *Furioso* (1971) and *Fracasso* (1973).

24 Joel Rosenberg, *Not Exactly The Three Musketeers* (1999). This is the first in a trilogy, and does not really stand alone.

25 Stephen Brust, *The Phoenix Guards* (1991); *Five Hundred Years After* (1994); *The Paths of the Dead* (2002), *The Lord of Castle Black* (2003), and *Sethra Lavode* (2004).

26 'Aramis, vous le savez,' continua Athos, 'est naturellement froid.' ('Aramis, you know' Athos continued, 'is naturally cold'. Translation by KLM.) Dumas, *Twenty Years After,* Chapter 16.

27 Georges Méliès, *Les Mousquetaires de la Reine* (1903); Gaumont Pictures, *Le Collier de la Reine* (1908); Mario Caserini, *I Tre Moschettieri* (1909). For a detailed examination of the musketeers in the cinema, see Philippe Durant, *Les Trois Mousquetaires: L'Histoire d'une Aventure Adaptée plus de 100 fois à l'Écran* (Ciné-Légendes 5 October 2000); Compère, *D'Artagnan*, pp.116–119, 148–51.

28 *A Modern Musketeer*, directed by Allan Kwan.

29 Apart from Diamant-Berger's version, the writers know only of the 1989 film, *The Return of the Musketeers*, directed by Richard Lester.

30 This film, which was directed by Lewis Allen, is known as *At Sword's Point* in the USA.

31 It is curious that, aside from Europe in the silent era, only the 1970s seem to have been able as a decade to confront the adultery theme. The same arc is noticeable in films about the King Arthur legend.

32 *The Three Musketeers* (2004)

33 *The Two Mouseketeers* (1952); *Touché Pussy Cat* (1954); *Tom and Cherie* (1955); *Royal Cat Nap* (1958).

34 *The Three Musketeers* (1974) directed by John Halas and Franco Cristofani. This is probably the best of the animated versions.

35 *The Three Musketeers* (Hanna Barbera 1968).

36 'Étrange destinée de ces homes d'airain!' Dumas, *Vicomte,* Chapter 79. Translation by KM.

Maps

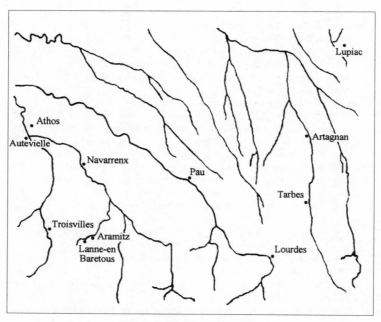

Gascony of the Musketeers

France in the time of d'Artagnan

Select Bibliography

There has been a great deal written on seventeenth-century France, and there are many interesting and fascinating books on almost every aspect of it. As far as Charles Castelmore d'Artagnan, his friends and his regiment are concerned, however, there is relatively little in English. Recent scholarly biographies of Charles are all in French, as are the few histories of the musketeers as a company. The following books, however, provide a good introduction to the times in which he lived, the people he knew, the wars in which he served, and the nature of the army in his lifetime; plus some works on Dumas.

IN ENGLISH

Richard Bonney, *The Thirty Years War 1618–1648* (Oxford 2002).

Wendy Gibson, *A Tragic Farce: the Fronde (1648–1653)* (Exeter 1998).

F.W.J. Hemmings, *The King of Romance: A Portrait of Alexandre Dumas* (London 1979).

Ruth Kleinman, *Anne of Austria: Queen of France* (Columbus 1985).

John A. Lynn, *The French Wars 1667–1714: the Sun King at War* (Oxford 2002).

—, *Giant of the Grand Siècle: the French Army, 1610–1715* (Cambridge 1997).

David Parrott, *Richelieu's Army War, Government and Society in France 1624–1642* (Cambridge 2001).

Michael Ross, *Alexandre Dumas* (Newton Abbott 1981).

Guy Rowlands, *The Dynastic State and the Army under Louis XIV: Royal service and private interest 1661–1701* (Cambridge 2002).

G.R.R. Treasure, *Seventeenth Century France* (2nd ed. London 1981).

—, *Mazarin: the Crisis of Absolutism in France* (London 1995).

—, *Louis XIV* (Harlow 2001).

IN FRENCH

Odile Bordaz, *D'Artagnan: Capitaine-Lieutenant des Grands Mousquetaires du Roy* (Baixas 2001).

Jean-Christian Petitfils, *Le véritable d'Artagnan* (2nd ed. Paris 2002).

Further references, to works in English and in French, will be found in the notes.

List of Illustrations

MAPS

Index